THE FIRST NAPOLEON

NAPOLEON AS FIRST CONSUL
From a miniature by Isabey

THE
FIRST NAPOLEON

SOME UNPUBLISHED DOCUMENTS
FROM THE BOWOOD PAPERS

EDITED BY

THE EARL OF KERRY

Lansdowne, H.W.
II

ILLUSTRATED

BOSTON AND NEW YORK
HOUGHTON MIFFLIN COMPANY
1925

Printed in Great Britain by R. & R. CLARK, LIMITED, Edinburgh.

TO

E. K.

CONTENTS

PAGE

I. AT SCHÖNBRUNN 1

    A Conversation between the Emperor and the
    Comte de Flahault in October 1809 . . 2

II. 1812 11

    (i.) Napoleon's Views on Poland . . 12
    (ii.) Flahault's Correspondence with his Mother 16

III. NAPOLEON AND HIS AIDE-DE-CAMP . . . 29

    (i.) The Cavalry 30
    (ii.) The Artillery 34
    (iii.) Orders for Eugène Beauharnais . . 35

IV. THE LUSIGNY NEGOTIATIONS 49

    (i.) Flahault's Report to the Emperor (February
    1814) 50
    (ii.) Two Letters from Napoleon . . 61

V. THE FIRST ABDICATION. 65

    Flahault's Letters from Fontainebleau (April 1814) 66

VI. THE SOVEREIGN OF ELBA 79

    A Conversation between Napoleon and two Eng-
    lish Members of Parliament (December 1814). 80

VII. THE HUNDRED DAYS 107

    (i.) Flahault in charge of Personnel . . 109
        Letter from the Emperor (April 18)
    (ii.) Napoleon and the Tenth Regiment
        (May 14) 110
    (iii.) Flahault becomes a Peer of France . 113
        Letter from Napoleon (June 2)
    (iv.) The First Day's Fighting . . 114
        Flahault to Madame de Souza (June 15)
    (v.) Quatre Bras and after (June 16-17) . 114
        Flahault to Brialmont, and to Lavalette
    (vi.) Waterloo (June 18) . . . 124
        Flahault to Thiers, and to the *Moniteur*
    (vii.) The Scene with Davout (June 28) . . 132
        Flahault to Larabit

PAGE

VIII. THE *BELLEROPHON* 137

The Journal and Letters of Admiral Viscount
Keith, commanding at Plymouth (July-
August 1815) 138

IX. ST. HELENA 179

Letters from Lady Malcolm during Napoleon's
captivity 180

X. THE EMPRESS JOSEPHINE 207

An Appreciation, by Madame de Souza . . 208

XI. LOUIS BONAPARTE 217

A Correspondence with Madame de Souza (1800–
1802) 218

XII. QUEEN HORTENSE 229

(i.) " The Frogs ask for a King " (1806) . 230
(ii.) " Ma Cousine Henriette " . . . 232
(iii.) Jean Hyacinthe de Morny . . . 260
(iv.) A Letter to Madame de Souza (1825) . 265
(v.) A Visit from Madame de Flahault (1829) . 267

XIII. THE NAPOLEONIC CORRESPONDENCE . . . 271

(i.) The First Commission for its Publication . 272
(ii.) An Unpublished Letter . . . 285

APPENDIX 289

Original French versions of Translated Documents (Nos. 1 to 25) 290

GENEALOGICAL TABLE 343

INDEX 345

LIST OF ILLUSTRATIONS

Napoleon as First Consul. From a miniature by
Isabey . . . . . . *Frontispiece*

FACING PAGE

Général le Comte de Flahault. From a miniature after
Gérard 16

Map to illustrate Napoleon's orders in March 1813 . . 38

A page of Napoleon's orders dictated to Flahault in March
1813 42

The Battle of Hanau (October 29, 1813). From a picture
by Horace Vernet 48

Napoleon as Emperor. From a drawing by Innocent
Goubaud 78

Admiral Lord Keith. From a miniature by George
Saunders 138

Napoleon's pocket-handkerchief (Plymouth, 1815) . . 156

The transfer of Napoleon from the *Bellerophon* to the
Northumberland (August 1815). From an oil painting
by T. Luny 174

Madame de Flahault (afterwards Madame de Souza) and
her son Charles. From a portrait in oils by Madame
La Bille Guiard 208

Plate used by Napoleon at St. Helena, with portrait of the
Empress Josephine by Isabey 214

Louis Bonaparte. From an etching by André Dutertre . 222

" Henriette " (Queen Hortense). From a miniature by
Isabey 232

Queen Hortense's music - book, given to the Comte de
Flahault 236

Seal given by the Comte de Flahault to Queen Hortense . 240

La Duchesse de St. Leu (Queen Hortense). From a water-
colour drawing by Isabey 268

A Letter from Napoleon to Talleyrand (August 5, 1797) . 286

LIST OF ILLUSTRATIONS

INTRODUCTION

WE are authoritatively informed in the preface to the *Correspondance de Napoléon I*, that, before the year 1854, there had already appeared more than ten thousand volumes of "Napoleana"— a number which has of course since steadily increased, and may by now have been doubled or even quadrupled. Nevertheless I hope that the papers now given to the public may seem to those who read them sufficiently interesting to justify the addition of yet another volume to the Napoleonic series. If they do not contain a great deal which is historically new, they provide at any rate some curious side-lights on well-known episodes of the Napoleonic period, and (with the few exceptions which are noted) they have never been published. Moreover, they were for the most part written at the time by persons who happened to come into actual contact with the great Emperor, and were eye-witnesses of the events related.

Some of these persons were ancestors, English and French, of the present Lord Lansdowne; others were the correspondents of those ancestors. It is thus that the documents have found their way into the collection of family papers which are now at Bowood.

The first and principal contributor is the Comte de Flahault (Lord Lansdowne's grandfather), who, after fighting his way in a subordinate capacity through the earlier campaigns of the Grand Army, held a staff appointment which brought him into frequent relations with Napoleon. Flahault persistently refused to write any memoirs, but it would seem that he kept some notes of conversations held with Napoleon, and that, in his later days, he dictated and perhaps amplified these notes, in the form in which they appear in Parts I. and II. Included in Part II. will be found a number of extracts from letters written by Flahault to his mother during the course of the Russian campaign of 1812.

In the following year Flahault was appointed aide-de-camp to the Emperor. In Part III. I have given some of the orders which were dictated to him by Napoleon on the eve of the war in Saxony, and in Part IV. an account of the negotiations at Lusigny, in which he took a leading part, a month before the Allies entered Paris in 1814. Part V. deals with the First Abdication in April of the same year, when Flahault was with the Emperor at Fontainebleau for the three weeks preceding the departure for Elba. I have printed the letters written by Flahault at that time, and have supplemented them with some other material from works already published.

During the Hundred Days and up to the final *débâcle* Flahault was once more at the Emperor's side. In after years he would sometimes recall these days in conversation, but it was not till near the end of his life that he put anything on paper, and then mainly for the purpose of correcting misstatements made by others. It was in such circumstances that the letters printed in Part VII. came to be written.

Forty years after Waterloo Napoleon III. appointed a Commission for the purpose of publishing his uncle's correspondence. Flahault was one of its original members. He has left an account of his activities in this connection, and of the discussions which took place as to the suppression of some of the more compromising documents (Part XIII.). To this I have added an early letter from Napoleon to Talleyrand which, if it was not purposely withheld from the printed Correspondence, has at all events not hitherto been given to the public.

The 3rd Lord Lansdowne (the grandfather of the present Marquis) had become, at the early age of twenty-four, Chancellor of the Exchequer in the Ministry of all the Talents, and thereafter (for some fifty years) held a prominent position amongst the leaders of the Whig party. It was perhaps for this reason that two Whig Members of Parliament, Messrs. Venables - Vernon and Fazakerley, made him the repository—and as it would seem the sole repository—of a carefully compiled account of the interview given to them by the ' Sovereign of Elba ' in November 1814 (Part VI.).

Lord Lansdowne's great-grandfather, Admiral Viscount Keith (whose daughter, curiously enough, was subsequently to marry the ex-aide-de-camp Flahault), spent the better part of his life in carrying on the war at sea against France. In

1815 he found himself, at the end of a long career, recalled once more to service as Commander of the Channel Fleet. In July of that year the *Bellerophon* brought Napoleon from Rochfort to Plymouth, and Keith became directly responsible for the safe keeping of the illustrious captive, until such time as arrangements could be made for his removal to the island of St. Helena. Keith was thus, for a fortnight or more, brought into close relations, both personal and epistolary, with ' General ' Bonaparte. The Admiral, a typical old sea-dog of the eighteenth - century school, was probably more at home on the quarter-deck than at the writing-table, but his Journal and private letters (Part VIII.), only a few of which have hitherto seen the light, afford a vivid impression of Napoleon's short stay in British waters.

Flahault's mother is best remembered under the name of her second husband, M. de Souza, and as the writer of a series of romantic novels. Madame de Souza had been during the early days of the Empire on intimate terms with the Empress Josephine. She has left us a short but striking appreciation of the character of that ill-fated lady, and of her relations with her inconstant husband in the years preceding their divorce (Part X.). Through her also we get the curious little collection of letters from Louis Bonaparte printed in Part XI.

Lady Malcolm was a cousin of Madame de Flahault's, and as the wife of the Admiral commanding at the Cape of Good Hope, she became in 1816 and 1817 a resident at St. Helena. She was thus a personal witness of the " Last Phase ", and left a Journal which was printed *in extenso* not many years ago. In Part IX. will be found some private letters, written at the same time as the Journal, which have not hitherto been published.

It is well known that during the latter part of the Napoleonic period Charles de Flahault was in intimate relations with Hortense, Napoleon's stepdaughter, and sometime Queen of Holland. Auguste de Morny, the future protagonist of the *coup d'État* of 1851, was their son. It could scarcely be expected that the direct correspondence between Flahault and Hortense should have survived. I have, however, brought together a number of extracts from the unpublished letters of Flahault and his mother in which (though the names are invariably disguised) there is a good deal of fresh information on the subject of this liaison, of Auguste de Morny's infancy, and of his putative parents, whose identity has hitherto baffled all research.

Of the documents referred to above, in the case of Parts I., II., III., IV., V., VII., X., XI., XII., and XIII., the originals were in French, while in Parts VI., VIII., and IX. they were in English. In spite of the loss which must always be entailed in rendering French into English, it seemed desirable to avoid a bilingual publication. The papers which I have translated are, however, shown by an asterisk at the beginning and at the end of each passage (*), while the more important of these documents will be found in their original form in the Appendix at the end of the volume.

The several portions of the book, as will at once
be seen, deal with separate phases in Napoleon's
career, and are in no way related to one another.
Without attempting to connect them by a narrative of intervening events, I have prefaced each
part by a few remarks which, in conjunction with
the footnotes, may be sufficient to explain both
the subject-matter of the documents and the
circumstances under which they came to be
written.

I have added on p. 343 a genealogical table, in
order to make clear the somewhat complicated
relationships of the Flahaults and their col-
laterals. This will help to explain how, through
the accident of descent, a number of documents,
so varied in their origin, are to-day collected
under one roof.

The illustrations are all taken from portraits
and objects in the possession of Flahault's
descendants. With the exception of Flahault's
portrait after Gérard, which was used in a previous
publication (*The Secret of the Coup d'État*), and the
portrait of Louis Bonaparte, which is taken from
an etching by André Dutertre in the British
Museum, none of them have appeared before.

The miniature of Napoleon signed by Isabey
was given, according to family tradition, by the
ex-Emperor to Flahault at the moment of their
final parting at Malmaison in 1815.

The crayon drawing of the Emperor is signed
*I. Goubaud, Professeur de dessin au Lycée Charle-
magne.* I am indebted to M. Barat, *Proviseur*
of the Lycée Charlemagne, for the information

that its author, Innocent Goubaud, was also *maître de dessin* to the King of Rome. This drawing was in all probability likewise a gift from Napoleon to Flahault.

The picture of the battle of Hanau belonged to Flahault, and was left by him to Lord Lansdowne. This engagement took place on October 29, 1813, a few days after the battle of Leipzig. The French were retreating towards Mayence, and successfully disposed on this occasion of an Austro - Bavarian force under General Wrede, which had sought to block their way. Lord Lansdowne's picture is a small edition of a much larger composition by Vernet, which, with three other battle scenes by that artist, used to hang in the Palais Royal. These canvases were considerably damaged by the mob during the '48 Revolution, but were afterwards removed and disposed of at Louis Philippe's sale in 1851. They were purchased by Sir Richard Wallace, and are now at the Tate Gallery. The small picture of Hanau would appear to have been painted for Flahault. He had at the time just been promoted *Général de Division*, and is shown as the central figure in the foreground, surrounded by officers who seem to be taking his orders, while the *chasseurs* of the Old Guard in their *bonnets à poil* are close by repelling the attack of the Austrian cavalry on the French guns.

The portrait of Madame de Flahault (Souza) with her infant son, is from the brush of Madame La Bille Guiard, the contemporary of Madame Vigée Le Brun. It was painted in 1785, and exhibited (though without the name of the subject) in the Paris Salon that summer. Madame Le Brun had several portraits on view at the same time, but it seems that her work on this occasion was contrasted unfavourably with that of her rival. Le Brun's pictures, the critics said, showed a lack of modesty, while Guiard had succeeded in depicting a woman—" chaste comme Pénélope, et toute l'habitude du corps annoncait la vertu conjugale dans toute sa modestie la plus parfaite " (Pierre de Nolhac, *Madame Vigée Le Brun*, 1912). Such a comment reads curiously in view of the stories then current regarding the birth of the infant portrayed. The appreciation would perhaps have been somewhat differently worded had the identity of Madame Guiard's sitter been disclosed.

Napoleon's handkerchief was secured while he was on the *Bellerophon* at Plymouth in 1815. Keith's daughter, Miss Elphinstone, appears to have been the ' receiver of the goods ', for the place and date are endorsed in her hand—but our records discreetly omit to name the thief. The monogram on this handkerchief has been reproduced on the cover of this volume.

The oil-painting of the transfer of Napoleon from the *Bellerophon* to the *Northumberland* off Berry Head, was painted for Admiral Lord Keith by Thomas Luny, a marine painter of the day. The transfer, as recounted in Keith's Journal (*infra*, p. 174), took place at 1.30 P.M. on August 7, 1815. Luny's seascape shows the party, which consisted of Napoleon, the two Bertrands, two Montholons, Gourgaud, and Las Cases, with the Admiral in charge, approaching the *Northumber-*

land which was to convey them to St. Helena that evening. The escorting ships can be seen in the distance.

The Sèvres plate bearing the likeness of the Empress Josephine is stamped on the back " Peint à la Manufacture Impériale de Sèvres, par J. B. Isabey : Août 1807 ". It was used by Napoleon at St. Helena. On his death it passed to General Bertrand, and was left in the latter part of the nineteenth century by Madame Thayer, Bertrand's daughter, to Flahault's second surviving child, Madame de Lavalette.

The miniature of Queen Hortense is by Isabey, and belonged to Amélie, the daughter of Prince Eugène Beauharnais and wife of Dom Pedro, the Emperor of Brazil. It is probably the portrait which Queen Hortense left by will to her niece (*Revue de l'Empire*, 1ʳᵉ année 1842). The miniature was bought about the year 1870, when a sale of some of the Empress Amélie's effects took place.

The water - colour portrait of the ex - Queen by Isabey is that referred to in Madame de Flahault's will (*infra*, p. 268). She had destined it for " Auguste ", but Morny having predeceased her, it passed to her daughter, Madame de Lavalette. Both these portraits are now the property of Lady Emily Digby.

I have had reproduced the curious seal mentioned in Part XII. which, for the reasons stated therein (p. 240), I conclude must have been made for Queen Hortense, and afterwards returned by her to Flahault.

My thanks are due to many friends and relatives who have assisted me with suggestions and advice, and especially to my father, Lord Lansdowne, and my uncle, Lord Fitzmaurice, both of whom have interested themselves throughout in the compilation of this volume. Also to Mademoiselle Bauer, whose assistance in deciphering the French script of a hundred years ago has been invaluable.

KERRY.

Bowood, *June* 1925.

I

AT SCHÖNBRUNN

A Conversation between the Emperor and
the Comte de Flahault in October 1809

The Empire was nearing its zenith. The greater part of
Europe had already been brought under Napoleon's sway,
but Austria had had the temerity to rise against him. He
could have crushed her after Austerlitz, but had then held
his hand, and when at the beginning of the year 1809 it
became apparent that a large portion of the Imperial forces
were still engaged in Spain, she determined to make a bid
for freedom. The movement was launched under the guidance of the Archduke Charles, Austria's leading general and
a man of marked political ability, but some initial successes
on the part of his enemies soon brought Napoleon himself
upon the scene. Travelling post-haste from Paris he assumed
personal command on April 17, and within a few days his
presence had entirely changed the aspect of affairs. He
carried the war into the enemy's country, and by a rapid
series of victories was able to establish himself in their capital
(May 15). There followed (May 21-22) the bloody battle
of Aspern-Essling, which, though an Austrian victory, was
indecisive in results, and, after a six weeks' interval, that of
Wagram, when, owing to the failure of the Archduke John
to come to his brother's rescue, the Austrians were decisively
beaten. On July 11, an armistice between the contending
forces was signed at Znaim, and negotiations for a treaty
of peace were soon afterwards set on foot. Both parties,
however, were watching events elsewhere, and it was not till
the issue in Spain and Belgium had declared itself in favour
of the French, that the Austrians could be persuaded to
accept Napoleon's terms. The Treaty of Schönbrunn was
announced by him as complete on October 14 (1809), though
it was not signed by the Emperor Francis until a week
later.

The conversation given below must have taken place towards the end of these negotiations.

The document from which we have taken our translation is in the handwriting of Flahault's daughter, Madame de Lavalette. It is initialled by Flahault, and the last paragraph shows that it was dictated (probably between the years 1860 and 1870) by him, from a note taken at the time.

We have given elsewhere [1] a biographical sketch of Charles Comte de Flahault. He was at this time twenty-four years of age. Ten of these he had already spent in military service. He had begun as a trooper in the *Houssards Volontaires*, was transferred as a *sous-officier* to the *Ve Dragons*, and in 1802 became aide-de-camp to Murat. After five years' service with this cavalry leader he had reverted for a time to regimental duty, to be reappointed in 1808 as aide-de-camp to Berthier, Prince de Neuchâtel, Napoleon's Chief of the Staff. Berthier's office entailed his constant presence at headquarters, and as his aide-de-camp Flahault came into frequent contact with the Emperor. As a young *émigré* Flahault had been carefully educated in England and in Germany ; he was a good linguist, and had the advantage of pleasant looks and manners. He was thus by training as well as by birth better equipped than many of his self-made confrères for the informal negotiations which Napoleon was continually carrying on with his allies and his vassals, and Flahault's letters show that he was frequently so employed.

Writing to his mother (presumably from Schönbrunn) on the 19th of August, he tells her that he has just returned from Brunn, where he had no doubt been sent with letters to Davout, whose headquarters had been established at that place about a month earlier. He is to set out again, he says, at once for the Russian and Polish armies at Cracow, and he adds, " Je suis content d'avoir été choisi, d'autant plus que c'est une autorité supérieure qui m'a désigné ". We learn from his *états de service* that (in order perhaps to strengthen his position at the Russian court) he had been created by the same *autorité supérieure*, a few days before, *Baron de l'Empire*. A subsequent letter shows that he was back at Schönbrunn on September 10. It must, therefore,

---

[1] *The Secret of the Coup d'État* (Constable & Co., 1924), Introduction.

have been after this date that he was despatched to Dotis, near Altenburg, where the Austrians had their headquarters. We may suppose that Flahault's report of the Austrian attitude served to strengthen Napoleon's determination to insist on the terms which he had just drawn up; it may even have contributed to his characteristic action in announcing the treaty as complete before it had been signed by his adversaries.

England at this time was little more than an onlooker. Following the formal adherence, in February 1808, of Austria to Napoleon's Continental system, she had been for more than twelve months technically at war with that country. A convention, however, was made in April 1809 between the two Governments, and in order to create a diversion in Austria's favour, the British Administration planned the famous Walcheren expedition. But there was still much mutual distrust. The Walcheren expedition started too late to be of any possible assistance to Austria, even if it had been successful, and when its total failure had become apparent Napoleon was able to dictate his own terms to Austria in the Treaty of Schönbrunn.

An account of a conversation with the Emperor Napoleon I., who had sent me on a Mission to the headquarters of the Emperor of Austria at Dotis.

(*The Emperor.*) What did they say about me ?

(*Flahault.*) They spoke of you, sire, with the most profound admiration. Up to the moment when they heard of your having come to join the army they were hopeful of victory, and it seems that the Archduke Charles participated in this feeling. But as soon as they heard that you had assumed the command there was a complete change, grave despondency taking the place of the high hopes which the Archduke had previously entertained—a clear proof of the mastery which your genius has obtained over them.

(*Emperor.*) This is ridiculous, and the Archduke could never have entertained such a foolish notion. The truth was that he believed all my troops were in Spain and that I had none left to use against them. Under these circumstances he thought I should not myself assume the command, and when he discovered his mistake he realised that my forces were sufficient to put him in danger of defeat. Still it is quite natural that they should make the most of my personal influence, for they imagine that by doing so, and attributing to me all the merit of success, they are detracting from the valour of my army. They try to make out that if I had not been there their army would have been a match for ours, but this is not the fact. They say that in numbers our army is stronger by a quarter than theirs. This may be true, but it is true also that man for man it is stronger to the same extent.

(*Flahault.*) Every one that I saw at Dotis was loud in complaints of the Archduke John's conduct. They blamed him for the slowness of his march, which prevented his being present at the battle of Essling,[1] and they said that if one of our Generals had behaved in such a manner, you would have had him shot.

(*Emperor.*) One would like to know exactly how far the accusations made against the Archduke are justified, and in order to do so one

---

[1] *Sic*, but Wagram is surely intended. The Archduke John could never have been present at Essling, but at Wagram he failed to obey his brother's orders to march on Napoleon's unguarded flank, though his advanced scouts arrived on the scene at the close of the day.

would have to understand the conditions under which he was working. It is quite true that if one of my Generals had laid himself open to charges such as those now made against the Archduke, I should have sent him before a *conseil de guerre*, but the mistake was in giving a command of this kind to a Prince of the blood royal. Princes were intended only to hunt in their royal domains.[1] Either they have talent, when they may attain to high command and so become a public danger, or they are so stupid that they cannot be employed at all. A sovereign must always be in a position to try, and if necessary to shoot, the Generals whom he employs. When you are dealing with Princes this cannot be done, for by trying or shooting a Prince you jeopardise the safety of the throne.

History teems with instances of Princes who have been a source of anxiety to Kings. I say again, where there is a reigning dynasty Princes will always be either useless or dangerous.

My brother [2] proved himself to be unreliable. I deprived him of his command. I am sorry that King Joseph should have that of the army in Spain, but that cannot now be undone. Princes, when they are not strong enough to form a party of their own, are always sufficiently ambitious to champion one which has been formed by others.

(*Flahault.*) They complained a great deal at Dotis of the harshness of the Treaty, and said

---

[1] It was because he considered hunting an essentially royal diversion, as well as for reasons of health, that Napoleon himself occasionally indulged in this sport (*Le Comte Molé*, Marquis de Noailles, p. 134).

[2] *I.e.* Louis Bonaparte who, as titular Constable of France, had command of the army in the Netherlands at the time of the Walcheren expedition. He was replaced by Bernadotte.

that in so greatly weakening them you were actuated less by anxiety on your own account than by the desire that, when you are gone, France should have no cause to fear any other power.

(*Emperor.*) That goes to prove their intention of attacking us whenever an opportunity may occur. They can never forget that they once controlled both Germany and Italy. France and Austria have always been like two bulls, who have disputed these pastures.[1] I need Germany and I need Italy; for Italy means Spain, and Spain is a prolongation of France.

I will never again believe their promises. One may be fooled occasionally but not repeatedly. The Emperor of Austria assured me that it was his desire to hold his crown through me. He vowed eternal friendship, but when he thought me too busy in Spain to defend myself elsewhere he at once attacked me. I am not afraid of him, I despise him too much. He is not a knave; on the contrary, he is a simple soul like Louis XVI., but he is always under the influence of the last person to whom he has spoken. One can never trust him. His one passion is his jealousy of the Archduke Charles, and that man is the only one there that counts. He came to see me at R[aab] after Essling, and suggested sending me back Durosnel,[2] but that idiot would not allow it. I

---

[1] Cf. Napoleon's remark to M. de Bubna, aide-de-camp to the Emperor Francis, "Your master and I are like two bulls who wish to mate with Germany and Italy" (Napoleon to Champagnay, September 10, 1809. *Correspondance*, No. 15,778).

[2] General Durosnel, Napoleon's favourite equerry, was wounded (and captured ?) at the battle of Essling on May 22, 1809. The Archduke John was defeated at Raab three weeks later (June 14). I cannot, however, find any historical mention of an interview between Napoleon and the Archduke Charles on either occasion.

have talked with him, and I repeat it, he is the only man that counts. If he were to take his rightful place in the country I would be ready to give them back everything.[1] As it is, they will make a peace with every kind of condition, only to break it six years hence. I have told the plenipotentiaries that by merely talking of peace, while they could turn me out from Vienna, they would show themselves to be a set of cowards; it would be a shameful action, and the very fact that they are now negotiating, shows that they are at the end of their resources. So peace will be made. What matter to them if they give up a few provinces—they are so dishonest that they will seize them again whenever they get the chance. Now Galicia, it is quite true, would have meant a real loss to them.[2] They are hated in that country, they are in the midst of irreconcilable enemies. If I had had my Spanish army here I would have insisted on keeping this province and thus separating the three kingdoms, but that would have taken some time to bring

[1] Flahault often related that when Napoleon heard that the Archduke Charles had resigned his command he remarked, " Alors l'Empire autrichien a perdu ses généraux ". Napoleon seems nevertheless to have changed his opinion, for in his conversation with Lord Ebrington at Elba in 1814, he stigmatises the Archduke Charles as " un esprit très médiocre," while he contrasts the Emperor Francis of Austria favourably with the Emperor Alexander of Russia.

Wellington's admiration of the Archduke Charles was subject to no reservations : " A great officer ? Why, he knows more about it than all of us put together . . . aye than Buonaparte or any of us ! We are none of us worthy to fasten the latchets of his shoes " (*Croker Papers*, i. 328).

[2] Under the treaty which was about to be signed, Austria was compelled to cede to France parts of Friuli and Carinthia, Carniola, Trieste, and portions of Croatia and Dalmatia. She kept Galicia, however, with the exception of a small strip which went to Russia.

about. Business calls for my presence elsewhere, so I shall make peace. I know I am wrong, but I shall do it nevertheless, and besides it is a case of following the line of least resistance, which always suits a Frenchman.

(*Flahault.*) Those wretched Poles will be sadly maltreated.

(*Emperor.*) Well, on that point there must be conditions, but in any case I am a Frenchman first. I have been very successful in my dealings with Poland, and it was interesting making that country into a Grand Duchy, but it is not there that my interests are involved. Was there any mention made of Holland ?

(*Flahault.*) No.

(*Emperor.*) Monnet is a rascal, and he lost his head, for the fortifications were intact.[1] At all events my ships are safe, but should the English do so much injury to Holland that she can no longer exist as a separate kingdom, I shall make her a province of France. I could not have done so without their help—it would have been unthinkable to remove my own brother from the throne ; but if they choose to weaken the country so much that it can no longer form a separate state, I shall incorporate it once more with France.[2] I shall institute a customs barrier, with M. Callin's [3]

[1] The allusion is to the Walcheren expedition. General Monnet had surrendered Flushing to the British after a three-days bombardment (August 16, 1809).

[2] Holland was annexed to France on July 9 in the following year, but Louis had saved his brother the trouble of formally deposing him, by his flight to Bohemia a week earlier.

[3] Was this the M. Callin who is given as Napoleon's Comptroller of the Household in Capt. Ussher's list of persons who accompanied the Emperor to Elba ? (J. Holland Rose, *Napoleon's Last Voyages*, p. 107).

minions, and they will soon see what they have missed. My brother had neither my strength of character nor my determination. The English attack will have done me a good turn. They [1] would like to make a favourable treaty and then to say that they beat me. They will break the peace in six years, but meanwhile Westphalia will have had time to take shape. Naples will no longer require the presence of a French army, and Italy already finds me 60,000 men.

The above note of my conversation with the Emperor was made on my return from the Austrian Headquarters. I had been sent there by him and had just passed a week in the midst of the Emperor of Austria's court. I was at that time (1809) a Colonel, and Aide-de-camp to the Prince de Neuchâtel.* [2]

F.

---

[1] *I.e.* the Austrians.   [2] Appendix No. 1, p. 290.

II

1812

(i.) NAPOLEON'S VIEWS ON POLAND

* " THE Emperor, when he received me on my return, treated me with the utmost kindness, and kept me quite a long time. It is a delight to hear him talk, and to be given the privilege of being a listener. The quickness of his mind is indescribable, and he is quite unlike any one else.[1] He is amazing." *

So wrote Flahault from Königsberg on June 13, 1812.[2] He was then aged twenty-four, and still aide-de-camp to Berthier, Prince de Neuchâtel, Napoleon's Chief of the Staff. The Russian campaign had been definitely launched a few weeks before, and the Emperor was on his way to join his army on the banks of the Niemen. In the intervals of the brilliant functions with which he sought while at Dresden to dazzle Europe, Napoleon had been trying to obtain from Metternich a promise of active co-operation on the part of Austria in the campaign which was to follow. His efforts in this direction met with scant success, and Flahault (as we learn from an earlier letter, written by him on May 22 from Dresden) had been despatched to Lemberg, where an Austrian force of some 30,000 men, under the command of the Prince de Schwarzenberg, was at that time assembled on the southern or right flank of Napoleon's army of invasion. Flahault was no doubt the bearer of a direct appeal to the Austrian commander, but though he was well received by Prince Schwarzenberg on this (as also on a subsequent) occasion,[3] the Austrian contingent took little or no part in the military operations which ensued.

Napoleon was, however, at the moment primarily con-

---

[1] *Il a un esprit dont on ne peut se faire aucune idée, parce qu'aucun autre ne lui ressemble. Il vous étonne.*
[2] Flahault to Madame de Souza, Bowood Papers.
[3] See *infra*, p. 20.

cerned as to the attitude of Poland. The Abbé de Pradt had just been sent as his special ambassador to Warsaw (it will be remembered that Napoleon was afterwards inclined to attribute the ill success of his Russian campaign to de Pradt's diplomatic failure in that capital), and Flahault must have received special orders to travel via Poland, for though his route from Dresden to Lemberg lay far to the south we find him on May 27 writing from Warsaw.[1] Napoleon left Dresden on May 28, and Flahault, as appears by the letter we have quoted, rejoined him soon after he had reached Königsberg.

The note of his conversation with Napoleon, printed below, is in the handwriting of Madame de Flahault, with corrections made by Flahault. It is without date, but the incident can be placed by the Emperor's allusion to the first Partition of Poland (1772) as having taken place forty years before. There can be no doubt that it is an account of the interview of June 1812 mentioned by Flahault above. Napoleon seems to have spoken without reserve, and we may infer that the young officer, who was at such pains to keep a record of what he had said, was his only hearer.

* (*Flahault.*) Yes, Sire, there is great enthusiasm amongst the Poles, and something more than that—a national spirit which shows itself in their hatred of the Russians, their admiration for your Majesty, and a feeling of confidence that it is through you that their country is going to be restored to them.

(*The Emperor.*) Love of one's country is of all human instincts the most enduring. It is innate in every child, and it persists till death. No feeling is more difficult to eradicate. The Romans are the only nation who understood how to destroy it amongst conquered races, but they made use of methods which are repugnant to modern

[1] Bowood Papers.

thought. They would remove an entire population from one country to another, but who could do this to-day ?[1] I believe myself to be fairly powerful, but were I to give orders for such a thing to be done scarcely an officer would obey me ; the lamentations of the aged, of the women and children, torn from their hearths and homes, would be more than they could bear. Even Russians would shrink from so drastic a course, though Poland could be thus dealt with more easily than any other country. It would be a case of forcing one or two of the great land-owning families to leave the country, and the rest, like a flock of sheep, would allow themselves to be transplanted and dealt with as one might choose. Indeed the Russians are perhaps the only people in Europe capable of enforcing so drastic a plan, and they would be quite ready themselves to replace those whom they were removing from their own country ; but even they have demurred to the suggestion. Moreover, what have we seen ? Forty years have passed since the first Partition of Poland,[2] but the national spirit of the Poles has remained as strong as ever, and whenever there appears to be a chance of re-establishing their country, the entire population is ready to rise in a cause which they regard as sacred.

But this war is not going to be a matter of a single campaign. I shall pursue the Russians and establish myself on the Dwina and the Dnieper. I shall form a sort of ' bridge-head '

[1] It was done, nevertheless, in 1923 by the Treaty of Lausanne (cf. Treaty Series, No. 16, 1923, p. 175).

[2] The first Partition of Poland took place in February 1772.

between the two rivers, and behind this I shall
establish 120,000 French troops. I shall raise
200,000 Poles, for it is with Polish blood that the
price must be paid for re-establishing Poland. I
shall spare the blood of Frenchmen, which is too
precious to be thrown away.*[1]

The foregoing conversation may be usefully compared
with another which, although covering a much wider field,
deals amongst other questions with Poland and the Emperor's
intentions in the 1812 campaign. It had taken place in
Paris four months earlier, between Napoleon and the Comte
de Narbonne (who was afterwards to be the bearer of his
ultimatum to the Russian Emperor), and is related by
Villemain in his *Souvenirs contemporains*. Villemain's
account is admittedly given at second hand ; indeed he tells
us that it was dictated to him by Narbonne *rapidement*,
between an afternoon visit and a dinner engagement, and
that in doing so Narbonne used *des mots expressifs plutôt
que des phrases complètes*.[2] Under the circumstances it
is hard to resist the suspicion that, even if correctly given
in essentials, the conversation, in the hands of so skilful a
writer, may have been considerably written up before it
appeared in print more than forty years afterwards. We
may therefore give the preference for probable accuracy to
Flahault. His story is short and unadorned, but it was at
any rate set down (as there is reason to suppose at the time)
by one who himself heard Napoleon's words.

In both conversations the cynical attitude of the
Emperor towards the Poles becomes apparent. He loved
and admired them, but their country was to be " a camp
and not a forum ".[3] Their bodies were to furnish the
' cannon fodder ' necessary for the attainment of his
object, but theirs was not to be the reward of ' self-
determination '. In his talk with Flahault we find
Napoleon dilating on the Polish spirit of nationality, and

---

[1] Appendix No. 2, p. 293.
[2] *Souvenirs contemporains d'histoire et de littérature*, M. Villemain,
1854, chap. xiv. p. 181.
[3] *Ibid.* p. 165.

stressing the fact that only for the restoration of their country would the Poles consent to take up arms. He expressly admits that he was contemplating a campaign in which they were to play the major part. Yet only a few days later, after carefully arranging through de Pradt that a Polish deputation should wait upon him, he refused to give the pledge they demanded as the price of their assistance.

He tells Flahault that he expects the help of 200,000 Poles, but that he did not intend to risk the blood of Frenchmen. Nevertheless about a month later he was to plunge his army into the heart of Russia, and that without effective Polish support.

We may note a remarkable difference between Napoleon's intentions as reported respectively by Narbonne and by Flahault. To the former (in March) he stated categorically that he meant in the forthcoming campaign to go to Moscow (pp. 163, 165). But in June we find him talking to Flahault of a bridge-head between the Dnieper and the Dwina, and of a second campaign for the attainment of his real objective.

The conversation furnishes one more proof that the Emperor remained undecided on this point up to the very last moment.

(ii.) Flahault's Letters to his Mother

We will conclude this section by some more extracts from Flahault's unpublished correspondence with his mother during the second half of the year 1812. The writer shows himself as a rule somewhat reticent on military matters. " Pas d'inquiétude ! " is a phrase which often recurs, and anything which was likely to add to a fond mother's anxieties is carefully excluded. He, however, occasionally permits us to get a glimpse of the actions in which the army had been engaged, and such sidelights as we may thus obtain derive an added interest from the fact that he was throughout closely associated with Napoleon's Chief of the Staff, and was probably reflecting the Prince de Neuchâtel's opinions.

GÉNÉRAL LE COMTE DE FLAHAULT
From a miniature after Gérard, 1812

By December the Grand Army had virtually ceased to exist. " Of the 600,000 men who had proudly crossed the Niemen for the conquest of Russia, only 20,000 famished, frost-bitten, unarmed spectres staggered across the bridge of Kowno in the middle of December." [1] Flahault was with them and remained in East Prussia until, towards the end of January 1813, he was suddenly recalled to Paris to take up the duties of aide-de-camp to the Emperor.

Flahault to Madame de Souza, *1812*

KOWNO, 24 *June.*

* We are the other side of the Niemen, [2] my dear mother, as you will see by the heading of this letter. The crossing of the river was not contested, and all your friends are well, though very tired after the long marches and the great heat. We are buoyed up by the hope that it will soon be all over, and that we shall meet again. Please don't be anxious.

WILNA, 29 *June.*

You can never have expected to receive a letter from Wilna, without a shot worth mentioning having been fired. Nevertheless this is what has happened. Except for a skirmish or two with the Cossacks, we have reached the capital of Lithuania, without striking a blow. It is very tiresome to have to go so far in pursuit of our enemies, and they might well have had the goodness to wait for us, but I don't believe they will run the risk. . . . It is a glorious feat on the Emperor's part to have gained so much territory without spilling a drop of his soldiers' blood.

---

[1] J. Holland Rose, *Life of Napoleon I.*
[2] War had been formally declared against Russia on June 22.

C

WILNA, 7 *July*.

I am being sent to Minsk [1] and shall probably be several days on my journey.

WILNA, 15 *July*.

Still at Wilna! We have been " booted and spurred " for the last three days, but I trust that by to-morrow we shall no longer remain in this state of stagnation [2]—it bores me terribly! We are going to advance to the Dwina, where we shall find out at last if these cursed Russians intend to wait for us and allow us to win a victory. It would be a very charming action on their part!

26 *July*.

At last we have met our enemies, and I am now writing to you—after seven or eight hours' fighting—in the middle of a field on the Witebsk road. . . . I escaped with a shot on the chest which my aiguillette turned off, and uncommonly lucky it was, for it was only fired ten paces off. The King of Naples was good enough to say that he was well satisfied with my conduct, and the Emperor remarked that I had had a very narrow escape.[3]

[1] It seems probable that Flahault was the bearer of the despatch to Davout (who was then at Minsk) which placed Jérôme Bonaparte under Davout's orders. This so much disgusted Jérôme that he incontinently left his command and retired to his kingdom of Westphalia. In the confusion which followed, the Russian army under Bagration was enabled to effect a junction with that of Barclay in the north, an event which had far-reaching effects on the ultimate result of the campaign.

[2] Napoleon advanced from Vilna on July 17.

[3] *Que j'avois été tué de près.*

WITEBSK, 1 *August.*

We have been resting here for a few days, as I have already told you. We had to do so after the amazing marches which we had made, marches which I can well imagine have astonished those at home. But though we are resting, there is no rest for the Emperor.[1] He is engaged in every sort of plan for victualling his army, and it is a splendid thing to see this great man enter into such details as the supply of cooking stoves, flour, ambulances, etc. We have a parade every morning at 7, and on these occasions all the heads of departments are present. This morning the Emperor gave special attention to questions affecting the wounded, and showed himself better informed as to their requirements and the supplies available, than those whose sole duty it is to see to such things. There are indeed some facts which, though they will probably never be mentioned in history, are not less noteworthy than his great victories, as for instance the care which he takes in maintaining his communications and in safeguarding his sources of supply. Even when he has won the most signal victory, all arrangements have been made for a possible reverse.[2] For eight years I have followed him in all his campaigns, and I would rather be attached to him in my present rank than obtain any other form of promotion. I am sure I should serve him well, for I have no other ambition.

The Russians continue to flee before us. It

[1] Cf. Ségur, *Histoires et mémoires*, Book V., for Napoleon's activities at Vitebsk, July 31 to August 13.

[2] *Lorsqu'il emporte la plus grande victoire, il a toujours tout prévu pour un revers.*

seems that they are afraid to risk a fight. They
have abandoned Poland without striking a single
blow. The Emperor's pride should surely be
satisfied, no enemy could have ever paid him a
more striking tribute. It is probable that this
state of things will not last much longer. Since
the Russians have seemingly made up their minds
that fighting is no good, the Emperor of Russia
will certainly now ask for peace. In the contrary
event, we are perhaps approaching a supreme
crisis for Europe and its peace. For this can only
continue under the sole autocracy[1] of the Emperor.

Kosow, near Slonim, 8 *August*.

I got here yesterday, and once again I have
been wonderfully received by the Prince de
Schwarzenberg[2] : an admirable, gallant, and
honourable man. This did something to cheer
me up after the appalling fatigue resulting from
a journey of 160 leagues, made throughout in
springless carts. Well, here I am, and I can only
look forward to returning in the same delightful
manner as I came !

Smolensk,[3] *August* 20.

I was close to Marshal Ney yesterday, during
a pretty hot affair in which he was engaged. I
cannot tell you how greatly I admired this gallant
man, and how splendid he is under fire. It is a
pleasure to be with him.

[1] *La toute puissance.*

[2] Schwarzenberg, who had advanced to Kosoff from Lemberg (where
it will be remembered Flahault had already paid him a visit in May),
was now being appealed to to help the Saxons under General Reynier
(Thiers, xliv. p. 187).

[3] Smolensk had been taken on August 18.

Viasma, *August* 30.

What a shameful thing it is for an army to abandon its territory—burning towns, villages, and the houses of the wretched inhabitants, ruining it in fact—and never to have the courage to risk a blow for the saving of their country. It would seem to me an awful thing to behave in such a way if we were in France. In spite of all this our forces move forward some ten leagues a day, and manage to find resources for their support. One hears the men singing on the line of march, and when these past-masters in the art of retreat [1] at length give us the chance, they may be certain the confidence which our army has in its commander will assure us a victory which will finish the war. Then I shall be able to come home, I shall give you a kiss and shall tell you all about my campaigns, while you with delightful patience will listen to my tale. Meanwhile I must tell you that the Emperor has spoken to me several times and in a most friendly manner. I felt very grateful to him.

Ghyat, *September* 2.

They say that the Tartars are going to stand. By God's help, and with that of our army, and especially of our General, we shall defeat them, and then peace will be made. . . . I was in the saddle yesterday for twelve hours. The Emperor was on horseback at 9 o'clock in the morning and only dismounted at 9 at night. How can a man like that ever be otherwise than victorious ? In

[1] *Ces généraux de retraite.*

the midst of all these gigantic plans of his, he actually turns his mind and gives his personal attention to seeing that the baggage train does not interfere with the artillery.[1] Every detail receives his attention and, busily occupied though he is, he neglects nothing. I am sure that if he spoke to me as M. de Chevert [2] did to the grenadier, I would not only do as that grenadier did, but I should believe him also. I give you my word, there is not a single soldier in the army, down to the youngest conscript, who is not confident of victory. Never I am sure has this confidence been more marked, and when you think that we are 700 leagues from our own country, it is really astonishing. I am most fortunate in being so situated that my duty takes me near His Majesty. He treats me most kindly. Yesterday after procuring for him some little canteens, which carry food for five or six persons, I was standing on one side. He saw me, and had the goodness to invite me to lunch with him. This mark of favour delighted me. To be noticed by the Emperor, to be known and appreciated by him, is in my eyes the highest form of reward.

THE BATTLE FIELD OF MOZAISK, *September* 6.

The end of the campaign is drawing near. Yesterday a redoubt was taken from the Russians,

---

[1] It was about this time that Napoleon, finding a private carriage encumbering the road on the line of march, ordered it to be burnt where it stood. Nevertheless Flahault himself appears to have kept a carriage up to the crossing of the Beresina.

[2] François de Chevert (1695–1769), a very gallant general, who with his grenadiers greatly distinguished himself at the siege of Prague.

and many of them were killed.[1] I expect that
soon all will be over. It will be a splendid thing
to be able to say, " I was close to the Emperor
in the battle near Moscow ".[2] I do not know if
his aides-de-camp realise how honourable a post
they hold, but I must confess that I can conceive
no position more enviable than theirs.

MOZAISK, *September* 10.

We are 20 leagues from Moscow. We have
defeated the Russians, who are retreating and
leaving their wounded behind them. So it is
inconceivable that when they realise their plight
they will not ask for terms of peace. The
Emperor will not forget his friendship for the
Emperor Alexander ; and thus war will prove
itself the road to peace.

Moscow, *September* 15.

What do you think of this heading, my dear
mother. Does it not seem to you unbelievable,
inconceivable, astonishing, surprising, incompre-
hensible, etc., etc. ! Well, we got here yesterday
after an arrangement under which our advance-
guard followed the Russian rear-guard without
fighting. If it fell to my lot to form part of
a rear-guard under such conditions in Paris, I
think I should die of shame ! Russian prisoners
are arriving in quantities, and the number of their
wounded is considerable. One cannot imagine

[1] The redoubt of Schwardino, which covered the approach to
Borodino, was captured on the evening of September 5, but the
principal battle was only commenced two days later.
[2] The phrase appears to be borrowed from Napoleon's proclamation
before the battle of Borodino (cf. Ségur, *Histoires et mémoires*, Book VII.
chap. vii.).

that they will not soon crave for peace at any price. The Emperor has found here immense resources for his army. There is enough to keep it for four months, let alone the convoys which may come in.

Moscow, *September* 19.

The Russians have just treated us to the most awful sight that can possibly be conceived, they have committed a crime unheard of heretofore. The Governor of Moscow left behind him a large number of brigands armed with incendiary bombs, and gave them an order to set the place on fire in all directions.[1] They did their work so well that half this wonderful but unfortunate town is at the moment devoured by flames. They are sure to try and lay the responsibility of this infamy on us, and this makes me dreadfully unhappy. It is an abomination which we could never have perpetrated. . . . The fire is nearly out and we have come back to the town. It is so huge that there are still a good many houses left, and we shall contrive somehow to manage, if only these vile and cowardly rascals leave us alone.

Moscow, *October* 8.

We had a parade this morning. The Emperor reviewed the Young Guard. It was some time since I had seen him. He is wonderfully well. There are hardly any sick in the army and the weather is magnificent.

[1] The great fire of Moscow commenced on the 15th, and raged for three days.

DESNA, *October* 10.

Three days ago the Prince sent in a very good and satisfactory report of me to His Majesty, and asked that I might be given the rank of General while remaining attached to him. This was refused by H.M., which was astonishing, especially after the kindness he has shown both towards me and in speaking of me.[1]

MOZAISK, *October* 28.

We had a glorious affair at Maloyaroslavetz— I hope you will be able to read and to pronounce the word! It was the Viceroy only, with his corps, who was engaged, and he did not spare himself. There was only one opinion as to what he had done, and admiration was unstinted. What a brave man! The fight was a hot one and the Russians were well beaten.[2]

SMOLENSK, *November* 11.

The war has taken a turn which disgusts my soul. It is cruel to a degree beyond endurance. Incendiarism, murders, pillage are rampant. All this is hateful to me, but it is the daily practice in both armies.

[1] Flahault had for some time considered himself hardly treated in being denied promotion. That he was not alone in this opinion is shown by the following extract from some recently published *Souvenirs sur Napoléon*, by the Comte de Sainte-Aulaire : " Nous avons vu Flahaut traité pendant très longtemps avec une malveillance prononcée. Il a fini par en triompher parce qu'il a été bien servi par ses amis et surtout parce que lui-même a observé sa conduite avec le plus grand soin " (*La Revue de Paris*, June 1, 1925, p. 493).

[2] The battle of Malojaroslavetz had been fought on October 24, and the brunt of the fighting fell on the vanguard of Italian conscripts commanded by Prince Eugène. Though part of the Russian army was defeated, the road to Kaluga (the Emperor's objective) remained blocked, and Napoleon was forced to retreat by the way which he had come. This finally settled the fortunes of the campaign.

KRASNOI, *November* 16.[1]

The Prince and the Emperor are in the best of health, and the Russians, who have been counting on their abominable climate and their savage country for our destruction during the winter, will be fairly astonished, if they refuse to make peace, when they find us taking our revenge on Petersburg next year.

OCHMIANA, *December* 6.

Here is a copy of a letter which I have just received :

SMORGHONI, *December* 5.

Monsieur le Baron Flahault,

I have the pleasure to inform you that the Emperor, by his decree of this date, has promoted you to the rank of *Général de Brigade.* His Majesty's intention is that you should still be employed under my orders. You will therefore receive your instructions forthwith.

Le Prince, Major Général,
ALEXANDER.

What do you think of this letter,[2] my dear mother ?

KOWNO, *December* 12.

Whilst we were at Wilna, I heard shouts in a house. I went in with a staff officer, and found

---

[1] The Niemen was crossed this day.

[2] *Es-tu content de ce poulet, ma chère maman ?* Flahault's promotion must have been almost the last act of Napoleon before leaving Smorghoni incognito for Paris on the evening of December 5. He had imparted his intention only to Berthier, Eugène, and Murat. Flahault was no doubt unaware at the moment that he had gone.

about 100 Hessians from Pappenheim, pillaging, stealing, and beating the inmates. We drove them away, but when we were outside in the courtyard I saw one of the soldiers with a drawn sword attacking the staff officer. I seized a musket from one of them, and with it gave the ruffian a blow full in the face. I was going to do it again, when I got one myself on the head, which made a wound three inches long. . . .

GUMBINNEN, *December* 18.

The Russians are no longer pursuing us. It seems that the cold does not agree with them any better than it does with us ! [1]

KÖNIGSBERG, 26 *December.*

We are impatiently awaiting the news of the Emperor's arrival in Paris.[2] It must have given the keenest delight, especially after so long a time without news.

KÖNIGSBERG, *December* 30.

I have kept quite well, I should have been in despair had I gone sick. There are times in which it would be, for a good soldier, a terrible misfortune not to keep all his strength, and when one has the good fortune to serve under the eyes of the Emperor, it would be better to die than even to seem to give in.[3] I have often felt terribly exhausted. The cold weather gave me an awful

---

[1] They followed the French none the less. They occupied Königsberg on January 5 and were in Berlin in March.

[2] Napoleon arrived in Paris on December 19.

[3] *De céder au malheur.*

cough with which I am still troubled, but I have contrived all through to wear a cheerful countenance and I have never left a duty unperformed.

POSEN, *January* 17.

The King of Naples has left for his State and the Viceroy has been entrusted with the command of the army.[1] . . . I am quite naked, my dear mother. I don't dare to show myself, for my uniform is a mass of holes, especially under the arms, and I am quite ashamed of it. I don't want more than one, but please send me a coat, with which to cover myself, some trousers and a pair of boots. Anything else I should not know what to do with.

POSEN, *January* 20.

Since the King's departure the Viceroy has taken the command of the army, pending the appointment of a commander-in-chief by the Emperor. During the short time he has been in control he has put our affairs in good shape. He is a hard worker, so unlike his predecessor, who did nothing at all. He has won esteem, respect, and devotion on every side.*

[1] Murat deserted his post on January 8. He was succeeded in the command by Prince Eugène, who forthwith commenced to concentrate the remains of the French army in the neighbourhood of Berlin.

III

NAPOLEON AND HIS AIDE-DE-CAMP

(i.) THE CAVALRY

FLAHAULT, as we have seen, returned from Prussia at the end of January 1813 in order to assume the post of Aide-de-camp to the Emperor which he had so long coveted.

His papers and correspondence during the succeeding weeks give us some idea of the multifarious activities, apart from personal attendance, which Napoleon required of his subordinates. Thus we find Flahault during the month of February ordered to make a careful inspection of the *Dragons de la Garde de Paris*, and to select from amongst their number such officers and non-commissioned officers as would be suitable to form the *noyau* of a new regiment of 1000 men. He was also to report on the state of their uniform, both in use and in store, in order that Napoleon could decide whether or no it was desirable to change its pattern. A few days later he was commissioned to make a similar inspection of the *Légion de Gendarmerie Impériale*, which had only that moment returned from Spain—they were however allowed two days "afin de leur laisser le tems de se reposer"—after their march of something over five hundred miles. In this regiment the older men were to be immediately transferred to the *Service de Paris*, the younger to the *Cuirassiers*, and other mounted corps. Next we find some instructions as to the constitution of a corps of *Gendarmerie d'Élite attachée à ma Garde*, the formation of which would appear to have been likewise entrusted to Flahault, and lastly there are a number of short notes with messages to Maret, Duc de Bassano, the Foreign Minister, and to others, as to stores and clothing for the advanced depots in Germany, directions as to the payment of the troops at the front and as to the " répartition du million, destiné par Sa Majesté au paiement des gratifications des officiers généraux et d'État Major ".

Early in March come the dictated orders which we print

below. We can well believe Comte Molé when he tells us that Napoleon, in giving these out, let fall such " an avalanche of words and ideas " [1] that only two members of his staff (Maret and Méneval) were able to keep pace with him. We have ample evidence in the *brouillons* which Flahault has left behind him that he could not do so. He has fortunately, however, provided us in two instances (the orders for the cavalry and the artillery *infra*) with transcripts of his own notes, so that their interpretation is in no doubt. We print these below in translated form. They are a good example of Napoleon's all-pervading activity, of his grasp of detail, and of the almost superhuman efforts which enabled him, within a few months of the termination of the 1812 campaign, to put into the field another army scarcely inferior in numbers to that which had perished on the plains of Russia.

7 March 1813.

* Flahault is to obtain from the offices of the War Department a state of the Cavalry. The Cavalry must be dealt with under four heads : Men, horses, saddlery and harness, and accoutrements.

Men. Find out how matters stood when the last reports were received and how each regiment stood. How many of the 1813 conscripts have they received ? How many of the Four-year men ? [2] How many from the Reserve companies ? How many from the Cohorts ? How many each regiment should receive from the volunteers who are offering their services ? How many they had received, and how many they had still to receive, when the last state of the forces was made out ? He must ask for a similar statement from the Minister for War.[3] He must also ask for the distribution of the officers and

---

[1] *Le Comte Molé*, Marquis de Noailles, i. 170.
[2] *Des quatre années*.   [3] General Clarke.

under-officers of Gendarmerie in the various corps.
On what date did those, who have already been
sent, leave ?   Lastly, he must obtain information
as to the strength and as to the time of arrival
of the Cadres of the Grand Army, and as to the
Cadres from Spain, both those already formed
and those to be formed.

Of the *Horses* there are three categories.   An
agreement has been made for the purchase of
4000—has it been executed ?   Find out their
distribution amongst the regiments.   15,000 are
to come from the Departments ;   find out by
which Department each regiment is to be provided, also the places and the depots to which
these horses are to come.   The same applies to
the 16,000 given by the towns and cantons.
Besides these there have been 3200 horses promised by individuals ;   where and how are they
being allocated ?   These four categories make up
an aggregate of 38,000 horses, which with the addition of those at the depots gives a total of over
40,000.   Amongst the latter must be reckoned
not only the depots of the Grand Army, but also
those of the army of Spain, that is to say, of
the 88 regiments.   The Minister of War and the
Minister in charge of administration [1] must have
all the information on this subject.   See the
Minister of the Interior, in order to get information as to who has given horses and to whom
they have been given.

Then *Saddlery.*   How many saddles for Magdeburg have left France ?   On what date will these

---

[1] General Lacuée, Comte de Cessac, *ministre directeur de l'administration de la guerre.*

leave Mayence ? This I must know, otherwise if any enemy marauders were to cross the Elbe it might all be lost. Lastly, when will the 40,000 saddles from the interior be finished ?

Similarly with the *Accoutrements*, (promised) to the amount of 500 sets from France. Get information in short as to the various depots of the Grand Army. When did they send goods to the service squadrons ? On what date did these leave ? When will the regiments get them ?

Tell the Minister in charge of administration and his assistants that I have not been satisfied with their reports. (1) When did the Minister write to the Intendant-General to dispose of stores at Magdeburg, and what stores were there there ? (2) On the 17th the Minister ordered the administrative councils to send stores to the service squadrons : What was their reply ? and how were they sent ? How do they go from Mayence to Magdeburg ? I must know this, for the line of communication may be interrupted. He must send me General Duvergier's letters in which he states that most of the accoutrement stores from Hanover are already available. I have received letters which contradict each other. When shall we get the accoutrements for the 500 men ?— there should be time enough for 900. The artillery train of the army of Italy had received nothing by the 4th of March. When will these stores arrive ? Go to the transport office and find out. These delays make it impossible for the Italian Corps of Observation to start. The 9th Transport battalion can do nothing, since the cloth necessary for the uniform has not yet left.

D

Send a despatch to tell them to procure it from Plaisance.*[1]

The foregoing orders may be usefully compared with those issued on the same subject to the Minister of War three weeks later. These will be found in a letter written by Napoleon to the Duc de Feltre on March 26,[2] and show the development of his plans. The Emperor kept his aides-de-camp fully employed. Flahault was sent from Paris to Leipzig on March 12 (*infra*, p. 36). He could scarcely have got back from his mission when he was, on the 26th, named as one of five Generals who were to be despatched forthwith, *sans délai*, to inspect and report on the fifty-two cavalry depots of the Grande Armée scattered throughout France and Germany. We do not know how many days were allotted for this operation, but Flahault's papers show that he was again busy with messages to all the heads of departments in Paris on March 30, and three weeks later he was once more sent off on a journey of 500 miles—this time to Ratisbon with a letter for the King of Bavaria.[3]

(ii.) THE ARTILLERY

7 March 1813, 7 P.M.

*The Minister of War must repeat his orders for the recall of the 17 companies of Artillery which are now at Magdeburg. This must be done through the special messenger who is to start to-morrow morning, and who will travel via Wesel. The steps which have been taken are not enough. There must be two companies of artillery at Mayence, to act with the two first divisions of the Rhine Corps of Observation. By the 10th of March there must be two companies and four

---

[1] Appendix No. 3, p. 294.   [2] *Correspondance*, No. 19,762.
[3] *Ibid*. No. 19,880.

batteries for the two divisions. It is contrary to the practice of artillery to put the matériel in one place and the personnel in another—all should be together. Therefore it is of the first importance that these 17 companies should get there. Should it happen that the Erfurt route becomes unsafe and that some of the enemy cross the Elbe, these companies would have to go to Cologne, and in any case they must recross the Rhine. Since they have no wheeled transport with them, they will have no difficulty in making their way—there are plenty of roads.

I must have states for the artillery drawn up in columns, so that from day to day I may see where the convoys are. These states have been supplied in such a way that I am unable to judge which of the convoys are liable to be cut off. It is probable that just at first nothing will be able to get through from Magdeburg to the Oder, and possible that soon communication between Frankfurt and Magdeburg will no longer be maintained. Thus the two Corps of Observation must in the last resort depend only on Mayence, while the artillery and engineers, the generals and officers, must all come from the interior.* [1]

(iii.) ORDERS FOR EUGÈNE BEAUHARNAIS

There was nothing to help towards the elucidation of the papers which follow. They were scrawled on un-numbered sheets,[2] with neither date nor heading, and it seemed at first almost impossible to guess what they were

---

[1] Appendix No. 4, p. 296.
[2] See the specimen page reproduced (p. 42).

about. A key to the riddle was, however, furnished by the
following letter which we reprint from Napoleon's published
correspondence.

** Napoleon to The Viceroy of Italy, commanding in chief
the Grand Army at Leipzig* [1]

TRIANON, 12 *March* 1813.

My son,

I have sent my aide-de-camp, Brigadier-General Flahault,
to talk to you about the position of affairs, and to explain to
you my plans and how I wish you to make use of your army
corps, on the lines which I have already communicated to
you in my various letters. When he has been with you for
twenty-four hours, send him back to me with all the particulars which may help me to form an opinion on the
general position.   NAPOLEON.*

The occurrence of the letters " V.R. " in our manuscript
showed that Prince Eugène Beauharnais was concerned. It
soon became clear that Flahault's notes were, in fact, a dictated draft of the orders to the Viceroy of which he was the
bearer. A further study of Napoleon's printed correspondence [2] showed the sort of instructions which the Emperor
was sending to his stepson at this time, and by collating these
instructions with Flahault's *brouillon*, it gradually became
possible to decipher the manuscript—though not, it must be
confessed, without a considerable amount of guess-work.

The circumstances may be briefly recapitulated. Eugène
—always addressed by Napoleon as " mon fils ", in compliment, we must suppose, to his mother, whom the Emperor had divorced a few years before—had been in December
1812 left in eastern Germany, in command of the remnants
of the army which had escaped from Russia. The Cossacks,
whom the French had learnt to fear during the retreat from
Moscow, were not for the time being in a position to press
the pursuit beyond the Vistula. Eugène was thus able to
profit by a temporary breathing space, in friendly (or it
would perhaps be more correct to say in *subject*) territory,

---

[1] *Correspondance*, No. 19,701.

[2] Letter No. 19,702, in which Napoleon transmits his written orders
to Prince Eugène on the day that Flahault was sent with his verbal
directions.

during which he could consolidate his scattered and attenuated forces. But in February 1813 fresh trouble arose. Bands of Cossacks began to penetrate into Germany, and the Prussians, encouraged by the weakness of the French forces, took heart of grace and rose in revolt. Thus it came about that early in March, Eugène (who according to Thiers [1] had then only some 10,000 men at his disposal) was forced to leave Berlin, and at the moment of which we write he was heading for Leipzig with a Prussian army not far behind him. All this, of course, thoroughly upset the Emperor's plans. He had determined, in spite of the terrific losses of the year before, to carry the war once more into Russian territory, and he characteristically refused to recognise the difficulties which beset the small remnant of the army which he had left behind him. He wished to start operations on a line as far east as might be, and in his endeavours to persuade the Viceroy to hold that line, we can see that he was prone to magnify the numbers which his lieutenant had at his disposal for this purpose, and to minimise those of the enemy.

In the event Napoleon did not succeed in preserving the line of the Elbe. That river was crossed by the Cossacks under Tettenborn, and Hanover was for a time overrun. The invaders were, however, dislodged by Davout before the Emperor himself appeared upon the scene. This incursion had the effect of retarding his operations, and instead of starting, as he hoped to do, about the 1st of April, he did not leave Paris till the 15th, and his first battle (Lützen) was not delivered till May 2.

The original orders, as already stated, are on loose sheets of paper without any indication of their sequence. We have assumed that they are complete, and have endeavoured so to place them as to make a continuous document. It is nevertheless possible that some sheets may be missing and that they were not all dictated at the same time. The reader can, however, form his own opinion on these points by a study of the original notes which are printed sheet by sheet with our translation.

In his letter to Prince Eugène of March 13 (*Correspondance*, No. 19,712) Napoleon states that Flahault had left

---

[1] Book xlvii. 326.

Paris for Leipzig on the previous day. The orders would probably therefore have been dictated on March 11.

The sketch map which accompanies this section will serve, by showing the position of the principal places mentioned, to make the orders intelligible. They constitute, of course, only a fragment of Napoleon's plans, but may help to throw some fresh light on the preparatory phase of the 1813 campaign.

(11 *March* 1813)

* Flahault is to leave for Leipzig, where he will probably find the Viceroy. He will go to Wittenberg, or to Magdeburg, should the Viceroy have moved thither in response to my orders.

The object of his mission is as follows : The Viceroy has informed me of his retirement from Berlin to Wittenberg. This was contrary to my wishes, which were that he should base himself on Magdeburg. I wrote on the 2nd to General Lauriston [1] in order to explain my intentions. The letter reached him on the 6th of March, the Viceroy having left Berlin on the 4th. I wrote also to the Viceroy on the 5th,[2] but he will not have received my letter till the 9th. The

[Flahault] parti[ra] p[our] Leip[zig] où il tr[ouvera] p[robablement] le Vice Roi il ira à W[ittenberg] ou à M[agdeburg] si en c[onséquence] de m[es] ordres il s'e[st] porté sur M[agdeburg] voici l'objet de la mis[sion] le V[ice] R[oi] [m']a ap[pris] sa re-[traite] de B[erlin] sur W[ittenberg] ce n'était p[as] mon int[ention] elle était qu'il s'ap[puye] sur Mag[deburg] j'ai écrit le 2 au gé[néral] Lau[riston] p[our] lui faire con[naître] m[es] int[entions] la le[ttre] est arr[ivée] le 6 mars le V[ice] R[oi] était part[i] le 4 de B[erlin] j'ai écrit au V[ice] R[oi] le 5 aussi il n'aura reç[u] ma let[tre] que le 9 je n'ai écrit que le 5

---

[1] *Correspondance*, No. 19,641. The Comte de Lauriston was at this time in command of the new *Corps de l'Elbe*. He afterwards became a Marshal of France.

[2] *Correspondance*, No. 19,664.

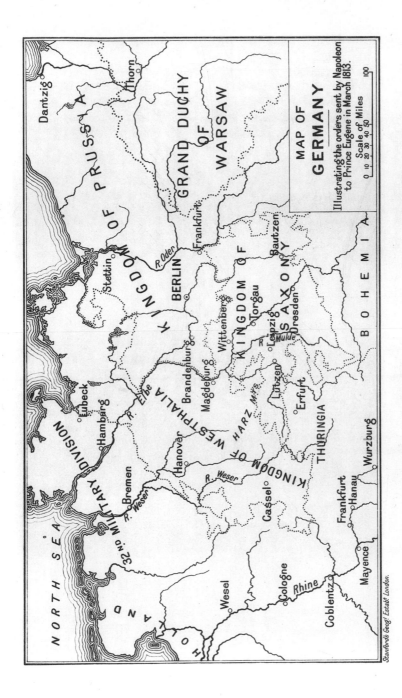

MAP OF
GERMANY

Illustrating the orders sent by Napoleon
to Prince Eugène in March 1813.

Scale of Miles
0 10 20 30 40 50   100

Stanfords Geog.¹ Estab.¹ London.

reason why I only wrote on the 5th was that it was necessary that my letter should be ciphered ; but I take it Lauriston will have written to him on the 7th, and thus the Viceroy will have been able to carry out my orders and to march by the left bank to Magdeburg. I merely informed Lauriston of my plan in outline, explaining to him that the Viceroy should cover the 32nd Division [1] and the river Elbe, and that he should cover Wesel and not Mayence. I am annoyed that in his letter of the 2nd he never said a word on such important matters as these.

My letter to the Viceroy [2] will have given him my plans in detail. He should have the cipher, unless he has lost it ; it is the one used by the Prince de Neuchâtel. If he had lost it, he can only learn my plans through Lauriston. I explained this to Haxo,[3] who

parce q[ue] j'avais bes[oin] de chiff[rer] ma lettre mais je sup[pose] que Lauriston lui aura écrit le 7 et qu'ain[si] le V[ice] R[oi] aura pu remplir mes intentions et se porte[ra] par la rive gauche sur Magdeburg je n'ai fait con[naître] à Lau[riston]mes intent[ions] que légèrement en lui disant que le V[ice] R[oi] devait couvrir le 32ᵉ D[ivision] et la ri[vière] et devait couvrir W[esel] et non May-[ence] je suis mécontent que dans sa lettre du 2 il n'ait dit aucun mot sur des ch[oses] si imp[ortantes]

ma lettre au Vice Roi [lui] d[onnera] détails là-dessus il a ce chiffre ne l'a t-il pas perdu c[elle] du P[rinc]e Neuchâtel s'il avait perdu le ch[iffre] il ne conn[aîtrait] que par Lau-[riston] mes inten[tions] je l'avais dit à [H]axo qui

---

[1] The *32ᵉ Division Militaire*, *i.e.* that part of northern Germany which with the towns of Bremen, Hamburg, and Lübeck was annexed by France in 1810.

[2] *I.e.* Napoleon's letter of March 9 (*Correspondance*, No. 19,688), in which he deals with Prince Eugène's letter of March 2.

[3] General François Benoît Haxo, commanding the *Corps du Génie*.

must have met the Viceroy on the 8th or 9th, telling him that I could not deal with such important matters except in cipher. Flahault should therefore be sure that he thoroughly understands my despatches and should explain them to the Viceroy.

The movement towards Mayence lays open to the enemy Holland, the Scheldt, Westphalia, and the 32nd Military Division —it hands over to the Cossacks a large portion of the Empire, with 15,000 horses in the Cavalry depots, and the line of defence which covers Wesel. The Viceroy, with the 35th and 36th Divisions, the four divisions of the Elbe Corps of Observation, and the Guard Division, is to establish a camp a mile in front of Magdeburg, demolish its buildings, and quarter one Division in its streets.

He should protect his camp with two redoubts. We must begin to make war in earnest. Entrenched in such a camp and supported by Magdeburg, with its garrison of 20,000 men, he would have some 80,000

a dû rencontrer le V[ice] R[oi] le 8 ou le 9 en lui disant que je ne pouvai[s] pa[s] s[ans] ch[iffre] f[aire] conn[aître] des choses si importantes le but donc de Fl[ahaut] est de bien comprend[re] mes dépêch[es] et les fair[e] conn[aître] au V[iceroi] le mouv[ement] sur May[ence] découvre la Holl[ande] l'Escaut la W[estphalie] la 32e D[ivision] M[ilitaire] et livre aux Cossaques une gr[ande] part[ie]de l'Empire et donne les dépôts de Cavalerie [et] 15,000 che[vaux] [et] la ligne qui couvre Wesel. Le V[ice roi] avec le 35e et 36e D[ivision] les 4 D[ivisions] du Corps d'ob[servation] de l'Elbe la d[ivisi]on de la Garde prendra un camp une lieue en av[ant] de Magde[burg] dém[olira] les maisons et baraque[ra] [les] rues d'une

d[ivision] qu'il couvre le camp de 2 red[outes]. Qu'on commence enfin à f[aire] la g[uerre] renf[ermé] dans ce camp app[uyé] à Mag[deburg] place dont la g[arniso]n seule ex[cède] 20,000 h[ommes] ce qui dit que

men and guns. He could scarcely be driven out by the whole of the Russian army, and the Russian army is now before Dantzig and Thorn and the Austrians, and in the valley of the Oder. 6000 cavalry sabres have already been got together, and Bourcier[1] has promised 12,000 more in March. From a position on the right bank, the Viceroy threatens Brandenburg and Stettin, and can fall on the enemy should he attempt to cross the Elbe. His position is such that, while giving him time to get his army together, it will enable him to win every engagement.

General Reynier[2] with the 7th Corps will hold Dresden as long as he can, and will then fall back on Torgau. Torgau is a strong position

80,000 y seraient bien avec de l'artillerie toute l'armée Russe ne peut pas l'en forcer et l'arm[ée] Ru[sse] est devant Dan[tzig] [et] Thorn et les Autric[hiens] et les plaines de l'Oder. Déjà 6000 h[ommes] de la cav[alerie] sont ralliés et Bour[cier] ann[once] 12,000 p[our] mars de cette posit[ion] sur la r[ive] dr[oite] menaçant Br[andenburg] et St[ettin] de tomber sur l'en[nemi] qui voudra passer l'Elbe le V[ice] R[oi] est dans une pos[ition] qui per[met] de rall[ier] son ar[mée] et de remp[orter] tou[tes] les bat[ailles], le Gén[éral] Reynier [avec le] 7ième Cor[ps] gardera Dresde aussi longtem[ps] qu'il le pourra et se rep[liera] sur Torgau. Torg[au] est une pl[ace]

and has a garrison of 6000 Saxons. If Wittenberg is in the same state as it was four years ago, 2000 or 3000 men could be left there, and

forte qui a une g[arnison] de 6000 Sax[ons] [si] W[ittenberg] [est] dans le mêm[e] état qu'il y a 4 ans, on p[eut] y laisser 20[00] ou

---

[1] Antoine Comte Bourcier (1760–1828) a cavalry general of distinction. He was entrusted with the reorganisation of the mounted branch in 1813.

[2] Jean Louis Ebenezer, Comte Reynier. He was afterwards taken prisoner at Leipzig.

guns (light artillery of 12 or 6 inches) could be obtained from Torgau, while care should be taken to guard the small posts on the left bank against the Cossacks by palisaded tambours. Then Bellune [1] can guard the left bank as far as Wittenberg, and the Prince d'Eckmühl with 6 Battalions can guard the left bank from Magdeburg to Hamburg. The King of Westphalia could draw in towards Magdeburg in order to help the Viceroy, if he were to be engaged. General Reynier, when he has crossed the Mulde, will withdraw towards Cassel and Magdeburg, and his right will hold the Hartz mountains.

It would be an absurd idea even to suppose that the enemy could shut themselves up on the Rhine, leaving in their rear a body of 100,000 men ; for the forces of Reynier, the King of Westphalia, of the Viceroy, of the Prince d'Eck-

3000 h[ommes] en faisant venir can[ons] de Torgau petit calibre [pièces de] 12 ou de 6 [pouces] en ayant soin de couvrir les petits points sur la r[ive] g[auche] par des tambours ser[vant] de paliss[ades] contre les Co[saques] enfin Bellune p[ourra] garder la r[ive] ga[uche] jusqu'à W[ittenberg] le Pr[ince] d'Eck[mühl] avec 6 B[attalions] peut g[arder] la r[ive] g[auche] dep[uis] Mag[deburg] jusqu'à Hamb[urg] le r[oi] de W[estphalie] peut s'ap[procher] de Magd[eburg] pour ven[ir] au sec[ours] du V[ice] R[oi] s'il dev[ait] liv[rer] bat[aille] le gén[éral] Rey[nier] ap[rès] avoir passé la Moldau se v. . . . le général se rep[liera] sur Cassel et Magdeburg sa droite occup[era] les montagnes du Harz

ce ser[ait] avo[ir] d'étranges id[ées] m[ême] que de supp[oser] qu'ils s'enferm[ent] sur le R[hin] laissant derrière eux un corps de 1000[00] car [les forces de] Reynier du [Roi de] W[estphalie] le V[ice] R[oi] du Pr[ince] d'Eck[mühl] et

[1] Marshal Victor, Duc de Bellune.

A PAGE OF NAPOLEON'S ORDERS

Dictated to Flahault in March 1813

mühl and of Bellune, make up at least that total. This disposition of our forces will make all safe and will give me time to wait for the month of April. By the 1st of April the Prince of Moskova will be at Wurzburg, and will occupy the outlets of Thuringia. The enemy must be aware that the Guard has returned to Frankfort, that the Italian Corps is on its way from the Tyrol, and the 2nd Corps of the Rhine is on their other side. If therefore they were to shut themselves in between the Elbe and the Rhine, they would be, like the Prussians, outflanked. Nothing of the sort can happen, but what is probable is that a corps will advance towards the lower Elbe, and seeing it is not held,

will contain Magdeburg and throw small forces against Hamburg, Cassel, and Hanover. If the Viceroy is already in position the situation can be easily rectified, wherever it may be that he may have to retake the river from them, since Holland and the 32nd Military Division must be protected.

Bellune ne font pas moin[s]. Cette pos[ition] peut tout assurer et me donne le temps d'att[endre] avril. Au 1er av[ril] le Pr[ince] de M[oskova] sera à W[urzburg] [il] occup[era] les déb[ouchures] de la Th[uringe] au 1er av[ril] l'ennem[i] ne peut pa[s] ignorer que déjà la g[ard]e [est] reve[nue] à Fr[ankfort] que le corps d'It[alie] est en marche du Tyrol et que le 2e corps du Rhin est de l'au[tre] côté. Si donc il s'enferme entre l'Elbe et le R[hin] ils seraient com[me] les Pruss[iens] débordés. Rien de tout cela n'es[t] poss[ible] mais ce qu'ils feront c'est qu'un corps s'appro[chera] de la basse Elbe et voy[ant] tout dég[arni]

masquera Mag[deburg] et jette[ra] des partis sur Hamb[urg] Cassel et Ha[novre] si déjà le Vice Roi a pris sa pos[ition] remède à tout. Dans quelq[ue] p[ar]t qu'il trouve l[a] R[ivière] à reprendre puisqu'il faut couvrir la H[ollande] la 32e D[ivision]

If the enemy were to reach Leipzig, they would not have reached our line of communication through Mainz; and if he did, there is an alternative line through Cassel, and there is always the line from Cassel to Coblenz and to Wesel. That is the advantage of getting nearer home; every place then becomes a shelter, and every road a communication; while an advancing enemy has one line only, and if he loses that, loses all.

Lauriston must have spoken to the Viceroy and Haxo and quoted the Emperor's letters. It is Lauriston's cipher. He can communicate by its means with Reynier and with the Major-General.[1] It is therefore Flahault's duty to consult with him and help him to understand the code.

m[ilitaire] l'ennemi qui serait à Leip[zig] ne serait pas arrivé sur la ligne d'op[érations] de May[ence] parce qu'il y a celle de Cassel. Il y a toujours la ligne de Cassel à Coblence et Wesel voilà l'avan-[tage] de s'approcher de chez soi c'est que tou[tes] les pl[aces] sont des retraites et sont des com-m[unications] tandis que l'en[nemi] qui av[ance] n'en a qu'une et perd tout s'il la perd.

Lau[riston] doit avoir dit au V[ice] R[oi] et [H]axo et cité les lettres de l'Em-p[ereur] c'est le chiffre de Laur[iston] il com[munique] par le ch[iffre] avec Rey[nier] et le m[ajo]r Gé-n[éral] c'est donc par me prenant p[our] conf[érer] avec lui et lui f[aire] b[ie]n comp[rendre] le système. . . .

[The three pages which follow are written on different paper from those which precede them. Since they repeat to some extent the previous orders, it would seem that they may have been dictated by Napoleon on a different occasion.]

The Viceroy arrived at Wittenberg on the 7th; the

[Le Vice Roi est] arrivé le 7 à Witten[berg], la garde

[1] Berthier, Prince de Neuchâtel, Chief of the Staff.

Guard left for Leipzig on the 9th. I hope he will have received my letter telling him to leave about the 10th. Even if he has not acted on it, he will know that I wish him to move towards Magdeburg. If General Flahault finds him at Magdeburg, he will inspect his corps, and return by post-chaise to tell me the state of affairs. He must make full inquiries as to the best route to take. He will observe whether the commandant of Erfurt has palisaded the gates of the town with a tambour, in such a way as to enable the garrison of the citadel to hold the town by means of detached posts and to ensure its safety against a flying column. I cannot believe that the Viceroy could be driven out (of Magdeburg) unless the enemy were able to bring 150,000 men against him. He has got plenty of munitions, and as many guns as he could wish—150 in Magdeburg, 92 more in rear of the town. How could the enemy venture to place himself astride of the river, against an adversary with 80,000 men ? He would

[est partie] p[our] Leip[zig] le 9. J'espèr[e] qu'il aura reçu ma lettre lui com[mandant de] partir v[ers] le 10 il n'en aura rien fait. Il aura app[ris] par [cela] qu'il doit se porter sur Mag[deburg]. Si le gén[éral] Flah[aut] le trouve à Mag[deburg] il verra son corps reviendra m'ins[truire] de l'état des choses en diligence s'il passe il s'inf[ormera] bien de la route qu'il d[oi]t prendre il verra [si] le command[ant] d'Erf[urt] a palissadé par un tambour les portes de la ville afin que la g[arnis]on de la citadelle occupe par des postes la ville et en réponde contre des troupes légères. Je ne comp[rends] pas que le V[ice] R[oi] pu[isse] être forcé à m[oins] que l'enn[emi] ne marche avec 150,000 h[ommes] encore ay[ant] des mun[itions] et des p[ièces] tant qu'on en veut 150 pièces dans Mag[deburg] 92 à l'arr[ière] ville. Com[ment] l'enn[emi] oserait-il se mettre à che[val] sur la riv[ière] contre un enn[emi] de 80,000 il se ferait p[ren]dre

run the risk of being taken in detail. When the enemy has discovered my plan, he will take up a position opposite Magdeburg, keeping the town under observation. He will thus lose time, while we shall gain the time that is essential to us.

Besides, the Viceroy will have 12,000 mounted men —as many as the enemy. In a theatre of operations which has been stripped as this has, they will never be able to cut him off from his camp at Magdeburg, and if he were worsted he would always have Magdeburg behind him. They are not likely to give battle under such conditions. There is however a chance that the enemy, wishing to establish himself on the lower Elbe, might unmask Magdeburg, but he will be afraid of doing this, since it would weaken his forces. If, however, in the last resort, Magdeburg had to be evacuated, the Second Division of the 1st and 2nd Corps could be left there under General Haxo, while the army of the Elbe could cover Cassel and Hanover, preserving communication

en détail. Quand l'enn[emi] aura [connu] ce projet [il] se mett[ra] vis à vis obs[ervant] Mag[deburg] et perdra du temps nous gagnerons le temps que (nous) devons gagner.

enf[in] le V[ice] R[oi] aura 12,000 h[ommes] de Cav[alerie] tout autant qu'en a l'enn[emi] sur un théâtre aussi détruit [on] ne pour[ra] p[as] le coup[er] de son camp [à] Magd[eburg] le V[ice] R[oi] battu serait sous les glacis de Magd[eburg]. On ne donne p[as] des bat[ailles] de cette manière. Il y a une chance c'est que l'enn[emi] fera des étab[lissements] sur le bas Elbe il faudra démasq[uer] Mag-[deburg] on craindra [de] le faire. Il faud[ra] des forces et s'aff[aiblir] il craindra de diminuer ses for[ces] enfin dans tout état de choses Mag[deburg] évacué on y laisserait la 2e D[ivisi]on du 1er et [du] 2e Corps sous les ordres du Gén[éral] [H]axo et l'armée de l'Elbe couvrirait Cassel et Ha-[novre] gard[ant] les com-

with Wesel ; and by April the 1st there would be a large army on the enemy's left flank, were he to debouch by Dresden.

Flahault must bring back to me a clear statement of the position and tell my son that I am vexed not to have had a clear and true account. Things have been happening, I want to know all about them.

I have told him of the V cypher, which is the one I mentioned in my letters of the 5th to the 11th of March.

The V cypher is different from the army cypher, I wish to be able to make use of it for important communications. General Lauriston, Reynier, and the others have got it. Be very careful that, if it were found out, a V.A.M. cypher (which can never be found out) should be substituted for it.*

m[unications] avec Wesel gardant le 1er avril une grosse armée sur son flanc gauche s'il débouchait par Dresde.

Flahault m'app[ortera] des états claires et dira à mon [fils] que je suis mécontent [de ne pas avoir] une relation claire et vraie il y a eu des affaires j'en veux savoir des détails.

Je lui ai com[muniqué] le sy[stème] V la même que mes lettres du 5 au 11 mars [sont] chargé de f[aire] connaître, un chiffre autre que le chiffre de l'arm[ée] général le système V afin que [pour] l'important je puisse m'en servir le Gé[néral] L[auriston] [et] R[eynier] et les autres l'ont. Tenez bien alors s'il était surpr[is] — instruisez pour le changer [pour] un ch[iffre] de V. A. M. [?] qui ne peut jamais être surpris.

THE BATTLE OF HANAU
(October 29, 1813)
From a picture by Horace Vernet

IV

THE LUSIGNY NEGOTIATIONS

(i.) FLAHAULT'S REPORT TO THE EMPEROR
(FEBRUARY 1814)

DURING the campaigns of 1813 Flahault was present at all the principal engagements and won considerable distinction; notably at Hanau (October 29), when after their defeat at Leipzig the French had to cut their way through an enemy force which barred their retreat to the Rhine. He was then *Général de Division*, and had recently become *Comte de l'Empire* and *Commandeur* of the Legion of Honour.

Before this he had been employed in the responsible office of French Commissioner at Neumarck, where he was charged with the duty of settling the details of the armistice, signed on June 4, which divided the first from the second Saxon campaign of 1813.

In November Flahault returned with the Emperor and the remnants of his army to France. In the January following they set forth once more, for that short but amazing campaign in which for more than two months Napoleon succeeded in disputing the possession of his capital with forces four or five times as numerous as his own. In this campaign, we are told [1] that Flahault was three times wounded, though he seems never to have been put out of action.

It will be remembered that after the battle of Leipzig Napoleon had shown a disposition towards peace. Pourparlers began with the famous interview at Frankfort in November 1813, between Metternich and the Baron de St. Aignan, brother-in-law to Caulaincourt, who had not long before replaced Maret, Duc de Bassano, as French Minister

[1] John Cam Hobhouse, *Letters by an Englishman resident at Paris during the Last Reign of Napoleon.*

for Foreign Affairs. These led to nothing, though Napoleon afterwards alleged that he was then offered terms—the *bases de Frankfort* — which he could and would have accepted, if they had not been subsequently withdrawn. Negotiations, however, continued, and in February 1814 they became focussed at Châtillon-sur-Seine, where a Congress had been brought together. Here the Allies, in whose favour the tide was now steadily flowing, formulated a definite stipulation that if France wished for peace she must return to her old limits of 1791. This demand spurred Napoleon to a fresh military effort, and within a week he succeeded by a series of brilliant victories in entirely changing the aspect of affairs.

It was after the battle of Montereau (February 18) that Prince Schwarzenberg, who was in command of the Austrian army operating against Napoleon, sent Prince Wenceslas of Liechtenstein to the Emperor's headquarters at Troyes for the purpose of obtaining an armistice.[1] No progress had been made at Châtillon, and Napoleon thought, no doubt, that an opportunity was here presented of securing, under the guise of a temporary cessation of hostilities, the terms on which he hoped to base a final peace. He acceded, therefore, to the Austrian proposal so far as to appoint Flahault as his representative at the negotiations, which it was arranged were to be held at Lusigny, only a few miles from his own headquarters. The Allied Commissioners were de Languenau (who fell ill and was almost immediately replaced by General Ducca) for Austria, Schouvaloff for Russia, and Rauch for Prussia.

We will now give the Instructions which Flahault received from the Emperor. These have been translated from the French version as it appears in the Napoleonic Correspondence, for the publication of which under Napoleon III., Flahault was one of those responsible. It seems probable that he himself supplied the information, and that the document which follows had been dictated to him by Napoleon, for (as we shall see) Flahault expressly states that he was given verbal instructions only.

[1] February 23, Thiers, lii. 383.

*Instructions for General Flahault, Aide-de-camp to the Emperor [1]

BOURG DES NOËS. TROYES
24 *February*, 1814.

Flahault will repair to Lusigny with the authority of the Chief of the Staff to negotiate, conclude and sign an armistice between the two armies.

It must be thoroughly understood that, as long as the Conference is in progress, there shall be no armistice; so that both the French and the Allied troops will be at liberty to fight and to move where they will. The armistice will only become operative from the moment that it is signed and ratified by both parties. This is a matter of the first importance, for I do not intend to be fettered by these negotiations.

In the present state of affairs, and while a new situation is in course of development, I cannot consent to a cessation of hostilities unless I am sure that it will lead to peace. I can only be sure of peace, if there is agreement to accept the basis suggested by Prince Metternich at Frankfort in the presence of Count Nesselrode and Lord Aberdeen.

General Flahault has seen the copy of the *Moniteur* which was suppressed, so he is aware of that basis. This is first condition.

Stress should be laid by General Flahault on the letter in which Prince Schwarzenberg has asked for an armistice and has insisted on the necessity of peace, as also on the reply made

[1] *Correspondance de Napoléon Ier*, No. 21,359.

thereto by the Prince de Neuchâtel, and on the letter in which Prince Schwarzenberg reiterates his request for an armistice. This correspondence will be placed in General Flahault's hands.

The preamble should be somewhat in the form which follows :

" The High Contracting parties, after bringing their plenipotentiaries together at the Congress of Châtillon for the purpose of discussing a treaty of peace on the basis proposed at Frankfort, have now, in order to facilitate the aforementioned negotiations and to save the public from further distress resulting from the war, resolved to arrange for a suspension of hostilities, and with this object in view they have appointed Messrs. —— as their commissioners."

Difficulties will be raised as to this condition. General Flahault will say that without it, nothing can be done. He will point out that at a moment like the present when a surprise attack may be launched at any moment on their rear and when other forces are hanging on to their flanks, the enemy cannot expect us to hold our hand. He will point out that it is only on the Frankfort basis that peace can be accorded.

General Flahault will refuse to commence the discussion until this condition has been assented to. If they have not got the necessary powers, these gentlemen can easily send to ask for them. General Flahault will remain dumb until this is done. When it has been done, General Flahault will propose a cessation of hostilities on the following lines :

The Allies to evacuate the 18th, 19th, and 7th

Military Divisions, as well as the department of the Aube. They will assemble their forces in Franche Comté, in Alsace, and in Lorraine. They will evacuate all Belgium, and their line will be along the Meuse from its mouth to its source, passing thence between Vesoul and Langres, and ending in Switzerland near Franche Comté. During the entire period covered by the suspension of hostilities, our garrisons will receive supplies. The question of supply for the Northern garrisons, since these are to be withdrawn, will not arise. In the case of the Meuse garrisons, we can make the necessary arrangements to supply them from the side of the river which will be once more ours. In the case of the garrisons in Lorraine, Alsace, and the Franche Comté, French Commissioners will be appointed for the purpose of supplying these with provisions. Geneva, being included in the 7th Division, will be evacuated.

General Flahault must be straightforward, and at the same time firm. " We are aware of the enemy's strength ", he might say, " but not much is known about ours ". We are joined every day by 10,000 men equipped and armed, of whom 2000 are cavalry soldiers. Our army is upwards of 300,000 strong. The Old Guard, composed of men with not less than sixteen years' service, has been tripled, and now forms three divisions, each of sixteen battalions. All the men who had served in the Guard and had been retired, have been recalled. This has so much increased the strength of the Guard, that it now numbers some 30,000 men. Though it is true that we have nearly 50,000 men who are not yet equipped, most of the equipment is on its way, and is expected at any moment. These men, moreover, have excellent weapons and are quite efficient. Finally the entire population of France has been excited to the point of frenzy by the unspeakable outrages committed by the Cossacks, and it is all under arms. Besides this, we believe that the chances are all in our favour, and it is only because we are determined to make peace (if it can be negotiated on the Frankfort basis) that we are now ready to consider a suspension of hostilities.

As to prisoners, it must be stated that up to the present we have taken 50,000, while we have captured eighty guns and eight hundred wagons. When all these matters have been settled, General Flahault may add that in view of the fact that the surrenders of Dresden and of Dantzig were concluded in accordance with the laws of war, they will be ratified. It follows that their garrisons will be brought back to the Rhine: there to be exchanged, agreeably to the terms of those surrenders, for an equal number of the Allied troops.* [1]

An account of the conference which ensued has been given by Thiers,[2] but the full story would appear never to have been made public. It is contained in two documents left by Flahault amongst his papers. The first and shorter of these ends with the words " Tel est le dernier état de choses à la connaissance de Sa Majesté ", which makes it sufficiently clear that it was written by Flahault for the Emperor at the time. The second document (in which the first is included and amplified) is corrected in Flahault's hand. The paper on which it is written bears the watermark " 1844 ". It

[1] Appendix No. 5, p. 297.   [2] Book liii. pp. 402 ff.

was evidently prepared for historical purposes, and may
have been given to Thiers, with whom, as we shall see
later (*infra*, Part VII.), Flahault had several communications
when that historian came to write of the events in which
his informant had played a leading part.

We reproduce the later account below, with the addition
of the final paragraph from the earlier document which deals
with the attitude of Austria during these abortive negotiations. This paragraph contains the most interesting commentary on the proceedings, for it shows that the Austrian
Emperor had been genuinely anxious to come to terms, and
that Napoleon had only himself to blame when, by pushing
his father-in-law to extremities, he brought disaster upon his
own head.

An Account of the negotiations at Lusigny : February 24 to 28, 1814. By the Comte de Flahault

* The first communications concerning the
negotiations for this armistice took place on
the 24th of February 1814. The French Commissioner, the Comte de Flahault, had received
merely verbal instructions, these, however, were
given by the Emperor in person. He was
expressly ordered to inform the Allied Commissioners that his authority to treat was
dependent on the condition that it should be
definitely stated in the preamble of the armistice,
that the aim of the convention was to facilitate
a peace on the Frankfort basis. The Commissioners of the allied armies replied that this
proposal went beyond their instructions, and that
a condition of this sort could not be inserted in
a treaty for an armistice, whose purpose was
merely to arrange a suspension of hostilities and
to fix the line to be occupied by the opposing
forces during the continuance of that suspension.

Nevertheless it was only after a discussion (the length of which indicated to the French Commissioner a keen desire to arrive at a settlement) that they decided to refuse to negotiate on this basis, and to send a message to their headquarters with the news of this unexpected difficulty and a request for further instructions.

The messenger returned on the 25th. He brought instructions to the Commissioners to refuse this preliminary condition as being in the sphere of diplomacy, and to confine their efforts to the military question of a suspension of hostilities. He was directed to add, that the propriety of this course was clearly indicated by the fact that the English were not represented at the negotiations.

The Emperor Napoleon accepted this view and sent orders to the French Commissioners to commence negotiations. Valuable time had, however, been lost. The anxiety caused by our successes at Champaubert, Montereau, etc., had had time to become allayed. It seems probable that if the Comte de Flahault had held more extended powers at the outset, he could have secured better terms. The Emperor, however, had given him the most stringent orders not even to enter into any discussions without a preliminary agreement on the question of this preamble.

The discussion of the line of demarcation then commenced, and the Commissioners prepared the following line : The old frontier between France and the Low Countries from the sea to Maubeuge, thence the road through Avesnes to Laon, thence to Rheims. From Rheims to Châlons, whence the line was to follow the Marne as far as St. Dizier. From there down to Colombey,[1] crossing the road between Troyes and Chaumont, thence by Châtillon-sur-Seine, Montbard, and Autun, rejoining the Saône at Chalon, following this river as far as Mâcon, and the road from this town to Bourg. Thence rejoining the Rhône at Lagnieu and following it as far as St. Genix, where that river rejoins the ancient boundary of Savoy, which, in accordance with this arrangement, would have been occupied by the Allied troops. As to the duration of the armistice, it was suggested that it should be for a fortnight, with a respite of six days from the time when it might be terminated.

The principal point of disagreement lay in the fact that His Majesty did not wish that either Belgium or Savoy should be included in the Allied sphere. After five hours' discussion, which brought agreement no nearer, the Commissioners decided to send a messenger once more for the purpose of obtaining further instructions on this point.

The messenger left on the 25th and returned on the 28th. He brought back to the Allied Commissioners new instructions. These, however, made no change in the conditions, already refused by the Emperor, as to Belgium and Savoy, while the line of demarcation was only slightly altered by establishing it as follows :

The ancient boundaries of the Low Countries from the sea to the outskirts of Maubeuge, thence a line crossing the Sambre near that place and rejoining the Avesnes road, leaving the town on

[1] Colombey des deux Églises, Haute-Marne.

the right, and thus reaching the road to Paris which was followed as far as Laon. From Laon by the main road to Rheims, from Rheims by the road to Châlons-sur-Marne, thence up the Marne, passing near Vitry, St. Dizier, and Joinville, as far as Chaumont. From Chaumont by the road to Langres, from Langres the road to Dijon, from Dijon by the canal as far as Mâcon, from Mâcon by the road to Bourg-en-Bresse, from that place to the Rhône by the Ain bridge at Lagnieu, and ascending the river as far as St. Genix. Thence the line was to pass to the ancient frontier of Savoy, which used formerly to separate the province from France, and was to follow this frontier along the Alps and the boundary of the Valais [1] as far as the Swiss frontier.

All the places on the line of demarcation were to be occupied by the troops of the Allied powers. The armistice was to apply also to the armies in Italy and to that of Lord Wellington. In these armies the line of demarcation would be fixed in accordance with the *status quo* at the moment when the messenger should arrive. The armistice was to continue for a fortnight, plus six days after its formal termination.

This line might for the most part have been accepted, but in the matter of its termination in Switzerland, it was quite impossible to arrange it agreeably to the Emperor, who had given explicit directions to the Comte de Flahault in no event to yield territories in the occupation of French troops. In the departments bordering on Switzerland the inhabitants had had some successes

[1] Now Vaud.

against the Allied troops. They would consequently have suffered, had they been placed by the armistice in the power of the enemy. At this stage the Emperor made up his mind to attack General Blücher, and on the morning of February 27th he wrote to General Flahault the following letter :

The letter which Flahault intended to, but did not, insert in this account, was no doubt the second of those which are printed below (p. 63).

The departure of the Emperor had two unfortunate results, one that the French Commissioner was left without instructions, the other (which was more serious) that the command of the force acting against the Prince de Schwarzenberg and the main army of the Allies devolved in consequence upon one of his Marshals. The secrecy with which he hoped to veil this change could not be maintained, and the feeble manner in which our forces made their attack at Bar-sur-Aube at once revealed the Emperor's absence. The Allies once more assumed the offensive, drove back the French forces, and the Prince Schwarzenberg after returning to Troyes declared the negotiations at an end. Thus the last chance of re-establishing peace and of maintaining the Imperial power faded away.

(The paragraph which follows is taken from Flahault's contemporary account of these negotiations.)

General Ducca, the Austrian Commissioner, has been frequently in confidential communication with General Flahault. He has expressed on behalf of the Emperor of Austria a sincere desire to put an end to the war. He has asserted that his master never had the intention nor the desire to go to Paris, and has cited the slowness of Prince Schwarzenberg's advance in proof of this statement. He has often repeated that, if only a cessation of hostilities could be arranged, he had no doubt that peace would soon be concluded; that such was the wish of the Emperor of Austria, whose views leant strongly towards moderation. He recurred to this subject day after day, asking in so many words that the Emperor should receive assistance in his efforts to compass peace.

" Try to arrange ", he said, " that hostilities should cease on the 28th, and make it easy for us to secure peace. I can swear to you that the Emperor of Austria and England both wish that it should be an honourable one for France ". In view of the exchanges which had previously taken place with General Ducca, there was no possibility of misunderstanding such a statement when made by him. At the last, when on the evening of the 28th the Commissioners were putting forward their final proposals, they all agreed that peace depended only on an armistice, and that they were sure it could be concluded on lines which would be satisfactory to the Emperor.*[1]

(ii.) TWO LETTERS FROM NAPOLEON

It was while Flahault was engaged in these negotiations that he received from Napoleon two letters, the originals of

[1] Appendix No. 6, p. 299.

which have been found amongst his papers. The first was duly printed by the Commission of publication with the addendum " Communiqué par M. le Comte de Flahault ". We reprint it here for the purpose of comparison with the second and unpublished letter.

* Napoleon to Flahault

TROYES, 27 *February*, 1814, 7 A.M.

Monsieur le Comte de Flahault,

You gave me no news yesterday. Let me know how you stand. I imagine that the enemy commissioners may have come nearer to accepting your line. You must on no account give way with regard to the districts of which we are in occupation, such as Bourg, Mâcon, Chambery, and Châlons-sur-Marne. This must be well understood by these gentlemen. How would it appear to the inhabitants of these places if they found themselves deserted ? Should, however, the difficulties of the situation point to their keeping Langres and Chaumont, you should agree, since they are in actual possession of these places. Try to bring matters to a conclusion ; it is the only way towards peace. I have already let you know that you might allow them to cross our line to the extent of keeping Breda and all Dutch Brabant. Lastly if, in order to reach some measure of agreement, you find yourself compelled to abandon the line which has been indicated, be sure that the value of such a concession is appreciated by the Emperor of Austria's aide-de-camp, and try to extract from him a positive undertaking, or some-

thing like one, that his master will consent to make peace on the " basis of Frankfort ".
May God preserve you in his safe keeping.* [1]

N. I.

The second letter, written only two hours after the first, has not hitherto seen the light.

* Napoleon to Flahault

TROYES, 27 *February* 1814, 9 A.M.

Monsieur le Général Flahault,

Try and make the plenipotentiaries think that I left last night to establish my headquarters at Bar-sur-Aube. I am going to Arcis-sur-Aube to operate in rear of Blücher, York, and Wintzingerode, who are advancing towards La Ferté Gaucher. You will appreciate how important it is that the Commissioners and the enemy should not suspect this move. As soon as you have received this letter, send me a courier to inform me how affairs are going.

May God preserve you in his safe keeping.* [2]

N. I.

This presumably is the letter referred to (though not given) in Flahault's story of the negotiations (*supra*, p. 60).

That it was omitted from the *Correspondance* is perhaps not surprising, since it shows that the Emperor, under cover of his negotiations, was deliberately trying to deceive the enemy, and to steal a march upon them. We shall see later on (Part XIII.) that when the Napoleonic correspondence came to be published, care was taken to omit anything " de nature à porter atteinte à la considération du Grand Homme", and this was assuredly a document deserving of such a description !

[1] Appendix No. 7, p. 303, and *Correspondance*, No. 21,389.
[2] Appendix No. 8, p. 304.

Napoleon did move to Arcis-sur-Aube on February 27, but (as Flahault has explained) his absence from Bar-sur-Aube was soon discovered, while his presence " sur les derrières de Blücher " did not produce the hoped-for results. That astute old general eluded his clutches and managed to join forces with the Northern army of the Allies under Bulow.

The disasters of Craonne and Laon followed soon afterwards, and on March 31 Paris capitulated.

V

THE FIRST ABDICATION

Flahault's Letters from Fontainebleau

* You should certainly write your memoirs of the campaigns, but you are such a lazy person! You must see how very interesting in your old age would be the story of your stay at Fontainebleau at the time of the First Abdication, and of those midnight conversations which you told me were so fine, so noble, so resigned.[1]

On my side I would contribute an account of affairs in France when he landed at Fréjus. I would show how his very faults—alarming as they were for the rest of Europe— were the source of some of the most glorious episodes in the history of the French race.

From the way things are now going I am convinced that, when he has ceased to be, France will mourn his loss. History will perhaps give as his motto those lines of which ' papa ' is so fond :

" Whose sons shall blush their fathers were thy foes." *[2]

So wrote Madame de Souza to her son in January 1816.[3] She had remained in France after Napoleon's fall, but

---

[1] *Ces conversations la nuit, que tu me mandois être si belles, si nobles, si résignées.*

[2] " Say, shall my little bark attendant sail,
Pursue the triumph and partake the gale ?
When statesmen, heroes, kings in dust repose,
Whose sons shall blush their fathers were thy foes ;
Shall then this verse to future age pretend,
Thou wert my guide, philosopher and friend ? "

The *Essay on Man*, towards the end of which these lines occur, was addressed to Bolingbroke, but Pope's eulogy of that statesman's character was scarcely endorsed by the verdict of history.

" Papa " (M. de Souza) was a fervent admirer of the poets, and spent many years of his life in re-editing the famous *Lusiads* of the Portuguese poet Camöens. It is, however, clear from the Flahault papers that Souza's acquaintance with the English language was of the slightest.

[3] Bowood Papers.

Flahault, to whom the Royalist atmosphere of Paris in the latter half of 1815 was scarcely congenial, had sought refuge in England, where he was soon to find a wife and a home.

It was a pity that Madame de Souza's suggestion was never acted upon, more especially as regards that episode to which she particularly refers. Flahault was at the Emperor's side throughout the weeks which immediately preceded the departure for Elba in April 1814. He was likewise with him during the shorter period which covered the Second Abdication at Malmaison in 1815. He apparently was one of the few persons admitted on these two occasions into any sort of intimacy with Napoleon, and could have told us much about his sayings and doings during those moments of adversity, much which would have been of the highest interest to those desirous of forming a true estimate of Napoleon's character. There are, however, amongst Flahault's unpublished letters to his mother a few which were evidently written at the time of the First Abdication. They show the part which Flahault played, and serve to reflect something of the atmosphere of Fontainebleau at that memorable time.

During the campaign of France (February and March 1814) Napoleon, whose forces were greatly inferior in numbers to those of the Allies, was compelled to operate on the flank and rear rather than in front of the enemy. But while he was thus engaged, their main body marched on the capital, and Paris had capitulated before he could come to its rescue (March 30). The Emperor rode forward, accompanied by Flahault amongst others, through Fontainebleau, and as far as Athis, only to learn that he was too late. The party then returned to Fontainebleau, whence (during the next three weeks) Flahault sent the notes from which the following extracts have been taken.

* Flahault to Madame de Souza

FONTAINEBLEAU, 1814.
[? *March* 30].

My God, how anxious I am at the prospect before us ! I cannot believe that the enemy will

not get into Paris. What will they do ? What
shall we do ? We have given them a good beating, but only a part of their army was involved.[1]
At any rate we showed them that there were still
Frenchmen worthy of the name, for our soldiers
behaved splendidly. . . . How interminable this
month seems to be. . . . I must leave you to
get a little sleep.

[? *April* 4.]

A great event is in the making—may it be the
means of restoring quiet to my unhappy country.
If the foreigners are as good as their word, it will
do so.[2] I have behaved all through, as I shall
always do, in a straightforward manner. I have
said what I thought, however hard it might seem.
I have been an eye-witness and a sharer in events
of the greatest moment. The *Grand Écuyer* [3] has
revealed himself in a finer character than ever.
What a noble soul !

April 7.

Well, all our efforts and our determination
have been thrown away. After persuading the
Emperor to make the greatest sacrifice which a
man could make, we must now bow the head under
a foreign yoke and put our country to shame. It
can never more be said " I am proud to be a
Frenchman ", and for my part I have thoroughly

[1] This seems to be an allusion to the action at St. Dizier on March 26
when Napoleon defeated and took 4000 prisoners with 30 cannon from
Wintzingerode (Thiers, liii. p. 617).

[2] The allusion is evidently to the Conditional Abdication, signed on
April 4, by which the Emperor surrendered his claims to the throne in
favour of his son. This was rejected by the Allies, and Napoleon was
forced, on April 7, to make his abdication unconditional.

[3] Caulaincourt, Duc de Vicenza.

made up my mind to keep nothing but my nationality, and to take no part in the affairs of a country so degraded as ours.

Please send this letter somehow or other to Henriette [1]—you might wrap it up in some silk—anyhow try and get it to her.

April 8.

The Emperor has given us full liberty to serve the new Government. But how could one bring oneself to serve it, with our standards draped in black, with the shame which we have earned added to the hatred which was felt for us before. Well, I rely on you to arrange things so that I may live in my own country and by your side. This for me is indispensable.

I don't know if *M. Bégo* [2] will condescend to help me in this matter, for since all these things have happened, he has shown me no sign of life through our mutual friends. I do not grudge him his good luck. I trust that he may always enjoy it—but I have my doubts. We are giving ourselves over to the enemy bound hand and foot.

I shall in all probability follow the Emperor to the place where he is to go. I feel I ought to do this, and if duty calls I have no second thoughts. When there comes an end to all these doings (which some call acts of infamous treachery and others describe as noble deeds), he who emerges without a stain on his escutcheon may consider himself a lucky man.

[1] *I.e.* Queen Hortense, who is always thus referred to in Flahault's letters to his mother (*vide* Part XII.).

[2] Talleyrand : he also is frequently thus disguised in the Flahault-Souza correspondence (*vide* p. 234).

[*April*] 9.

I have not sent in my resignation, and since you wish it—in spite of the signs of mourning now covering our standards, in spite of the depths to which we have sunk—I will continue to wear my uniform and to give my services to my country. I have served it faithfully throughout the time which is past. I had some share in saving it from a civil war, though in so doing I was acting against my own interests. But what are personal interests when set against those of one's country! I would have given my life to save it from the humiliation which has come upon it—but, alas, this humiliation is complete.

I shall stay here till the Emperor leaves. I shall even go with him, if he wishes it, to the place where he is to embark, after that I shall come back to you. I asked him (as I felt bound to do) to give me his opinion and his wishes as to the line of conduct which those who were attached to his person should now follow. "I desire, Sire, to preserve your good opinion and so I should like to have some guidance for my conduct, and this no one but your Majesty can give me." His reply was that "he wished us to be happy, that anything which might prevent this would be contrary to his desire; that all was over, and that every man owes himself to his country. . . ."

I have sent a short but carefully expressed letter to M. de T[alleyrand]. I have asked him to do the best he can for me. I don't know whether he still takes an interest in me—his own good fortune does not seem to excite in him consideration for others! At any rate, I can

look every one in the face, and I can hold my
head erect. It is not every one who is in a
position to do so!

[*April* 15.]

Here is my act of adherence [1]—I will only go
with him if he insists upon it. It is hard to refuse
a thing which you feel inwardly prompted to do,
when moreover it is something which an honourable (if unfriendly) critic might fairly blame you
for leaving undone. . . .

What a miserable time it has been here, my
dear Mother, you can scarcely imagine it! Well,
it must have an end. . . . Send this letter to
Henriette, if a good opportunity should present
itself.

[*April* 16-19.]

I expect I shall accompany the Emperor either
to the frontier, or to the place where he is to
reside. This is a duty which I mean to perform,
for my feelings towards him are not estranged by
his misfortunes. He had intended, and it was
his desire to keep me with him, but I told him
that I owed myself to you before every one.

The insults which are being showered on him
by the public press, draw me nearer to him. I
have spent with him most of the nights, since the
blow fell,[2] and never have I seen a calmer or more
courageous spirit. " I regret nothing," he said

---

[1] *Mon adhésion*—*i.e.* to the new Government. The Comte d'Artois
had arrived in Paris on April 12. Flahault's *soumission* was presented according to Masson on April 16. We can guess that his
mother would have lost no time in sending it in, and have therefore
dated this letter April 15.

[2] *Depuis ces derniers jours.*

to me, " and I should have been a sadder man
than I am, if I had had to sign a treaty taking
from France one single village which was hers on
the day when I swore to maintain her integrity."

When at last I have fulfilled this final duty, I
shall (if the Russians have delivered us from their
odious presence) return to your side, without
shame and without regret, and ready if Henriette
will agree to make a happy life with her. . . .
Have you sent her my letter ? . . .* [1]

*   *   *   *   *   *

The last extract is important and suggests some interesting
speculations. The letter from which it is taken will be found
in extenso in the Appendix. It has no date, and can only be
placed by means of such evidence as its contents afford.

A clue is given by Flahault's enquiry as to the note for
Queen Hortense which he had enclosed in a previous communication to his mother. Two of these were sent, on April 7
and April 15, but the allusion must, I think, in the light of
the context, be applied to the second. When Flahault says
that he has been with Napoleon *depuis ces derniers jours*,
he must surely be using the words in the same sense as
does Ségur when he refers to the Treaty of Fontainebleau,
signed by Napoleon on April 13.[2] The Cossacks, who were
bivouacked on the Champs Élysées, had only entered Paris
on March 31 ; and there could have been no question of
a " deliverance from their odious presence " until the Treaty
had been concluded. We can therefore date this letter
with some confidence as written between April 16 and 19.

Flahault lays stress on Napoleon's fortitude under adversity, and denies all reports to the contrary. He could
surely not have done so, if it was true that Napoleon had,
on the night of April 12, attempted to put an end to his life by
taking poison. This allegation was first made definitely in
the *Manuscrit de 1814* published by Baron Fain in 1823. It

[1] Appendix No. 9, p. 304.
[2] *Un Aide-de-camp de Napoléon*, 1813, 1814, 1815, p. 536.

would appear to rest mainly upon the evidence of one Hubert, a valet, who was on duty with the Emperor at the time. The story was afterwards taken up and embellished, notably by Thiers, who relates the incident with much picturesque and apparently circumstantial detail (Book liii. p. 803), and by degrees it seems to have obtained general acceptance. The tale of a young servant, admittedly on night duty for the first time, might well under all the circumstances be received with caution. It is also worthy of remark that the prescription—the same, we are told, as that which killed Condorcet twenty years before—proved in this instance quite inefficacious ; for Fain expressly states that Napoleon rose and dressed at his usual hour on the morning of April 13. Lastly, both Maret and Caulaincourt, who are stated by the same authority to have been present, are known to have afterwards denied the whole story.

If our deductions as to the date of Flahault's letter are correct, it would afford an implicit contradiction of the tale from one who was present at Fontainebleau throughout, and who had spent most of the nights there in close proximity to Napoleon.

Madame de Souza could scarcely have urged her son (less than two years afterwards) to write for posterity an account of his midnight conversations with the Emperor —" si belles, si nobles, si résignées "—had either of them believed this tale (*supra*, p. 66).

Then there is the evidence of Captain Ussher, who commanded the *Undaunted* which conveyed Napoleon from Fréjus to the Island of Elba. Ussher relates how, soon after the formation of the Provisional Government, one of Napoleon's entourage had suggested suicide to him as a way out of his difficulties. To this the Emperor replied, " Yes, I might do so, but it would do no good to my friends, and it would delight my enemies ".[1] Now Ussher must have got this story from one of the officers who accompanied Napoleon to Elba, and it seems in the highest degree unlikely that such a conversation would have taken place in May if Napoleon had really tried to poison himself in April 1814.

[1] *Oui, je puis faire cela, mais ceux qui me veulent du bien ne pourraient pas en profiter, et à ceux qui me veulent du mal cela ferait plaisir* (*Napoleon's Last Voyages*, edited by T. Holland Rose, p. 113).

Finally we have John Cam Hobhouse, who tells us of a similar discussion that took place at Malmaison between "Count —— " and the Emperor in June 1815. Napoleon on this occasion is quoted as saying that " whatever might happen he would not attempt to anticipate the fate that might be in store for him, by a single hour ".[1] Was a man who had deliberately attempted to take his own life in the preceding year likely to use words such as these ?

The valet's tale has, we believe, always been considered suspect. We venture to suggest that in the light of the passages quoted above it should be definitely discredited.

*   *   *   *   *   *

Amongst Madame de Souza's closest friends was the Comtesse d'Albany, as the widow of Charles Edward Stuart, the Young Pretender, preferred to call herself. The two women appear to have kept up a constant correspondence, a part of which has been printed in *Le Portefeuille de la Comtesse d'Albany*. We will give one of these letters, which helps to fill in some of the blank spaces left by Flahault. It reveals the fact that there had been a difference of opinion between mother and son, the former in her worldly wisdom being obviously anxious that Charles should at once embrace whole-heartedly the new régime—while Flahault had with difficulty been dissuaded from sharing his master's exile.

Madame de Souza to the Comtesse d'Albany

PARIS, *May* 1814.

* Since I last wrote to you, my best of friends, I have been through a terribly anxious time. I was indeed for the space of three weeks in such an agony of mind that I could not wish my worst enemy to suffer as I did even for a day ! I was so much afraid of Charles's high principles. You

---

[1] *Quelque chose qui arrive, je n'avancerai pas la destinée d'une heure* (*Recollections of a Long Life*, i. p. 292).

will realise how well founded was this anxiety.[1]
Anyhow all is now arranged for the best. He has
been straightforward and open with his former
General, who has released him from his oath.
He first sent in his adherence [2] and then stayed
with him till the eve of his departure. He afterwards came back here, was presented to the
Princes, and now we are living once more a
wonderfully lazy existence, which seems to him
delightful, but which I do not want to see too
much prolonged. This is between ourselves, and
please do not even mention the matter when you
reply. He is so fond of you that he might ask
to see your letter, and if he were to read my
guilty thought he would never forgive me. He
really imagines himself to be past all forms of
ambition, and he believes that even at his age one
knows what one will think ten years hence. . . .* [3]

Madame de Souza then goes on to suggest that her friend
should make interest for Charles with M. de Blacas, *le favori
de notre nouveau Roi.* But Flahault was no party to any
of these proceedings, and his mother schemed in vain, for
during neither the First nor the Second Restoration would
he consent to have any dealings with the Bourbon dynasty.

It seems that his meeting with " the Princes ", of which
his mother told her friend, was not an unqualified success.
In Hobhouse's *Recollections* [4] we find an account of a conversation with the Duc de Berri, which presumably took place
on the occasion in question.

" What rank have you held ? " asked the Duke. " I was
aide-de-camp to the Emperor Napoleon," Flahault replied.
" In what campaign did you serve ? "—" In all." This was

---

[1] *Je craignois si fort les vertus de Charles ; vous comprenez jusqu'où
mes craintes pouvoient aller.*
[2] *Son adhésion*—*i.e.* to the new Government.
[3] *Le Portefeuille de la Comtesse d'Albany*, L. G. Pélissier, 1902, p. 193.
[4] *Recollections of a Long Life*, J. C. Hobhouse, i. 251.

more than a Bourbon Prince could stand, and the Duc de Berri
" turned up his nose and walked off ". It was a bad beginning from Madame de Souza's point of view, and explains
perhaps why (according to the same authority [1]) Flahault
was afterwards " cut at court ", an insult which evidently
rankled in his mother's mind.

Hobhouse must have taken a strong fancy to Flahault,
whom he describes as " a charming person, who has been
wounded nine times ".[2] He is frequently mentioned both in
his *Recollections* and in the *Letters*,[3] to which we shall have
occasion to refer later.

We will give in Hobhouse's own words an account of
another interesting conversation, which must have taken
place almost immediately after Napoleon's departure for Elba :
" The other evening at Talleyrand's General Flahault and
Pozzo di Borgo had, in the presence of Talleyrand, a long
argument as to the military talents of Napoleon. Flahault
. . . contended that his last campaign was his masterpiece,
and asserted that in all he had never more than 75,000 troops
under him and his Generals—excepting Soult and Suchet
from the number. Pozzo di Borgo said his movement to
St. Denys [4] was that of a madman : he was sure to lose Paris.
Flahault said that the occupation of Paris by the Allies was
contemplated by Napoleon, who thought they would weaken
their army so much to preserve it, that they would be more
easily attacked afterwards. ' He ought to have known the
people were against him,' rejoined Pozzo di Borgo. ' To
be sure,' said Flahault, ' he did think Paris would have
stood true to him, he did not take treachery into account.'
He did not know that Talleyrand had corresponded for several
days with the Emperor of Russia ! " [5]

From another English visitor to Paris a glimpse may be
obtained of Madame de Souza's *salon* at a later period of the
same year. We quote from Lady Bessborough's letters to
Lord Granville Leveson Gower.

---

[1] *Recollections of a Long Life*, J. C. Hobhouse, i. 249.
[2] *Ibid.* i. 251.
[3] *Letters from an Englishman resident in Paris during the Last Reign
of Napoleon.* Anonymous, 1816.
[4] *Sic*, but Hobhouse surely meant St. Dizier.
[5] *Recollections*, i. 121.

" We went to Mme de Souza's which was very pleasant. Sebastiani, Macdonald, and Talma were there. After they went, Madame Ney and General Flahault sang several pretty romances, and he ended with some old national songs, which drove Madame Girardin, Madame Ney, and Madame Souza herself out of the room—all really, or affecting to be, frightened. The latter perhaps was, for she is not *en bonne odeur* at Court, and it is wonderful *comme on jase de tout ici*. I have already had three notes to enquire whether it was really true that General Flahault had sung *La Marseillaise* and *Ça ira*." [1]

A week later Lady Bessborough, after dining with a party at Véry's, seeing Mlle. Mars act in "La Coquette corrigée", and attending a concert at the Duchess of Wellington's, " ended at Madame de Souza's, where there were some Marshals, some Savants and some singing ".[2] Flahault and the pretty wife of Marshal Ney were again the principal performers, and Lady Bessborough amusingly recounts how she succeeded in obtaining a surreptitious glance at one of their *romances* which they had tried to conceal from her. It was entitled *Le Vaillant Guerrier français*, and the reason for the mystery became apparent when she discovered that the subject of the song was the invasion of her own country, and each verse ended with the refrain :

> *Les guinées des Anglais dans nos bourses,*
> *Les charmes des Anglaises dans nos bras.*

We may wonder if Lady Bessborough ever recalled this incident to Flahault after his marriage, three years later, to a lady of British birth and considerable fortune.

It is clear that Flahault's conduct at this time would of itself have destroyed any hopes of advancement which his fond mother may have founded on Louis XVIII. and M. de Blacas. But such manifestations of loyalty to the Napoleonic régime were then allowed to pass. It was only after the Second Restoration, when the 'Ultras' had begun to assert themselves, that they provoked reprisals.

[1] *Lord Granville Leveson Gower*, ii. 509.
[2] *Ibid.* ii. 511.

NAPOLEON AS EMPEROR
From a drawing by Innocent Goubaud

VI

THE SOVEREIGN OF ELBA

A CONVERSATION BETWEEN NAPOLEON AND
TWO ENGLISH MEMBERS OF PARLIAMENT IN
DECEMBER 1814

In the following pages will be found an account of a hitherto
unpublished conversation with Napoleon on the island of
Elba.

The time must have hung somewhat heavily on the
Emperor's hands during his enforced residence on the island,
and he was always ready to talk, whether with Sir Neil
Campbell, the British Commissioner,[1] or with casual visitors.
Four such interviews have already been made public, in
whole or in part : with Lord Ebrington on December 6
and 8, 1814;[2] with Lord John Russell on December 25,
1814;[3] with Mr. John Macnamara on January 13, 1815;[4]
and with a Mr. Douglas in January 1815.[5] The present
interview was anterior in date to all these, and took place on
November 18, 1814, Napoleon's interlocutors being Messrs.
Venables-Vernon and Fazakerley.

George Granville Venables-Vernon was the eldest son of

[1] *Napoleon at Fontainebleau and Elba*, by Sir Neil Campbell.

[2] *Memorandum of two Conversations between the Emperor Napoleon
and Viscount Ebrington at Porto Ferrajo* (James Ridgeway), 1823.

[3] There is a short account of this, taken from Lord J. Russell's *Diary*,
published in Spencer Walpole's *Life* (vol. i. p. 74), and a longer one
written subsequently to Mr. Van de Weyer was privately printed in
1868.

[4] In *Recollections of a Long Life* (J. C. Hobhouse), vol. i. p. 178.

[5] An account of this interview was given in February 1815 to the
Marquis of Huntly (afterwards Duke of Gordon), and by him to Albert
Gallatin, United States envoy to France (1813–27). It is printed in
the *Diary of James Gallatin* (Heinemann, 1914), pp. 53 ff. Douglas
probably was Frederick Sylvester North Douglas, the son of Sylvester
Douglas, Lord Glenbervie, who was member for Banbury from 1812 to
1819.

Edward Vernon, sometime Archbishop of York. He later took the name of Harcourt, on succeeding to the Nuneham estates, which on his death in 1861 passed to his brother William, the father of the famous Liberal statesman. George Vernon was a member of the House of Commons, as was his companion, Mr. Fazakerley; so were also Lord Ebrington, Lord John Russell, and Mr. Douglas. All, except perhaps Douglas, were Whigs. It seems that members of this party were more anxious to seek audiences with the Emperor than the Tories, while Napoleon (though apparently in this case unaware beforehand of the politics of his visitors) was perhaps more prone to unbosom himself to members of the party amongst whom he had some sympathisers, than to those who, as pledged supporters of the Tory Administration, were directly responsible for his downfall.

The circumstances under which the Vernon-Fazakerley interview came to be given are sufficiently explained in Vernon's covering letter. This is addressed to Lord Lansdowne—Henry, the third marquis—who was later to be known as "the Nestor of the Whigs". Lord Lansdowne had held the post of Chancellor of the Exchequer in the Ministry of All the Talents (1806-7), and was already counted amongst the leaders of his party ; he was besides a personal friend of both Vernon and Fazakerley.

There was therefore a double reason for confiding this document to his charge. Perhaps its compilers may have expected him to undertake its publication, but if so they were disappointed, for it remained buried for upwards of a century amongst a mass of correpsondence at Bowood and was only rediscovered a few years ago.

The conversation (as stated therein) lasted, like the Ebrington interview, nearly four hours. Of both, therefore, only a portion can have been actually recorded, but the salient facts of each have no doubt been preserved in the accounts which survive.

It is not without interest to place them side by side, and to see how far Napoleon repeated himself in the two interviews.

We may note particularly the similarity in the Emperor's account of his admission to the Mohammedan faith and in his

G

explanation of the failure of the Russian campaign. In each
we may further observe his admiration of the position held
by the British House of Lords, his desire to build up a new
French aristocracy in emulation of that existing in England,
his curious receipt for securing colonies with a black population by means of polygamy, and his distinction between the
pride of Englishmen and the *vanity* of his own adopted race.

But when this had been said one may marvel, as his
visitors did in both instances, at the grasp of his mind, at
the accuracy of his memory, and at the readiness with which
he was willing to discuss the epoch-making events in which
he had been so recently a protagonist, with men whom he had
never seen before.

WHITTON TOWER, *March* 1, 1815.

My dear Lord,

I have endeavoured to comply with your
request that I should give you some account of
our recent visit to the " Sovereign of Elba ", but
you will readily conceive that I can pretend only
to furnish you with an imperfect sketch of a long
and very desultory conversation, which lasted
nearly four hours, and during which he talked
occasionally for a considerable length of time
without intermission ; for he was by no means
inquisitive, except on the subject of Egypt, but
very willing to enter freely and largely upon
almost any topic that was proposed to him. I
had heard formerly from M. de Metternich that
this was his disposition, "qu'il aimait beaucoup à
causer, et à se faire écouter"—this was all that we
could wish, and our part therefore in the dialogue
was almost limited to the endeavour of leading
him, as opportunity offered and civility permitted,
to speak on such matters of interest as occurred
to us at the time.

I have wished to retain in French such passages of our conversation, as I recollected most distinctly. With Fazakerley's assistance I could probably remember more, especially of the first part relating to Egypt, which was entirely addressed to him. What regarded European politics and the events of the campaign, 1813–14, was chiefly addressed to myself; as I told him that I had been for some time at the Head Quarters of the Allies at two different periods of the campaign, and he might suppose therefore that I was more accurately informed of the events that occurred there than F., who had not been on the Continent, at least not in those parts of it, during that year.

Perhaps at a future day, when he returns to England, I may be enabled to improve my narrative and you shall then have the new edition. In the meantime, if you find any amusement in these recollections of our audience, I shall not regret having occupied two mornings in committing them to paper for your perusal.— Yrs. very truly,   G. V. VERNON.

The Marquis of Lansdowne.

I landed at Porto Ferrajo on November 18, 1814, accompanied by Mr. Fazakerley, and furnished by the kindness of Sir Neale Campbell [1] with a letter of introduction to General Count

---

[1] Colonel (afterwards General) Sir Neil Campbell (1776–1827). He had been sent to accompany Napoleon as British Commissioner to Elba.

Bertrand.[1] He, however, as we learnt with much disappointment on our arrival, was confined to his bed by illness. I wrote to him, therefore, enclosing Sir N. C.'s letter, and soliciting his assistance to obtain us the favour of presentation to Napoleon. I mentioned that I had been acquainted with the Empress Josephine, and had met at Malmaison the Viceroy and Queen of Holland—that I was a cousin of L^d: Holland, and, as well as my companion, a Member of Parliament. I added that he had travelled in Egypt and Palestine, and concluded by suggesting that we had engagements at Florence, which made an early audience very desirable to us.

I received in a few hours a note from the Governor, General Count Drouot,[2] who informed me that Count Bertrand had transmitted to him my letter, regretting that his illness would prevent him from making our acquaintance ; he assured me that he would place it *sous les yeux de l'Empereur*, and would give me an answer as soon as possible. He desired us in the meantime *de disposer de lui*, if he could be of any use to us during our stay in the island. We dined at a French *traiteur*'s newly established, where there was a daily Mess of most of the French officers— Napoleon had till recently kept a table for them, but in consequence of the non-payment of his promised pension he had reduced his kitchen

---

[1] Count Henri Bertrand (1770–1844), an officer of Engineers who succeeded Duroc as *Grand Maréchal du Palais*. He remained with Napoleon till his death.

[2] Count Antoine Drouot (1774–1847). He had gained great distinction during the Napoleonic campaigns and accompanied the ex-Emperor to Elba as governor of the island. At the Restoration he was put on his trial, but acquitted.

establishment to the service of one man and a boy. We slept in wretched lodgings, tormented by fleas.

Early the next morning Count Bertrand's secretary called upon us to offer us any assistance we might desire. I asked him to accompany and introduce us to the Governor. We found him a plain, well-mannered soldier, apparently between fifty and sixty, and were received with great civility. I expressed our anxiety for an early audience, which he said he would endeavour to procure for us, but that hitherto the Emperor had not given answers to such applications in less than forty-eight hours. He informed us that he was about to attend him to his country house, five miles distant from the town. As we returned from the Governor's with Count Bertrand's secretary, I said to him, in conversing about Napoleon : " On dit qu'il est beaucoup engraissé depuis son séjour ici."—" Oui, mais si j'avais été à sa place, je me serais engraissé avec un coup de pistolet "—he followed this observation with much complaint of the solitude and inanity of their new existence.

We determined to walk immediately along the road which leads to St. Martin, Napoleon's Villa ; where we should be certain to see him pass soon, and might have a chance of obtaining an interview. We conversed by the way with some fine old soldiers of the Imperial Guard, who talked to us willingly, and did not complain of their situation. I learnt however afterwards, that great precautions were taken to prevent desertion to the continent, which was not infrequent. There were altogether about 800 troops in the island, most of whom were of the Guard, the rest newly levied.

We had arrived within a quarter of a mile of St. Martin, when Napoleon overtook us in an open carriage, accompanied by Count Drouot, who sat uncovered. He was escorted by a few Dragoons and two or three men dressed like Mamelukes; but one of them was a black, and Mr. Fazakerley suspected the others not to be more genuine. We stopped and made a bow, which he returned, and apparently inquired of Count Drouot if we were the newly arrived English. The carriage passed on, but in a few minutes one of the Dragoons was sent back to inform us that the Governor had ordered the sentry at St. Martin to allow us to enter its enclosure, if we pleased. We now anticipated the success of our walk, and proceeded towards the house, near which the Emperor had alighted, and was giving directions to some workmen who were making a road to it, and dressing the adjacent ground; for he had placed his new residence in a retired situation, in the centre of a semicircular range of hills, which extend from each side of the Port towards the middle of the island. These rise behind it, covered with ilex, cork trees, olives, and pines, while its front windows look over the intermediate valley upon the beautiful port and the steep cliffs which shelter it from the sea. It is built with the greatest simplicity, has six windows in front and two stories.

The Governor was waiting for us, and told us that, since we had left him in the morning, he had written to me to inform me that I might be presented in the evening, and that Mr. F. would have been then informed that he should have an audience the next day, but that as we were anxious to be received as soon as possible, the Emperor would allow us an immediate interview. He was then advancing to meet us, and we were presented to him. He said to me that he understood my cousin, Lord Holland, was travelling in Italy, enquired what his plans were for the winter, and then asked about Mrs. Fox. He next questioned me about my seat in Parliament, what place I represented, what was the right of voting, what the number of my constituents, and whether any and what influence preponderated among them—then, addressing Mr. F., he said he believed he had been in Egypt, and proposed to us to walk into the house, where we should see some Turks and Mamelukes. We accordingly followed him through a small entrance hall into the dining-room, the walls of which are painted in fresco after some of Denon's engravings, representing Egyptian landscapes with Turks and Mamelukes on horseback, etc. He then addressed numerous questions to Mr. F. respecting the places he had seen and individuals whom he had known in that country, showing much accuracy of memory, and talking with much interest on this subject. He asked if they ever speak now of himself—Mr. F. answered, "Frequently," and that he knew a man who had given his name to one of his children.

"Et en général, qu'est - ce qu'on dit des Français ?—

On les admire beaucoup, Sire, comme militaires.—

Mais comme administrateurs ?—

On les aime mieux que les Turcs.—"

He smiled and began describing to us the battle of the Pyramids, which was a *beau spectacle*. He had experienced much difficulty at first from the superiority of the Mameluke cavalry, but had discovered that, although ten French Dragoons were unequal to ten Mamelukes, and 50 to 50, and 100 to 100, by moving them in stronger parties their compactness and discipline assured them the advantage. He had been obliged to conciliate the religious prejudices of the Turks, who had a very inconvenient aversion to be governed by Christians—for this purpose he caused an assembly of them to be convened, and desired them to consider of some arrangement by which scrupulous consciences might be reconciled to a Christian Government.

* " I am a good Catholic, but no bigot, and something had to be done to conciliate those people. Some were more difficult to deal with than others—the Turks have their Jansenists and Molinistes just as France used to have—but after weighing the matter, they all agreed to suggest to us two conditions. One was that the whole French army should forego the use of wine, the other that we should all be circumcised. I answered them that from force of habit the drinking of wine had become, for Frenchmen, a necessity of health, and as regarded circumcision, we believed that we were perfect as we stood, and there was no reason why we should be cut about. I asked them to come together once more and to think of some other means of adjustment. They had another discussion, and eventually they gave up the idea of circumcising us and insisted only that, for every bottle of wine that a Frenchman was allowed to drink, he should be expected to perform some good action. ' With pleasure, gentlemen, I readily agree '— and I thereupon began to build a mosque." * [1]

He enquired about the recent massacre of the Mamelukes which had happened when M. Fazakerley was at Cairo, and then informed us how he had quelled an insurrection there.

* " One had to take strong measures to crush it at the start. I knew that it was the priests who had instigated the people to rise. I caused two hundred of them to be assembled (they were Turkish abbés, belonging to the priesthood). I had them all shot within twenty-four hours, and as soon as people saw that weakness did not enter into my ideas of administration they became very fond of me." *

. Having dwelt some time on the subject of Egypt, he said to me : * " What party in Parliament do you belong to ? "

" I have been, Sire, in that which is opposed to the Government now in power."

" You cannot then have much to do ; your party is now powerless against the Government."

" It is quite true, Sire, that recent events have strengthened it considerably, while the opposition,

---

[1] Napoleon seems to have been fond of relating the circumstances of his conversion to Mohammedanism. Cf. his conversation with Captain Ussher on the *Northumberland* in 1815 (J. H. Rose, *Napoleon's Last Voyages*, p. 160), and his interview with Lord Ebrington.

for its part, has been somewhat discredited by the predictions they made as to the probable outcome of the war in Spain—which fortunately proved not to be true. They thought our troops would be driven out of the Peninsula."

" They should have been — my marshals suffered from divided counsels." [1]

" There was a general belief that Your Majesty would have gone there to take the command yourself."

" There were occurrences which prevented my going."

" I knew, Sire, that Your Majesty was carrying on the war in other directions, but most people had made up their minds that you would have left no stone unturned to drive us out of the Peninsula before you attacked the Russians."

" The Emperor of Russia compelled me to make war on him. There was a secret article in the Treaty of Tilsit that he was to break off relations with England. He did not do so; he failed in his engagement to me."

" Does Your Majesty think him an able man ? "

" He is not wanting in intelligence, but he is treacherous and cunning. It would seem that some people now believe he intends to re-establish the Kingdom of Poland—only those who do not know the facts could ever expect such a thing. The Emperor would never dare, even if he desired to do so. He would never dare give up the Russian provinces to Poland, unless Smolensk were given back to him. It will never be done

[1] Ney and Soult were at daggers drawn throughout the 1809 Peninsula campaign.

by him; but he does not even want to do it.
Quite the reverse, we shall soon see that he means
to lay down the law in Poland more than ever.
I like the Poles, they are brave, loyal, and good
soldiers. I was very anxious to re-establish them
as a nation. It was with that object that I took
the Illyrian provinces from Austria. They were
not necessary to France, but I wished to have
something which I could afterwards exchange
with Austria for Galicia, which I intended some
day to take from them in order to re-establish
Poland in its integrity."

"Perhaps if Your Majesty had remained in
Poland last winter instead of going to Moscow,
things might have turned out differently." He
hesitated and I continued : "Your Majesty perhaps believed that once at Moscow you could dictate terms, that the Emperor would be frightened
into submission ".

"It is true I might have relied to some extent
on such an expectation, and besides, I had no
reason to expect the fire at Moscow, such a thing
had never occurred in history before. It was
the Cossacks who burnt it; they dislike the
Russians. They set fire to the villages everywhere."

"I believe, Sire, that it was countenanced by
the Government, at any rate I know that the
Governor of the town, Rostopchin, gave the
example to the rest. An English general, who
was with him at the time, told me that he saw
him setting fire to his own house, which was
sumptuously furnished. He started with his
wife's room, where he set fire to the bed,

and he afterwards did the same in the other apartments."

" I know, it was General Smith " (I did not interrupt him, but it was Sir R. Wilson) ; " I know all about it. The Governor was in league with the Cossacks ; he had all the fire-engines taken away. I did all I could to stop the fire. I was on the Kremlin ; but the wind was too strong."

" I saw, Sire, at Paris the Abbé de Pradt, who was, I believe, Your Majesty's minister in Poland at that time. He told us one evening at Madame de Staël's how, during a conversation he had with Your Majesty, when you had stopped at Warsaw on your way back from Vilna to Paris, Your Majesty said to him, ' But for one man I should have been master of the world '. He said that that man was himself, that he should have shown more energy in making things move in Poland, that he had not managed to extract from that country all the resources he might ; in a word, that he was responsible for the ill-success of the campaign."

" It is true that, when I stopped at Warsaw to write some letters, this man came to report to me the progress of certain matters which I had entrusted to his care, and he went on to talk to me on military affairs. Conceive the Abbé trying to teach me ! I never spoke to him at all. I was writing at the time to my minister at Paris, and I gave him, amongst other instructions, the order to recall Monsieur l'Abbé. It may be that later on in Paris I said something about his incapacity. You say you saw him at Madame de Staël's ? "

" Yes, Sire."

" What is she saying about me now ?   Perhaps
at this very moment she is singing my praises
and abusing the Bourbons."

" She never spoke to me about Your Majesty,
and she does not want to antagonise the Government ;   for she has lodged a claim to recover
some money which was owing, I believe, to her
father."

" One must, however, do her the justice to say
that she is not a woman who seeks her own ends."

" I am well aware of that, Sire, and her friends
had so little confidence in her discretion that they
asked her to leave Paris while the question of
the Liberty of the Press was under discussion—
this question is very much to the fore in France
just now."

" I know it is ; but what may be good for you
is not good for France ; in her present condition
a constitution like yours would not suit her.   I
meant to do great things for France, but I always
said I required twenty years ; it would have
required twenty years to work out my plans.
You have a Government which is essentially
aristocratic.   Your aristocracy controls Parliament and can sway opinion ; it actually upheld
the Duke of York against his detractors.   This
sort of thing could never have happened in
France ; she has not got an aristocracy which
can make itself felt.   I tried to form one, but
that was a thing which required time.   Chemists
have a species of powder out of which they can
make marble, but it must have time to become
solid.   In England the aristocracy is revered

and powerful in itself, and if the entire House of
Lords were destroyed at one blow, their children
would soon fill the gap; the nation would scarcely
be a loser. In France our 'tail' is good, our
'head' bad ; in England your head is good, your
tail poor. The two countries differ also in their
national outlook. The English are proud, the
French vain. I attempted too much in their
interest. They would not support me. It was
you Gentlemen who won the day. England
was never so great as she is to-day; it is she who
plays the leading part. But her day will come ;
she will fall like all great empires."

"Your Majesty does not think that this day
will come soon ? "

"I do not know enough about the political
situation in England to form an opinion on this
matter. But meanwhile you will become extremely rich. The peace will enable you to pay
your debts, but you must not count too much
on it, for it will not last long. In order to ensure
a lasting peace Belgium should have been left
in the hands of France."

"But Your Majesty will allow that it has
always been held that the independence of
Holland could only be ensured by a frontier
between her and France."

"There is no necessity for this. The Prussians
will always be on the side of the Dutch against
France ; and besides you can send troops there.
An army of forty thousand English in that country
would be by no means negligible. They are brave
fellows, those English troops of yours ; they are
worth more than the others. Next to them, I

consider the Prussians the best, but I have always found myself able to defeat the Continental troops with very inferior forces—how often have I defeated the Allies between the Rhine and Paris with a mere handful of men. It is unfortunate for Europe that your Government is not a stronger one. If you had had a man like Lord Chatham at the head of affairs, he would have realised that it was a mistake to humiliate France too far. You had already humiliated her enough by saddling her with the Bourbons. She will never give up the hope of regaining Belgium. You will see, there will arise one of these days in the heart of the country, a Libyan wind [1] which will upset everything. For my own part, I am no longer concerned. My day is done—but wait and see. There are five hundred families in France, who are not liked—if you wished to keep her quiet, you should have allowed her to keep her natural boundaries. You know how air which has been too much compressed will burst through anything in order to escape.[2] You will see that war will break out once again on account of Belgium."

" It seems to me, Sire, that France is tired of war. However much she may regret the loss of Belgium, her prime necessity is peace."

" You make a mistake. France is not exhausted. I have always been careful of her

---

[1] *Un vent de Libecci, i.e.* an unhealthy disturbing wind, such as those known as the *simoom, sirocco,* and *föhn.* These winds were (and are still) popularly though erroneously supposed to originate in the great Libyan desert.

[2] Napoleon used the same figure in his conversation with Douglas, adding (as he did here) " Mais ce n'est pas mon affaire—je suis mort " (*Diary of James Gallatin,* p. 54). Cf. also his conversation with Ussher (*Napoleon's Last Voyages,* p. 84).

resources. It was in order to spare France that
I drew soldiers from Germany, Italy, and Spain.
I levied contributions everywhere with the same
object ; I had two milliards of money brought
to France from foreign countries. You would
soon have seen in the provinces a teeming
youth, improved agriculture, flourishing manufactures." * 1

He entered then into details about the progress
of the latter, speaking especially of the cotton
manufactures. He said that some persons concerned in these had recently come to him and
stated their apprehensions of the ruin of their
trade by the competition of the English, who
would insist upon a treaty of commerce dis-
advantageous to France ; that his refusal to make
one such as we wished had been the cause of our
breaking the Treaty of Amiens. I suggested to
him that his own measures at that time appeared
to us so little consistent with the repose of
Europe that we preferred a state of open war to a
precarious peace.

He said " No," that the real cause of our renew-
ing the war was his refusal to make a commercial
treaty agreeable to us ; that he had proposed one
on the principle that a million of French goods
should be exchanged for a million of English, but
that Mr. Pitt and Mr. Addington laughed at this ;
that for his part he had wished to keep the peace
and had not intended to invade his neighbours ;
that we sometimes complained of encroachments
which we compelled him to make. * " Holland,
for instance—it was you who forced me to incor-

1 Appendix No. 10, pp. 307-312.

porate that country with France. I knew that you
had made arrangements with the King of Holland
and the King of Naples to facilitate the importa-
tion of English goods, and that in spite of the
treaties I had made with them. It was I who
held the power; I was obliged to dethrone
my brother.* It was you, too, who compelled
me to occupy Holland after the battle of Jena.
Mr. Fox's Order in Council established a pretended
blockade of the whole coast from Hamburgh to
Brest; this made my Decrees necessary, and the
annexation of Holland."

He was going on, but I interrupted him (which
he civilly permitted) and observed that I thought
Mr. Fox's Order in Council only respected the
mouths of the Elbe and Weser, which were effectually blockaded.

"Vous vous trompez, mon cher," putting his
hand on my arm, and insisting on his statement,
which I admitted on recollection.

He proceeded to canvass the subjects of naval
blockade and right of search; not saying anything new upon them, but stating that these
rights must be the same by sea as by land, and
that we endeavoured to establish a particular
privilege for ourselves which we should deny to
others. He said we might probably be glad to
know that he had not made, as had been supposed,
any private treaty with America, but that he had
met with much firmness in negotiations on the
part of that Government.

* " Now, here is another instance of what I
have just been saying—that you do things yourselves which you will not allow others to do. You

H

have often accused me of ill-treating conquered countries, but look what you have just done at Washington. You have burnt public buildings, and done a great deal of harm to the people."

" I have heard, Sire, that the town suffered a good deal, but I know no details of this business."

" What are people saying about the Congress ? "

" I do not know anything at all about it. It would seem that splendid entertainments are being given at Vienna. I have many acquaintances in that country, amongst others M. de Metternich, who has the honour of being well known to your Majesty."

" Yes, I know him well."

" He seems to me to be very pleasant socially."

" Yes, he has wit, but a man must not lie continually ; he may lie once or perhaps twice, but not always—that is no use.[1] I do not place him very high as a statesman. As Austrian Minister, he made a mess of things ; he should have made peace at Frankfort. Austria never improved her position afterwards. It was the Russians and Prussians who found it to their interest to prolong the war. Italy had already been lost to France, and besides this, Austria was more likely to lose than to gain by going on. Italy is even now a source of weakness to her. Germans are not popular there, and they were already cherishing notions of independence. I had succeeded in imbuing them with some sort of

---

[1] Cf. Douglas interview, where Napoleon uses almost the same words about Metternich.

Talleyrand once said that the difference between the Cardinal de Richelieu and Metternich was that the first never told a lie and deceived everybody, while the second lied to every one and deceived nobody.

instinct of nationality, their young men were just beginning to cherish high ideals; strangers will not be received gladly in that country. England ought to have encouraged these tendencies, and should make the freedom of nations a cardinal principle at the Congress. But Italy will remain quiet—in three or four years' time passions will have calmed down." *

I observed that I thought it would be very difficult to unite into one kingdom so many states, long divided, and very jealous of each other; and then mentioned that I had met the Viceroy [1] at Malmaison, where I had dined with the Empress, who was very civil to me, and I added that her death was much regretted:

" Oui, c'était une excellente femme."

He enquired what would become of her statues and pictures—I said I believed they would be sold to pay her debts.

* " It is a pity for France's sake. I had given her some very beautiful things. She ought not to have got into debt. She had a large income, and, besides, I used to pay her dressmakers' accounts every year." *

He asked how long I had stayed at Paris. I said two months, and expressed admiration of what he had done for his capital; and I added that travellers were much indebted to him, as well as the north of Italy, for the road over the Simplon. He regretted that it would probably not be kept up, as the King of Sardinia and the Austrians would be jealous of that entrance into Italy, in a military point of view.

[1] Eugène Beauharnais.

I said that I had seen several of his Generals at Paris, among others Marmont, who appeared to be unpopular on account of the capitulation.

He spoke of him immediately, rather with feeling than asperity :

* " He is a man whom I have befriended since his childhood. He came of a good family. I thought he had generous feelings, but I made a mistake." *[1]

He had seen him not long before the capitulation ; he should not have surrendered his troops. The Allies might have entered Paris, but could not have remained there. If Marmont had joined him at Fontainebleau with the 10,000 men he commanded, he would then have had there 43,000 men, with whom he would have harassed the rear of the enemy, and should have had a chance of compelling him to retreat ; that even as it was, he might have fallen back on the Viceroy, and continued the war in the south.

I expressed my surprise that he had not consented to make peace sooner, and suggested that he might have had very good terms by agreeing with Austria in the negotiation at Dresden, of which, having been then at Vienna, I knew something.

* " It is true that I might have made peace at Dresden, and I should have done so, if the Austrians would have contented themselves with the Illyrian provinces which I proposed to give up to them. But they wanted to have Venice, and this was not in my scheme of things. Besides I had still the wherewithal for a good campaign ;

[1] Cf. the Douglas interview.

but Marshal Macdonald allowed Blücher, though his force was inferior, to defeat him in Silesia, and Marshal Ney made some bad mistakes in the neighbourhood of Berlin. I had believed that I could keep the line of the Elbe, and that there was no necessity for me to make peace. Nevertheless, I do not pretend that, if I had to do it all over again, I would not act differently." *

I then suggested that he might have made peace at Châtillon. He said that he could not do so honourably; that he was then willing to give up Italy, Spain, Holland, and Germany, but that he could not cede Belgium, which had belonged to France when he obtained the government; that he could not consent to cede anything within the natural boundaries of France.

I observed that these natural boundaries were assigned by his own fancy; that France had been great under the Bourbons, before these boundaries were heard of; that he might have reigned in it such as it formerly was, or that he might even have recognised Belgium in a few years.

* " No, I could not make a peace which would have involved France in dishonour. The Bourbons are ' Grand Seigneurs ', the things which appeal to them are their châteaux, their palaces, Versailles, Fontainebleau, and the rest. As for me, I was born a soldier; I have reigned for fifteen years. I have left the throne. Well, when one has lived through life's misfortunes, only a coward would complain." * [1] He had hoped that

[1] Cf. the Douglas interview, where Napoleon is reported as saying in this connection : " Ce serait une tâche qui ne pourrait pas soutenir l'existence ". The phrase should surely read " Ce serait un lâche ", etc.

when the Allies passed the Rhine, all France would have united to resist them.

* " I ask you whether it would not have been so in England if the French army had landed on her shores, whereas in France it was precisely at this moment that the Prince of Beneventum and Marmont began their intrigues." *

I mentioned the difficulties made by the French Government relative to the abolition of the slave trade, and a pamphlet of M. Sismondi on this subject, which I afterwards left for him.

He said that he would not have hesitated to consent to the abolition, that he considered it an *affreux brigandage* which ought to be prohibited. He thought France would never recover St. Domingo. He would not have attempted to do so, having learnt by experience the difficulty of this enterprise. His intention had been to propose to the black chiefs to allow France the exclusive trade with the island, and the establishment of factories on the coast, as she has in the East Indies. With respect to the latter, he thought our Government wrong in restoring to France her possessions there; that they are not considerable enough to be of real value to her, and may prove a source of jealousy and quarrel with us. The only mode of abolishing slavery altogether would be to permit polygamy. He had formed this opinion at Cairo, where he had observed that difference of colour does not affect the estimation which belongs to the individuals; he attributed this equality to the prevalence of polygamy. Men are *gourmands en amour*, and, when permitted, will prefer having wives of various colours. The customs of the East allowing this indulgence, females of different complexions frequently met together under the roof of the same husband from distant parts of the Asiatic and African continents. Thus the offspring of a white, a mulatto, and a black are brought up together, sit at the same table, and receive the same education; which removes the prejudices prevailing generally among the whites against persons of colour. He therefore had proposed once to a French bishop that polygamy should be permitted in the West India Islands, but Monseigneur would not hear of it.[1]

I suggested to him that it would be a good thing to attack the Turks and drive them out of Europe.

* " You are quite right. It is the English who could do so. England and France together could do anything they liked." *

After a pause, which would have permitted us to suggest a new topic, if any had occurred to us at the moment, and we had not felt somewhat fatigued by standing after our walk nearly four hours (as he also did, during this conversation), he proposed to show us his other rooms, observing : " Ce n'est qu'une bicoque, comme vous voyez ". The dining - room opens into a small drawing-room (from whose window he showed us a vineyard he had bought), and this communicates with his bedroom ; I remarked here a miniature of the King of Rome. He then walked out of the house, and being joined by Count Drouot, who had not been present at our conversation,

[1] Cf. Ebrington and Douglas interviews.

returned immediately in his carriage to Porto
Ferrajo.

We followed on foot—contrary to his intention,
—for when we first arrived at St. Martin he had
very civilly sent a dragoon to the town to order
one of his carriages for us. We learnt this in the
evening from Count Drouot, who resides in a
wing of the castle, which is occupied by Napoleon.
It is a small building, with a terrace in front
à pic over the sea, and looking upon the mouth
of the port. On the other side is the town ;
this has a place, but few tolerable houses. We
lodged in a wretched lane, called the Strada
d' Amore.

We had called on the Governor, to thank him
for his civilities to us. On our making some
enquiry into Napoleon's habits, he told us that
he writes a good deal, but did not say what. He
mostly dines tête - à - tête with him at six o'clock.
In the evening he visits his mother and the
Princess Borghese ; goes to bed at ten, rises
between one and two, and then writes till five,
when he lies down again for two hours. In the
middle of the day he frequently goes in his carriage
to St. Martin, otherwise he walks on the terrace
before his house.

I thought his countenance gloomy when he
passed us in the carriage ; in conversation it was
agreeable, and occasionally much animated. He
stood with his hat under his arm, in which was a
small cockade of his own colours, white with a
red stripe, and three bees. He wore a plain green
uniform and the Order of the Legion of Honour.
He took snuff frequently, and talked with much

cheerfulness, good humour, and civility of manner. His features are handsome; his figure ignoble, but less corpulent than I expected.

We sailed early the next morning and reached Leghorn in six hours, where we found the Duke and Duchess of Bedford, Lady Montagu, and Lord John Russell[1] in the Lazaretto.

[1] This meeting no doubt suggested to Lord John Russell his visit to Elba, which took place five weeks later.

VII

THE HUNDRED DAYS

The Hundred Days

" I am not at all flattered by your assimilation of me with these circulating conspirators (*sic*). I have never been concerned in any conspiracy and in 1815 only joined Napoleon when Louis XVIII. had left Paris."

The above is an extract from a letter written by Flahault to his wife in October 1849.[1] The Austrian Government, with the help of the Emperor Nicolas of Russia, were at that moment endeavouring to obtain the extradition of Kossuth and other Austrian revolutionary leaders, who had fled to Constantinople. Flahault was amongst those who held that these conspirators should be made to suffer ; but his wife, taking a leaf out of Palmerston's book, was inclined to condone their action. Madame de Flahault had, it would seem, been drawing unmerited comparisons between Kossuth's conduct in 1848 and that of her husband in 1815.

Flahault's repudiation of her 'assimilation' serves to explain his action after Napoleon's escape from Elba. It shows that however strongly his affections may have prompted him to return to his former master, he did not do so until Napoleon had once more become the *de facto* ruler of France, and he could fairly claim that he was no longer bound by the act of adherence which he had given to the Provisional Government ten months before (*supra*, p. 71).

So it came about that Flahault was amongst those who rejoined Napoleon on his entry into Paris on March 13. He was at once reinstated in his old position. The trust reposed in him may be measured by the fact that on April 4 he was sent off with a message to the Empress Marie Louise at Vienna, though he found himself stopped by the Allied authorities at Frankfort and was forced to

[1] Bowood Papers. The letter from which this extract is taken is printed in the *Secret of the Coup d'État*, p. 70.

return with his task unaccomplished. Soon afterwards, by Napoleon's written authority, he was given the sole charge of the military personnel, while on June 2 he was created a peer of France (*infra*, p. 113).

Through the whole period known as the Hundred Days he scarcely left the Emperor's side. He could no doubt have told us more than any one of the inside of events during this memorable time. It is unfortunate that with the exception of a single note to his mother, written on the eve of Quatre Bras (*infra*, p. 114), no contemporary material from his pen survives, and that it was only in later life, when accounts began to appear of events in which he had himself taken part, that he felt moved to break his self-imposed silence.

We have brought together in this section some letters and documents, for the most part unpublished, which have been found amongst his papers, and will leave them, as far as possible, to tell their own tale.

(i.) Flahault in Charge of Personnel

* *Napoleon to Flahault*

Paris, 18 *April*, 1815.

Monsieur le comte de Flahault,

* It is my intention to put you in charge of all matters of military personnel.

You are therefore to collect all the information you can as to the Generals and other officers, for should I make bad selections, I shall hold you responsible.*   Napoleon.

The original of this letter, signed by Napoleon, is amongst the Bowood Papers. It has been printed by Masson and others. Davout was at this time Minister for War, and was much hurt at the power thus given to Flahault to revise his selections. Perhaps the feeling thus engendered may have had something to do with the scene which took place between him and Flahault two months later (*infra*, p. 133).

Flahault, however, cannot have long continued to exercise these functions, for, after the middle of May, Davout appears to have enjoyed the sole responsibility in the matter of military appointments.[1]

(ii.) NAPOLEON AND THE TENTH REGIMENT (MAY 14, 1815)

After the escape of Napoleon from Elba, the army immediately, and almost to a man, forsook King Louis XVIII. and rallied to their former master. The notable exception was the Tenth of the Line. This regiment, which boasted the Duke of Angoulême as its colonel - general, was at this moment actually serving under its titular commander, and on April 3 it had attacked and defeated (at the Pont du Drôme) some of the troops who had already re-espoused Napoleon's cause. It was the only action in which a shot was fired by the Royalists, but the regiment very soon afterwards went the way of the rest and was brought to Paris.

The meeting of Napoleon and the Tenth Regiment took place on Sunday, May 14, 1815. The story is related by Thiers, *Histoire du Consulat et de l'Empire*, Book lix. p. 480. Amongst Flahault's papers there is a draft of a letter written by him to Thiers in October 1861, soon after the volume in question had made its appearance. In this letter, after congratulating the historian on the excellence of his work, Flahault goes on to say : " Je tiens de plus à vous dire que vous avez parfaitement rendu l'épisode que je vous avais raconté ". In the circumstances there can be little doubt that this was the ' episode ' to which Flahault refers.

The account which follows was dictated (presumably from a note taken at the time) by Flahault to his daughter, Madame de Lavalette. It shows that, outside the regiment in question, Flahault and De la Riboisière were the only witnesses of the incident in question. The story therefore deserves to be told in Flahault's own words :

[1] Houssaye, *1815, Waterloo*, p. 69.

* The Tenth Regiment had supported the Dauphin in the Midi, and encountering some troops which had taken the side of the Emperor they attacked them. The Emperor after his return to Paris was to inspect them in the Court of the Tuileries, and he had been made aware that there was a plot to fire a shot which would put an end to him. He ordered the regiment to form a hollow square, into which he advanced, followed only by his aide - de - camp, General Flahault, and his orderly officer, Monsieur de la Riboisière. Placing himself in their midst, he then addressed them as follows :

" Soldiers, you are the only troops who have not only refused to recognise, but have fired on, the colours which for the past twenty-five years have conducted you from victory to victory, from capital to capital. What I ought to do would be to erase from the Army records the number of your regiment, to cover your standards with crape, and to order every tenth man amongst you to be shot. But I want to give you an opportunity to repair your fault and to put yourselves right with the Army.

" It is said that you have had bad leaders, I will now give you good ones, and I will place you in the forefront of the battle. You shall see every shot which is fired, and the stain which rests upon you shall be cleansed with your own blood."

At the termination of this speech the men threw themselves at his feet, and with one voice shouted " Vive l'Empereur ! " *[1]

[1] Appendix No. 11, p. 312.

If the above story supplies an instance of Napoleon's power of inspiring enthusiasm amongst his troops, it might, in the light of subsequent events, be cited as a proof that the feelings he evoked were founded rather on the glamour of his name than on affection for his person, and that they were of a nature highly transient.

Whether during the brief campaign of Waterloo the Tenth Regiment found the opportunity which had been promised them to " *laver votre honte avec votre sang* " we cannot say. There is, however, sufficient evidence that as soon as Napoleon's final failure was apparent, they became once more ardent supporters of the Royalist cause.

Charles, Comte de la Bédoyère, one of Flahault's most intimate friends, had been the first officer of note to come back to Napoleon after the escape from Elba. He became in consequence after the Second Restoration a marked man, and figured prominently in the list of those who were proscribed by the famous ordinance of July 24, 1815. His friends advised him to seek safety in flight, as did many others similarly situated, but he insisted on returning to Paris to see his wife and was arrested. For some time his fate hung in the balance, for though he was technically guilty, so were hundreds of others in almost the same degree, and La Bédoyère had many friends in high places who were working for his reprieve. It was at this moment that there appeared from the Tenth Regiment the following manifesto:

* " La Bédoyère was the man who was responsible. It was he who gave the example which others followed. Nobody but he could have done so." [1] *

This indictment was widely circulated, and had the effect intended of causing the army to join in the clamour for La

---

[1] *Histoire des deux Restaurations*, de Vaulabelle, iv. 392. Cf. also *De la conspiration qui a obligé Louis XVIII de quitter son royaume*, published anonymously in London in the summer of 1815. The Royalist writer of this interesting pamphlet seeks to show that the various regiments, after being previously canvassed, had been carefully stationed along the line of Napoleon's route from Elba to Paris, in accordance with their readiness to desert to his side. Thus the defection of La Bédoyère's regiment was followed, first, by those at Grenoble, and then by others at Lyon and in Burgundy. Paris, Bordeaux, and the Midi followed suit, and Louis XVIII. soon found himself without any army.

Bédoyère's execution as a scapegoat. After going through the form of trial, he was shot on the Plain of Grenelle on August 20, 1815.

Thus perished one of Napoleon's most devoted and single-minded adherents, driven to his doom by the regiment which had been shouting "Vive l'Empereur!" at the Tuileries only two months before.

(iii.) FLAHAULT BECOMES A PEER

Napoleon to Flahault

[*June* 2, 1815.]

Monsieur le Comte de Flahault,

* By virtue of the Additional Act of the Constitution of the Empire, Article 4, section I., and in consideration of the services which you have rendered to our country, as also of the attachment you have always shown to our person and to the principle of a Constitutional Monarchy, which governs our Empire, we have created you a Peer of France. Our wish is that at three o'clock on Saturday you should repair to the Palace of the Peers, see our cousin the Prince Archchancellor of the Empire, to whom we have given the necessary orders to the end that your title may be confirmed, and that in virtue thereof you should take your seat in the House of Peers.

Such being the object of this letter, may God preserve you in His safe keeping.

Given at the Élysée Palace the second of June eighteen hundred and fifteen.*

NAPOLEON.

The Secretary of State,
Duc de Bassano.

I

(iv.) THE FIRST DAY'S FIGHTING

Flahault to Madame de Souza

Napoleon left Paris on June 12. On the 14th he was with his army near Beaumont. On the 15th his troops drove back part of Ziethen's force at Thuin, and he himself broke through the enemy line at Charleroi. General Letort, one of the most brilliant of the French cavalry leaders, died of wounds received that day at Gilly. The battles of Quatre Bras and Ligny were fought on the morrow.

15 *June* [1815].

* I have received your letter of the 13th. . . . I feel very low, although we have had to-day several pretty little fights. Poor Letort has been very seriously wounded, I feel quite sure that he will not get over it. He is a good officer, and one who will be much regretted. . . . You are perfectly right as to the enthusiasm of the troops. I have never seen anything like it. They are like men possessed.[1] . . . *

(v.) QUATRE BRAS AND AFTER (JUNE 16-17)

Flahault to Brialmont

A draft of this letter (though without the name of the person to whom it was addressed) was found amongst Flahault's papers. The contents make it clear that it was destined for Alexis Henri Brialmont, whose *Histoire du duc de Wellington* was published in 1856. We can date the letter from Flahault's quotation therein of a portion of his communication to the *Moniteur*, which will be found printed *in extenso* below (p. 128). The letter to the *Moniteur* was sent

---

[1] *Cela approche de la folie.*

on April 6, 1857; Flahault must, therefore, have written to Brialmont immediately afterwards.

[1857.]

*Sir,

I have just read the account of the campaign of 1815 with which you close the second volume of your history of the Duke of Wellington. Sad though it is to recall these events, I cannot refrain from telling you how much pleasure it gave me to read this chapter of history, distinguished as it is by the impartiality of your account of the events which took place and of your estimate of the persons concerned in them.

I hope you will not take it amiss if I now impart to you certain facts of which you can scarcely have been cognisant. These may perhaps modify the views which you have expressed as to the responsibility attributable to Marshals Ney and Grouchy for the outcome of this campaign.

Perhaps the best way to achieve my object would be to give you an account of events which took place under my own eyes and of which I can speak with personal knowledge. The Emperor, as you have rightly said,[1] dictated to me at Charleroi between 8 and 9 o'clock in the morning[2] a letter to Marshal Ney, wherein he apprised him of the manner in which he had divided the army between him and Marshal Grouchy. To the best of my recollection he informed him also of the movement which, in conjunction with the latter, Count Lobau's corps, and the Imperial

---

[1] *Histoire du duc de Wellington*, vol. ii. p. 386.
[2] *I.e.* of June 16. This letter is printed in the *Napoleonic Correspondence*, No. 22,058.

Guard, he was about to launch against the
Prussian army. But as regards orders for the
movement of troops, I was directed to give them
to Marshal Ney by word of mouth. I therefore
gave him as from the Emperor the order to move
to Quatre Bras, to hold this important point in
strength, and (should the enemy allow him to do
so) to support with every man at his disposal the
Emperor's offensive against the Prussian army.
After giving him (as I stated in the letter to the
Duc d'Elchingen which you quote) this order at
about eleven o'clock, I went forward, and not
far from Quatre Bras I met General Lefèvre
Desnouettes[1] with his cavalry. I stayed with
him pending the arrival of Marshal Ney's forces,
and we then saw opposite us, some way off,
some of the English staff, who seemed to be
taking stock of the position. General Lefèvre
Desnouettes ordered a few rounds of artillery to
be fired on them, although they were out of
range.

At length Marshal Ney came on the scene,
and the engagement started.[2] But there was no
cohesion in the affair. It was like attempting,
as the saying goes, to 'take the bull by the
horns'. Our forces were thrown into battle
piece-meal as they arrived upon the scene, and
in spite of the bravery they displayed no result
was obtained.

When night came, each side held its ground. I
had supper with Marshal Ney, and went off afterwards to join the Emperor. I reached Fleurus

---

[1] Charles Comte Lefèbvre-Desnouettes, *Général de Division* since
1808.   [2] This was about 2 P.M.

between 6 and 7 o'clock in the morning.[1] Marshal Ney had no time to make a report and ordered me to explain to the Emperor what had occurred. My account was far from giving him satisfaction.

About 10 o'clock we got on our horses, and after riding round the battle-field [2] we came back to the high road. At this point the Emperor took leave of Marshal Grouchy, using words which I remember as well as if it had been yesterday : " Now then, Grouchy, follow up those Prussians, give them a touch of cold steel in their hinder parts, but be sure to keep in communication with me by your left flank."

You can see therefore, sir, that as regards Marshal Grouchy it could not have been more strongly impressed on him that he must not lose sight of the Prussian army, and that he must be prepared to support the Emperor should the opportunity arise. It is clear, therefore, that His Majesty had no cause to expect the Prussians except with Grouchy at their heels.

As regards Marshal Ney, he knew at 11 o'clock in the morning of the 16th, how much importance the Emperor attached to his being in possession of the position of Quatre Bras.

As to the cavalry operations, which you rightly cite (p. 422) as having had so disastrous an effect on the battle of Waterloo, I have the honour to send you a copy of a reply to certain untruthful assertions of Marshal Marmont which I felt compelled to print in the *Moniteur*. This will tell you exactly what happened.* [3]

---

[1] *I.e.* of June 17.   [2] Of Ligny.
[3] Appendix No. 12, pp. 313-315.

Flahault here proceeds to quote the latter part of his letter of April 6, 1857, to the *Moniteur* (*infra*, p. 128).

Flahault to Lavalette

In October 1861 Flahault was once more roused into historical activity by the appearance in the *Revue des Deux Mondes* of some articles on the Waterloo campaign from the pen of M. Edgar Quinet.

His strictures on this writer are contained in two letters, the first addressed to Thiers, and the second to his friend Lavalette,[1] who had not long before been appointed French ambassador at Rome, though he was at the moment still in Paris.

The letter to Thiers has been already published, in part or in whole, by Masson[2] and others. We print below the letter to Lavalette, in which Flahault gives more forcible expression to the feelings aroused by M. Quinet's inexactitudes.

LONDON, *27th October* 1861.

* My dear Félix,

Do you know anything of M. Edgar Quinet, the author of the articles which have appeared in the *Revue des Deux Mondes* on the Campaign of 1815 ?

This is quite between ourselves and for your eyes only, but he appears to me to be a vulgar fellow, who writes about things of which he knows less than nothing, who is badly informed, and who, with the idea of establishing Ney's reputation, makes the most ridiculous accusations against the Emperor.

For instance, he says that it was two or three

---

[1] Charles Jean Marie Félix, Marquis de Lavalette (1806–81). He afterwards married Flahault's daughter Georgine.

[2] *Le Général Comte de Flahault : une rectification*, a brochure published in the journal *Le Napoléon* in 1881.

o'clock [1] before Grouchy was able to commence
his march, while in the same breath he says that
the head of Napoleon's column appeared at
Quatre Bras at two o'clock.   If this were so,
Napoleon must have taken leave of Grouchy
and left Fleurus some time before, for the two
places are a long way apart.

Again, he says that Marshal Ney sent me to
the Emperor [2] in order to obtain news as to
what had happened at Fleurus.   If he got this
from the Duc d'Elchingen, it proves that his
informant was as ignorant as the recipient of
the information !   I was close to Ney throughout
the Quatre Bras engagement.   Nobody could have
shown greater courage, I might even say greater
contempt for death, than he did.   But here my
praise of him must end, for the affair resolved
itself into a series of spasmodic attacks, delivered
without any semblance of a plan.

When it was all over, and I had had supper
with the Marshal, I departed about one o'clock
in the morning, not as the bearer of a message
from him, but for the purpose of rejoining the
Emperor at Fleurus.   I arrived there before
déjeuner and gave him an account of what had
happened on the previous day.   Soon after
déjeuner we got on our horses in order to take a
look round the battle-field.   After this we made
our way to the high road leading from Namur to
Quatre Bras, and it was there that the Emperor
gave his final instructions to Grouchy.   As to
what M. Quinet says about there being no possi-

---

[1] *I.e.* on the afternoon, June 17.
[2] On the night of June 16-17, *i.e.* after Quatre Bras.

bility of communication by any lateral road, I can on my honour affirm that the Emperor said to Grouchy, " Allons Grouchy, poursuivez les Prussiens, l'épée dans les reins ; mais communiquez toujours avec moi par votre gauche." Surely this was as good as telling him that the maintenance of communication was an essential point in his orders.

I can quite understand that M. Quinet, who seems to have been in close touch with the Duc d'Elchingen, should do his best to reconstruct these events in a way favourable for Marshal Ney, and I do not wish to say a word against that illustrious victim. But why should he display so unfair a spirit, and stray so far from the facts, in that which concerns the Emperor ?

Thus he applauds Ney's conduct, or at any rate thinks it quite natural that he refused to attack the English before he knew how things were going on on the Prussian front. Why then does he blame the Emperor so severely because he would not throw himself blindly against the Prussians, without knowing what was going on on the English front ? If such action was justified in the first instance, why not in the second ?

He finds great fault with him for his slowness in following up Blücher's army the next morning, but there is not a word of truth in this suggestion. After a pitched battle, and marches such as we had made on the previous day, our army could not be expected to start off again at dawn. What is really marvellous is that the Emperor should have been able to do as much as he did with the forces which he had at his disposal on this sad occasion.

Try as he may, M. Quinet, even with the help of all the papers left by Marshal Grouchy, will never clear that general of the error he committed (I do not say intentionally) in not keeping his left flank in constant touch with us. Besides, both Gérard and Excelmans specially urged him to do so.

Even a republican and an advanced liberal must, when he begins to write history, tell the truth. It is the only tiresome duty of a historian !

Besides all this, there are in his descriptions of events some things which make one die of laughter. Thus he says (on page 35 of the article of September 18) that some French lancers rode gallantly forward and made, with the shafts of their lances, a sort of palisade just in front of the enemy and only a short distance from their bayonets. Can you conceive anything quite so ridiculous ? It is a sort of burlesque imitation of Voltaire's " Tirez, messieurs les anglais ".

Further on (page 37) you will find the following : " Kellermann, at the head of his dragoons, charges down a road which is enfiladed by an English battery. He forces his way through their ranks, and in a moment the road is strewn with the corpses of the attackers. This great effort was useless, the charge gets broken up. Kellermann, whose horse was killed, remains for some time at the enemy's mercy. He escapes on foot by clinging to the bits of two of the troop horses." Can you imagine a more ingenious way of effecting one's escape ? For what was it he clung to—the manes, the boots, or the horses' tails ? Not at all ! He hung on to their *bits*, which would inevitably have prevented them from moving and caused them to fall. It is really a burlesque ; nevertheless it is sad to see the *Revue des Deux Mondes* admitting articles such as this in its columns. I trust in heaven that, in spite of party spirit, the public will have the good sense to treat such foolishness as it deserves.

By the way, I should like the Emperor to know all that I have just told you, and I authorise you to read him this letter or to put it in his hands— though it has been written in a great hurry.* [1]

The letters which we have cited show that whenever he thought that an injustice had been done to the Great Emperor, Flahault was ready to take up the cudgels on his behalf. At a later period he himself became the subject of criticism, but found an able defender in the person of the late Frederic Masson, to whose brochure (*Le Général Comte de Flahault : une rectification*) we already have had occasion to refer.

In one of M. Henri Houssaye's volumes, however, a charge is made against Flahault to which we believe no reply has yet been made.

Houssaye is dealing with the message from Napoleon to Ney, of which Flahault was the bearer on the morning of Quatre Bras (June 16). He remarks thereon : " We must observe, by the way, that Flahault did not hurry himself. Though he was on a fresh horse, he did not succeed in covering more than two short leagues in the hour." [2]

The implication is that Flahault could have carried Napoleon's message much quicker than he did, and that had he shown greater despatch, things might have turned out differently. It is now known that Ney could have easily seized the all-important position of Quatre Bras before it

---

[1] Appendix No. 13, p. 315.
[2] *Remarquons en passant que Flahault ne se pressait guère. Il faisait tranquillement, sur un cheval frais, ses deux petites lieues à l'heure !* (Houssaye, *1815, Waterloo*, p. 189 n.)

was occupied in force by the British on the morning of the 16th, though he was unable to do so later in the day. The allegation against Flahault therefore deserves close scrutiny. It is agreed that he left Charleroi at 9 A.M., and he himself states that he delivered the orders to Ney (at Frasnes) somewhere near 11 o'clock.[1] The distance between these two places is 17 kilometres—if therefore Flahault only reached Frasnes at 11, and if he had no occasion to stop on the way between Charleroi and that village, Houssaye would have been guilty of nothing more than a slight exaggeration in saying that he had only made *deux petites lieues à heure*.

But there are some further considerations, to which Flahault would no doubt have called attention had he been alive when this accusation was made. The first point is that he must in fact have reached Frasnes some time *before* 11 o'clock. For proof of this statement (and of the argument which hangs thereon) I am indebted to a letter addressed in the year 1899 by Colonel Baron Stöffel [1] to Flahault's daughter, Madame de Lavalette. The Colonel assures his correspondent that he has a copy of an unpublished letter from Ney (the only one written by him during the Waterloo campaign and still extant) to Soult, dated from Frasnes at 11 A.M. on June 16. In this letter the Marshal acknowledges the receipt of the Chief of the Staff's orders, which he says have just reached him, and explains that the Emperor's orders had been received some time before, and that he had already acted on them. This surely implies that Flahault must in point of fact have reached Frasnes nearer 10.30 than 11 o'clock, and thus the time that he had spent in the saddle is reduced to something like 1½ instead of 2 hours.

But this is not all. Ney's headquarters on the night of the 15th-16th had been at Gosselies, half-way between Charleroi and Frasnes. The Marshal had, however, gone forward to Frasnes at 7 o'clock that morning and had left

---

[1] *Vers onze heures* (*supra*, p. 116). Flahault's letter was, of course, written before any question had been raised as to the time consumed on this ride.

[2] Colonel Stöffel was military attaché in Berlin during the last days of the Second Empire. As such he sent in to the French War Office a remarkable series of reports warning them of the coming danger. No notice of these was taken at the time, but there was loud indignation when the fact became known after the fall of the Empire.

behind him at Gosselies General Reille, for the express
purpose of receiving and executing the Emperor's orders as
soon as they should arrive.

Flahault was reported by Reille to have handed him these
orders " about 10 o'clock ".[1] Whatever may have been the
precise hour of their delivery, it is clear that some time must
have elapsed while they were being read and copied for Reille,
before Flahault could proceed on his way to Frasnes. We
might concede a quarter of an hour at least for this operation,
and if this were so, Flahault could not have spent much more
(and might well have spent considerably less) than an hour
and a quarter in all to do his 17 kilometres. The road to
Brussels was presumably encumbered with troops and transport at the time, and the implication of tardiness would thus
fall completely to the ground.

(vi.) WATERLOO (JUNE 18)

Flahault to Thiers

During the reign of Louis Philippe, Flahault and Thiers
had been on the most friendly terms. These were, however,
interrupted under the Second Republic, for while Flahault
became increasingly identified with the *Parti de l'Élysée*,
Thiers, after assisting to secure the election of Louis Napoleon
as President, leant more and more towards the majority
party in the Chamber, which was soon at loggerheads with
the Prince President. December 1851 found Flahault a
protagonist in the *coup d'État*, whilst Thiers was among the
deputies who were on that occasion arrested and exiled. It
was, nevertheless, only a few weeks later that Flahault,
always a generous adversary, specially interceded on Thiers'
behalf with the Prince,[2] and it was probably due to his request
that the ex-Minister was amongst the first of the *exilés* to
return to France.

Ten years later the quarrel had been made up, for
after 1860 we find Flahault once more writing to Thiers

---

[1] *Vers 10 heures* (Reille to Ney, June 16).

[2] Flahault to Louis Napoleon, March 29, 1852 (*Secret of the Coup
d'État*, p. 280).

in the most friendly terms. We have already mentioned (*supra*, p. 110) his letter of October 1861, written after the publication of Thiers' Book LIX. We now give a second communication sent ten months later, Book LX. having meanwhile made its appearance. This letter has not been previously published, and although it covers the same ground as some of our other extracts, it is not without interest.

LONDON, *August* 27, 1862.

* My dear Thiers,

I have just finished reading your Book LX. which gives an account of the 1815 campaign. It has reawakened in me many sad memories of those mournful days, and I am still sad at heart while writing to tell you some of the thoughts to which it has given rise.

Your task, as a trustworthy historian, was indeed a painful one, and I feel bound to say that while showing up, as you had to do, the mistakes made, you have managed to keep for their authors the respect to which their services before, and their misfortunes since, those days have entitled them.

Your regard for the good name of the Emperor made it incumbent on you to show that our misfortunes must be charged to those who were responsible for them, and in this you have been remarkably successful. You were right also in asserting that at no period of his life did the Emperor display more energy, more authority, or greater capacity as a leader of men.

Grouchy was, as you say, under some kind of illusion during those two days, for he had it in his power to save France, for a time at any rate, and his action is the more difficult to understand in view of the words which the Emperor used as he left him. These were exactly as told you by Gérard ; [1] I heard them myself and they are graven in my memory.

As to Marshal Ney, his action at Quatre Bras was just as you state, and my own report to the Emperor, when I rejoined him the next morning, was also such as you describe.

Passing now to the battle of Waterloo itself, the account which you give is accurate, and if we had had a talk together about all this sad affair, I would have told you of an incident which would serve to confirm what you say [2] about the cavalry attack which Ney ordered. Seeing the enemy's position apparently denuded, Ney imagined that the Duke of Wellington had commenced a retirement ; for he forgot that the English never man the heights, but always use them as a curtain behind which to conceal their troops. I was close to the Emperor on a knoll, where he remained for the greater part of the day, and when he saw Ney beginning the movement by sending a corps of cavalry across the ravine, he exclaimed, " There is Ney hazarding the battle which was almost won " (these words also are fixed in my memory), " but he must be supported now, for that is our only chance ". Turning then to me, he bade me order all the cavalry I could find to assist the troops which Ney had thrown at the enemy across the ravine.

It is painful to resuscitate these things, and it

[1] General Comte Maurice Étienne Gérard, who was in command of a corps during the Waterloo campaign. He later became a Marshal and Minister for War under Louis Philippe.

[2] *Histoire du Consulat et de l'Empire,* lx. pp. 221 ff.

is no use trying to conceal the fact that you will, in all probability, incur the anger and ill-will of some who have inherited great names and who will feel wounded by statements, however well founded, which may tend to lessen their lustre. But those who undertake the writing of their country's history must always remember that truth is the first duty of the historian. FLAHAULT.

P.S.—I had before me, not long ago, the whole correspondence which the English Government and Admiralty had with my father-in-law, Lord Keith,[1] Sir H. Hotham and Captain Maitland, when the Emperor gave himself up in 1815 and suffered so hardly from treatment which, besides being both abominable and cruel, showed a complete lack of all generous feeling. You mention in your history those who advised him not to give himself up to the English. Nobody could have counselled him more strongly against this course than I did. I told him that no generosity was to be looked for from a party Government, responsible to Parliament, and I not only advised him to throw himself for choice on the Emperor Alexander, but I offered to go myself to arrange matters with that monarch. I pointed out that, in dealing with him, the Emperor Alexander would feel a sense of responsibility towards posterity, and I expressed my conviction that with him a safe refuge was to be found.*[2]

---

[1] Flahault had evidently been studying his father-in-law, Lord Keith's official correspondence, at the time of Napoleon's surrender (*vide infra*, Part VIII.). Sir Henry Hotham was Vice-Admiral under Lord Keith at the time, while Captain Maitland was in command of the *Bellerophon*.

[2] Appendix No. 14, p. 317.

Flahault to the "Moniteur"

We will now give Flahault's letter of April 6, 1857, to the *Moniteur*.   This was the document from which he quoted in his letter to Brialmont (*supra*, p. 114).

It was provoked by the glaring inaccuracies in Marmont's *Mémoires* which had lately been appearing in the same journal.   The letter was afterwards reprinted *in extenso* in Rapetti's *La Défection de Marmont* (Appendix, p. 460).   We shall, however, make no apology for inserting it in this volume, for it constitutes the principal if not the sole authority for Napoleon's doings on the night of Waterloo, and though frequently used by historians, it has seldom been acknowledged as their source of information.

LONDON, 6 *April* 1857.

* Monsieur le Directeur,

The *Mémoires* of Marshal the duc de Raguse have already given rise to a number of criticisms which have been published in the *Moniteur*, and I hope that you will be good enough to insert those which I now have the honour to send you.

Believe me, Monsieur le directeur, to be most faithfully yours,   COMTE DE FLAHAULT.

Dealing with the battle of Waterloo on page 121, vol. vii., Marshal Marmont writes as follows :

" During the course of the day Napoleon was so far away from the field of battle that he was unable to control the execution of his orders ; this prevented him from supporting in time the cavalry attack, which might otherwise have had such fruitful and decisive results.   Launched as this was prematurely and carried out as an isolated movement, it was useless ; though had the Guard been brought in at the outset the position could have been retrieved. When the rout took place Napoleon was seized with terror. He fled for several leagues at full gallop, and (it being then dark) he constantly thought he saw the enemy's cavalry around or beside him, and wished to have investigations made."

No one could fail to notice the rancour which inspires this account throughout. The Marshal would have us believe that he obtained it from General Bernard, but this is out of the question, for General Bernard was a gallant and honourable man, and would have been incapable of telling him such a tissue of lies.

The Emperor during the battle took up his stand on a hillock in the centre of the position. From this point he was able to take in the operations as a whole, and while there he saw the cavalry attack which Ney had ordered. He thought it indeed premature and ill-timed, and actually exclaimed, " *Voilà Ney qui d'une affaire sûre en fait une affaire incertaine ; mais maintenant, puisque le mouvement est commencé, il n'y a plus autre chose à faire qu'à l'appuyer* ". He then bade me take his orders to all the cavalry, to support and to follow the squadrons which had already crossed the ravine between them and the enemy—and this was done. Unfortunately the moment had not yet come for an attack of this sort to meet with success, and of this the Emperor had been perfectly aware. It was, however, impossible either to stop or to recall the troops which were already committed. In war there are sometimes mistakes which can only be repaired by persevering in the same line of action.

K

I will leave to Marshal Marmont all the credit (which I have no desire to share) of his endeavour to make comparisons between the commanders of the rival armies, and to apportion to each his due share of responsibility for the outcome of the battle. He is at pains to shower praises on the British General at the expense of the Emperor, and to lay to the charge of the latter all the mistakes which, as he thinks, contributed to the disastrous result. It might, however, have occurred to him that the unexpected arrival on our flank of a body of 20,000 Prussians—whose artillery enfiladed and tore up with its missiles the whole of our terrain—was the real cause of our losing the battle and of the disasters which ensued. The Duke of Wellington, in reporting to his own Government, was fair-minded enough to admit this.

As regards the panic which, as alleged by the Marshal, overcame the Emperor when the day was lost; this untruthful statement can best be refuted by an account of the events which took place before my own eyes, and no one is in a better position to give such an account than myself.

After taking part in the attacks of the Cavalry and of the Guard, I turned back, when the retreat had definitely set in, to find the Emperor. Night had then fallen. I found him in an infantry square,[1] and from that moment I did not leave his side. He stayed there for a time, but the day being now irretrievably lost, he moved off in the direction of the Charleroi road. We made our

[1] *Je l'ai retrouvé dans un carré.*

way towards it, not at a gallop, as is so infamously stated in these *Mémoires*, but at a foot's pace, nor would an enemy pursuit, had there been one, have inspired the fear to which the Marshal in his hatred would have us believe the Emperor was a prey. Of personal fear there was not the slightest trace, although the state of affairs was such as to cause him the gravest uneasiness. He was, however, so overcome by fatigue and the exertion of the preceding days, that several times he was unable to resist the sleepiness which overcame him, and if I had not been there to uphold him, he would have fallen from his horse.[1] We arrived the next morning at Charleroi, whence we posted [2] in order to get to Laon. He stopped there for the purpose of writing the bulletin in which he gave an account of this fatal day, and then after dining set out for Paris. That is the true story.

I hope it may be compared with Marshal Marmont's spiteful and untruthful account, and that every one will judge for himself between the two.

What a sense of indignation and disgust is aroused when one sees a person, who had every reason to wish himself forgotten, or at least forgiven, going out of his way to attack his former benefactor! He betrayed him alive—he now slanders him when dead.* [3]

Cte DE FLAHAULT.

[1] In conversation Flahault often drew a vivid picture of this midnight ride, *genou à genou*, with the Emperor. (Bowood Papers.)

[2] *Nous avons pris la poste.*

[3] Appendix No. 15, p. 319.

(vii.) THE SCENE WITH DAVOUT (JUNE 28)

Flahault to Larabit

In July 1867 a statue of Davout, Prince d'Eckmühl, was unveiled before a large gathering at Auxerre. In a speech made on this occasion, Monsieur Larabit, sometime President of the *Conseil Général de l'Yonne* and a colleague of Flahault's in the French Senate, had apparently attempted, for the benefit of the late Marshal's assembled admirers, to explain away the story that Davout had once threatened to arrest the Emperor Napoleon with his own hand. Hence Flahault's letter to Larabit. It was published by Frederic Masson in the brochure which we have already mentioned,[1] and is here given in translated form.

It will be remembered that after formally abdicating on June 22, 1815, Napoleon (on June 25) left Paris for Malmaison. There, with his mother, Queen Hortense, and a few of his more faithful adherents, he spent the four days that remained prior to his final departure. Fouché and the Provisional Government were anxious, quite as much for their own sake as for his, to get him out of the country. They had promised to provide him with two French frigates to convey him whither he would, but on the condition that he must not embark until a safe conduct had been obtained from the Allies. Napoleon, objecting to the delay, was insistent that the condition should be removed, and sent repeated messages from Malmaison to the Provisional Government with this object. His remonstrances were, however, at first unavailing. On June 28, a further attempt was made through Flahault.[2] This was the occasion of Davout's famous outburst.

The point at issue was conceded nevertheless, and late on the night of June 28 Napoleon was so informed by Fouché's emissaries, Admiral Decrès and Boulay de la Meurthe. He at once arranged his departure for the morrow, and at 5 o'clock on the evening of the 29th he left Malmaison for Rochefort—and St. Helena.

---

[1] *Supra*, p. 118 *n.*
[2] See " Le Lendemain de Waterloo," *Revue de Paris*, June 15, 1925, p. 730.

2 *August* 1867.

* I had been sent by the Emperor from the Malmaison to ask the Government that instructions might be given that the commanders of the two frigates which were at Cherbourg should place them at his disposal. My orders were to say that he would refuse to leave Paris until these instructions were given. I had just announced this decision to the Duke of Otranto, when Marshal Davout, who was standing near the fireplace—intervening quite unnecessarily—said to me, "General, go back to the Emperor, and tell him that he must leave, that his presence is embarrassing to us and will prevent any possibility of settlement, and that the salvation of the country demands his departure. If he does not go, he will have to be arrested—indeed, I will arrest him myself."

I was dumbfounded by these words, and in no uncertain tones I immediately replied, "Monsieur le Maréchal, he who frames such a message must be his own messenger. For my part I refuse to carry it, and if my refusal entails the resignation of my commission—I place it in your hands."

After this scene I was for some moments overcome by keen emotion, while the Duke of Vicenza and several others came over to speak to me, making no secret of their sympathy and indignation.

I then returned to the Malmaison, where I found the Emperor in bed. He told me to come in, but fearing to add to his anxieties, I had determined to make no mention of the scene in which I had just taken part. With his wonted acumen he soon saw that I was withholding something. He asked me to conceal nothing from him, endeavouring at the same time to impress upon me how essential it was that he should know all. I then told him exactly what had taken place—" Well," he said, with a movement of his hand towards his throat, " let him come ".

This is the absolute truth. I am far from wishing to revive this sad subject, for it is a painful task to say a word which might tend to discredit one of France's heroes. I cannot, however, pass over in silence the denial of a story, which alas is only too true.* [1]

A lengthy reply to this letter is preserved amongst Flahault's papers. It may be sufficient here to say that Larabit, unable to gainsay the account of an eye-witness, endeavoured to minimise the misstatements he had made. He tries to show that Davout's threat, made as it was in the presence of others in the Chamber of the Provisional Government, was less treasonable than it would have been if uttered (as had been previously alleged) in the Emperor's private room at the Élysée. It was Fouché, Larabit says, who was the villain of the piece. By concentrating in himself the powers of the Provisional Government, he had made it hard for Davout not to show some signal mark of his adherence to the new authority, and it was " une faiblesse malheureuse " which prompted the Marshal to use the language for which he had been condemned.

* * * * * *

We have printed above all the information as to the Hundred Days which is directly available from the Flahault papers. It may perhaps be supplemented from another source in order to give some idea of the part played by Flahault during the final scene in the Napoleonic drama.

[1] Appendix No. 16, p. 322.

John Cam Hobhouse, who has been already quoted,[1] was again in Paris in 1815 at the moment of Napoleon's fall. His experiences have been narrated in two books, the first published in 1816,[2] the second nearly fifty years later.[3]

In his *Recollections* Flahault is frequently mentioned, and an account is given of an interesting argument between him and the Emperor on the subject of Napoleon's abdication. " Flahault said he had a right to do it in 1814, but in the next year he compromised many of his best friends. Napoleon said that from the moment the Chamber declared itself permanent he felt he had ceased to reign, but Flahault said that the Chamber by that declaration had broken the pact under which they were assembled and Napoleon might have fairly dissolved them." [4] In Hobhouse's *Last Reign*, however, Flahault, though often alluded to, is only once spoken of by name. The reason for this is not far to seek. Hobhouse, as we have seen, had made Flahault's acquaintance in 1814 ; he subsequently became intimate also with Madame de Souza, and it seems obvious that much of his information must have been derived from one or other of them. At the time when the *Last Reign* was published Flahault was in England, and had already won the affection of Miss Mercer Elphinstone, whom he was to marry in the following year. Miss Elphinstone was also amongst the number of Hobhouse's friends. Now though he had never been officially proscribed, Flahault's position in England was a somewhat delicate one, as was his mother's in Paris, for in neither country were the more prominent adherents of Napoleon looked upon with favour by the powers of the day. The question of Flahault's marriage to a lady of British extraction, which both Governments (as well as the bride's father) did their best to thwart, was a further complication. Hobhouse, therefore, must have felt in honour bound

---

[1] *Supra*, pp. 74-76.

[2] *The Last Reign of Napoleon : Letters of an Englishman resident in Paris*. Anon. London, 1816. A copy of this book was sent to St. Helena by Hobhouse, with the inscription IMPERATOR, NAPOLEON. It was at once confiscated by Sir Hudson Lowe.

[3] *Recollections of a Long Life*, Lord Broughton-de-Gyfford, 1865.

[4] *Ibid*. iii. 164.

to say nothing which, by giving prominence to Flahault's past relations with "the prisoner of St. Helena", might serve to accentuate the difficulties of his friends or impede their marriage. So when he tells us that Count de Labédoyère and "another aide-de-camp" were the only "habitual visitants" during Napoleon's last stay at Malmaison,[1] we can readily guess that the unnamed individual was in fact Flahault.

The blank can also be filled in the passage already mentioned,[2] in which Hobhouse speaks of a discussion between the ex-Emperor and "his aide-de-camp Count ——" on the subject of suicide. It must have been to Flahault that Napoleon gave it as his opinion, that "whatever happened he would never attempt to anticipate his destiny even by an hour", and it can only have been Flahault or Madame de Souza who told the writer of this memorable conversation.

Lastly, we get from Hobhouse "on the authority of one who was present", a glimpse of the final parting on June 29. In this the unnamed aide-de-camp again appears, and we are told that the Emperor was so much affected at leaving him that he "embraced him four times before he could prevail upon himself to bid him a final adieu".[3]

Memories such as these must have been almost sacred to Flahault, and it is scarcely astonishing that in after years he neither talked nor wrote of the last days at Malmaison.

---

[1] *Recollections*, i. 289.

[2] *Ibid.* i. 293, and *supra*, p. 74.   [3] *Ibid.* i. 294.

VIII

THE *BELLEROPHON*

THE JOURNAL AND LETTERS OF ADMIRAL
VISCOUNT KEITH, COMMANDING AT PLY-
MOUTH (JULY TO AUGUST 1815)

THE letters and extracts in the ensuing pages are taken
from the papers of Admiral Lord Keith, who as Commander
of the Channel Fleet during the summer of 1815 was responsible for the dispositions which brought about Napoleon's
surrender, and also for the safe keeping of the captive from
the time of his arrival at Plymouth and until his departure
on board the *Northumberland* for St. Helena (July 24 to
August 7).

George Keith Elphinstone was a younger son of the tenth
Lord Elphinstone, and was born in 1746. He took his name
(and at a later date his title) from his grand-uncle Keith,
tenth Earl Marischal of Scotland, a Jacobite who, like his
more famous brother, Marshal Keith, was forced to fly the
country and to end his days on foreign soil.

Elphinstone went to sea at an early age, and for upwards
of half a century served his country with distinction in the
Royal Navy.

Though he was not destined to achieve an equal fame to
that gained by the great admirals of the eighteenth century
—for the opportunity of winning a notable victory at sea
never came his way—he left behind him a considerable
reputation as a commander and as an organiser of victory.
He was uniformly successful in carrying out the work committed to his charge, and the belief in his luck is said to have
been so strong that all ranks were eager to serve under his flag.

Keith may be chiefly remembered to-day by his share in
the capture and defence of Toulon in 1793, in the Cape
Expedition of 1795, and in the landing at Aboukir Bay in
1801.

At Toulon, as the officer entrusted with the defence of

ADMIRAL LORD KEITH
From a miniature by George Saunders

Fort La Malgue he encountered for the first time the future
Emperor, who was then Major Buonaparte of the French
Artillery. The Cape Expedition culminated in the capture
of that Colony and the surrender of the Dutch fleet in
Saldanha Bay the following year. The successful landing
at Aboukir proved to be the beginning of the end for the
French in Egypt and the East.

For these and many other services Elphinstone was
rewarded by the Knighthood of the Bath in 1795, by a Barony
in 1797, and finally in 1814, by a Viscountcy of the United
Kingdom. He had meanwhile advanced through all the
successive grades of his profession as Rear-Admiral, Vice-
Admiral, and Admiral, each in turn of " the blue ", " the
white ", and " the red ", while he had incidentally acquired
a considerable fortune through his share in the capture of
innumerable prizes of war.

He was twice married, first in 1788 to Miss Mercer, the
heiress of Meikleour and Aldie in Perthshire, and secondly
in 1807 to Hester Maria ("Queenie") Thrale, daughter of
Mrs. Piozzi—the little girl with whom Dr. Johnson used
to "play horses".

By his first marriage Keith had a daughter, Margaret, on
whom the name and estates of Mercer devolved at her
mother's death. Margaret Mercer married the Comte de
Flahault, and in due time their eldest daughter was united
to the son and heir of the third Marquis of Lansdowne. It
was thus that Lord Keith's papers have been transmitted
through three generations to their present owner.

Keith was first appointed to the command of the Channel
Fleet in 1812. At this time the French, who, after Trafalgar,
had deliberately adopted the method of a *guerre de course*,
as a means of training their young sailors, and of annoying
British commerce, could scarcely be said to possess a fleet in
being. The work of our own naval forces lay therefore
rather in the direction of blockade than in fighting. These
conditions made it necessary that the Admiral in command
should never be beyond the reach of the Admiralty. Keith
accordingly spent much of his time on shore or in the vicinity
of our southern ports, while detachments of his force were
harrying the enemy or assisting the British Army which was
at this time engaged in the Peninsula. So things continued

until the first abdication of Napoleon in April 1814 brought hostilities for a time to an end. Keith struck his flag at Plymouth in the following July; but he was soon to be recalled to duty, for in February 1815 Napoleon made his escape from Elba.

The extracts we print in this section have been selected with a view to giving in Keith's own words, both a narrative and a commentary on the events which followed his resumption of the command in April 1815. They have been taken from three sources :

(1) A MS. " Journal of the Proceedings of Admiral Viscount Keith, G.C.B., Commander-in-Chief of the Channel Fleet " (April 29 to August 19, 1815). This " Naval Journal ", if lacking in picturesque detail, may serve to make the narrative more clear, by supplying a faithful record of occurrences as set down by Keith or his secretary from day to day.

(2) Keith's private letters to his wife and to his eldest daughter.

(3) A MS. volume amongst Keith's papers, entitled " Proceedings relating to the surrender of Napoleon Buonaparte ". This was compiled (probably by Keith's secretary, Mr. Meek) immediately after Napoleon's departure to St. Helena, and contains copies of all the correspondence concerning Napoleon which passed at the time between Keith and the Admiralty. Some of these documents have already been published in Keith's biography.[1] We reproduce a few of the most important, as well as several private letters from Lord Melville which have not hitherto been published.

Journal

April 28th, 1815.

Orders from the Admiralty to proceed to Plymouth and hoist my flag on board the *Ville de Paris* ; taking under my command the ships and flag officers named, and directing the latter

---

[1] *Memoir of George Keith Elphinstone, Viscount Keith*, by Alexander Allardyce. This work has been characterised (by Professor J. K. Laughton in the *Dictionary of National Biography*) as " a clumsy, crude, and inaccurate compilation ".

to hoist their flags on board the ships against their names expressed.

May 22.

Issued a secret general order directing the detention of all French National armed ships.

Rear-Admiral Sir Henry Hotham ordered to proceed with the *Superb* and *Bellerophon* to assist the Royalists.[1]

May 25.

Issued a secret general memorandum directing the respective Captains, etc., to endeavour to intercept an American ship, said to be at Havre, receiving valuable effects on board, the property of Napoleon Buonaparte.

June 19.

Received from the Admiralty an Instruction on the reduction of ships of the Line and directing me to order the *Royal Sovereign* into Hamoaze, the *Ramillies* and *Vengeur* to Spithead, and not to consider either of these ships or the *San Josef* as being any longer under my command; and acquainting me that the flag of Vice-Admiral Sir Richard Strachan is ordered to be struck, and the command of Rear-Admiral Sir Graham Moore as Captain of the Fleet is recalled.

To Lady Keith

[*Royal Sovereign* : Plymouth Sound] *June* 19*th*.

Great changes, my dear ! My ships of the line are reduced to seven; Sir Richard Strachan and Graham Moore taken away, Hallowell and Hotham

---

[1] In La Vendée, the only district in which any support was forthcoming for the Bourbons, after Napoleon's escape from Elba.

only remain.   Fleming is not to come, Bonny[1]
having no ships.

I hear the Rascal is strong and our purse
weak. . . . I think matters cannot remain much
longer as they now are.   We must begin or make
a peace.

June 20.

A French frigate was seen off the Start Point
yesterday.   I have sent one out to look what she
is about, if she remains hovering on the coast to
conduct her in to me. . . . The Frigate is brought
in by two of Sir John Duckworth's ships.   She
came from Martinique with troops to join Bonny,
and they fired only a few shots at each other.
. . . Half of the *quarter men* cried out " Vive
l'Empereur ", the other half " Vive le Roi ".
Our captains told them they must determine who
was to be uppermost, or they would fire, and a
few shots decided in favour of Louis.

Journal

June 21.

Shifted my flag to the *Chatham* . . . the *Larne*
arrived from off Brest.

To Lady Keith

[*Chatham* : in Cawsand Bay.]   *June* 21.

I have nothing new to add from this quarter,
but that affairs in France are said to be going on
well, and will be conclusive, if the first battle goes
in favour of the allies.   But I do not believe all

[1] Lord Keith always spells it thus, instead of the more usual "Boney".

the Royalists tell me, for it always ends " give me money and arms ".

Journal

June 22.

Ordered a salute to be fired by the officers under my orders on the coast of France in honour of the late glorious victory.[1]

To Lady Keith

June 22.

There has been a great battle. I am anxious to hear the real event ; I am not satisfied with the account. We seem to have been taken by surprise at Ld. Wellington's ball.

Journal

June 23.

Ordered a vessel of war to receive on board 6000 pairs of shoes, and convey them to the Royalists in La Vendéc. . . . Shifted my flag to the *Ville de Paris.*

To Lady Keith

[*VILLE DE PARIS* IN HAMOAZE.] *June 24.*

Here is great news ! I shall call for you in a day or two on my road to Scotland " in piping days of peace ". We began the war yesterday only. Our poor nephews have suffered. James is wounded in two places, was a prisoner, but

[1] Waterloo, June 18.

when the French fled he made off.[1]   The ball is still in General Adam's leg.[2]   I hope it is up with Bonny.

Our affairs about Quiberon go well.   I send them arms, shoes, cannon, and a little money now and then ; but there are rogues Royal as well as Imperial !

June 26.

It is a sad suspense.   I am sorry for Uxbridge [3] and in trouble for all of them. . . . One cannot help being anxious to hear the French account, also of the general impression in France, upon which so much depends.   Our battle ended well ; but seems to have been bungled in the beginning, and the troops too wide. . . .

26th June (1815), ½ *past* 5 P.M.

I have only time to tell you that I have a message by telegraph to this effect :

" Buonaparte abdicated ".

June 27.

I am anxious to have the terms of abdication, or if he made any, or if it is the act of his people

---

[1] James Drummond Elphinstone, fourth son of William Fullerton Elphinstone, and grandfather of the present Lord Elphinstone. He was at this time a captain in the 7th Hussars. After being wounded and taken prisoner on the 17th of June, he was brought before Napoleon. The Emperor treated him with great consideration, and rebuked Flahault, who was standing by and had cast doubts on the truthfulness of the answers given by Captain Elphinstone to the questions addressed to him. Elphinstone was confined that night at Genappe, but released by the British advance the next day, when his guard retired with the salutation, " Mon Capitaine, je vous souhaite bonsoir ".

[2] Frederick Adam, fourth son of William Adam, M.P., Lord Keith's brother-in-law. He received a ball in the leg at Waterloo. In 1832 he became Governor of Madras.

[3] Lord Uxbridge lost his leg at Waterloo.

or perhaps the Jacobins. I suppose I shall be off very soon, and all us sea-folks ; but this is no post day and we can hear nothing. The weather too thick for telegraph.

Melville [1] *to Keith*

Private and Secret.

WIMBLEDON, 27th June 1815.

My Lord,

Reports have reached His Majesty's Government from various quarters that, in the event of adverse fortune, it was the intention of Bonaparte to escape to America.[2] If there is any truth in these statements, he will in all probability make the attempt now, unless he should be forcibly detained at Paris. If he should embark in a small vessel from one of the numerous ports along the coast of France, it may be scarcely possible to prevent his escape ; but if he should wait till a frigate or sloop of war can be fitted out for him, you may perhaps receive information of such preparation, and may thereby be enabled to watch and intercept her ; at any rate it is desirable that you should take every precaution in your power with a view to his seizure and detention, should he endeavour to quit France by sea.

I have made a similar communication to Sir

[1] Robert Saunders Dundas, 2nd Viscount Melville (1771–1851), son of the better-known Henry Dundas, 1st Lord Melville. He was at this time First Lord of the Admiralty in Lord Liverpool's Government.

[2] This appears to be the first intimation given to Keith of the possibility of Napoleon's attempting to escape by sea. The Government, however, had received a hint as early as May 14 (*vide* J. Holland Rose, *Napoleonic Studies : The Detention of Napoleon*).

L

John Duckworth, Sir Edward Thornborough, and
Sir Thomas Freemantle, and
    I have the honor to be, etc.,
                                    MELVILLE.

To Lady Keith
                                        June 29.

Here are the *Avant Garde* of the 5000 French
prisoners, said to be very unruly. . . .
    It is now said little Nap is assassinated at
Paris.[1] . . . I do not think matters can long continue as they are. The Assembly will wrangle
and jangle till the Allies are at the gates, and thus
throw away the opportunity of settling a reason-
able government. The French frigate is ordered
to be delivered up to Louis 18th.

Journal
                                        June 30.

Ordered the *Daphne* to convoy a transport
laden with arms in safety to Quiberon Bay.
    Ordered the *Helvus* to receive on board three
French officers and take under her protection two
transports laden with arms and clothing, and
proceed with them to the Gironde to assist the
Royalists in that quarter.

To Lady Keith
                                        June 30.

I am seeking for Bonny on the sea. In Vendée
things is not so well, but in Morbihan famous.

---

[1] Keith must have received this report from Quiberon Bay, whence
a despatch boat had arrived that day. Napoleon was in point of fact
just leaving Malmaison for Rochfort.

July 1st.

It is said Bonny is in London. I do not believe it, but I am seeking out for him on the water. . . . I suppose I shall linger on here till this second Congress [1] *confounds* matters again—for which I shall be very sorry.

Journal

July 2.

Wrote to Rear-Admiral Sir H. Hotham and his senior officers off Brest and l'Orient, apprizing them of Bonaparte's intention to quit France, and furnishing them with instructions as to the measures to be taken to intercept him.

To Lady Keith

PLYMOUTH, 2 *July.*

I am sending out all I have to look for Bonny if he takes to the sea. . . . It is hard to say what the French may do, but I do not think I can long be kept here.

Journal

July 3.

Ordered the Hon. Captain Duncan of the *Glasgow* to take the *Prometheus, Esk* and *Ferrol* under his orders and proceed to the westward of Ushant to endeavour to intercept Bonaparte.

Ordered the *Swiftsure* to proceed and cruise off Cape Finisterre, and the *Vengeur* in the track

[1] The Congress of Vienna, after deliberations extending over many months, had completed its labours by the Treaty of Vienna (June 9). A new Congress was now about to assemble in Paris, and the second Treaty of Paris was signed in November.

of the Channel, for the purpose of intercepting Bonaparte.

To Lady Keith

July 6.

I have not got Bonny yet, my dear, but a rumour ran that I had, and that he was at Windsor's Hotel, to which place all Plymouth and Dock repaired. Nothing new here. They write me from the Admiralty that it is reported there had been firing at or near Paris.

Journal

Orders from the Admiralty

June 7.

All ports in France which shall hoist the White Flag and declare for peace with Great Britain, shall be forthwith relieved from the pressure of all hostility by sea.

To Lady Keith

9th July.

Our Government think all things right and I trust it may be so. I have orders to stop hostilities in a certain degree ; but I do not like the Austrians making an armistice prior to us, or their having any knowledge of the great battle. Had all the Allies been up and staunch, I do not imagine Lord Wellington would have given such terms as I read. I think the Prussians have had some severe fighting on the left Bank of the Seine with Grouchy [1] and at Meaux too. . . .

---

[1] Grouchy with his corps (which should have been but was not at Waterloo) had succeeded in eluding the Prussians and had reached

Journal

Orders to Rear-Admiral Sir Henry Hotham

July 10.

To cause the entrances to the Ports of Rochfort and Rochelle to be closely watched, Bonaparte having quitted Paris and proceeding in the direction of those towns.

To Lady Keith

July 12.

Here is Bonny gone, as I suggested, to Rochfort,[1] but where I fear I am too weak to stop his two frigates. There seems nothing very decided in the papers, but I see these vermin Marshalls collecting around the elect King, planning no doubt his dethronement.

Thursday, 11 p.m. [*July* 13, 1815.]

My ships have got into the Gironde, taken the Battreys and are at the old anchorage. There was a battle in Bordeaux, but the Loyal were worsted ; but all will go well. It was the fear of the army on the South of the Loire. Nap was on board a Dane but left her, and was in the *Épervier* Corvette near Rochfort.

July 14.

I have letters from France of the 5th. It is astonishing how little impression the abdication of Nap has made. I begin to doubt the sincerity, indeed I never put much confidence in a French-

---

Laon. His rearguard had had a successful engagement at Namur. It is probably to this that Keith is alluding.

[1] Napoleon had reached Rochefort on July 3.

man. No white flags but near our ships,[1] and the Batteries fired on our ships in passing by them :—this or " Vive le Roi ". I have invited Mrs. Mostyn to come and condole with Nap at Dartmoor, and afterwards to attend Susan [2] to Paris to compliment Louis 18th.

Melville to Keith

Private.

ADMIRALTY, *15th July* 1815.

My dear Lord,

It appears by the letters which we have received from Paris during the last two or three days that Bonaparte was still at Rochfort. To-day we have letters from Lord Castlereagh of the 12th, which state that three vessels, the *Saale* and *Méduse* (which I believe are of the same class as our 38 gun Frigates) and an *aviso,* had been placed by the Provisional Government at the disposal of Bonaparte, and they seemed to think that at the date of their last accounts he was actually on board the *Saale* in Aix Roads or in the Charente, but afraid to sail on account of the English cruisers. I trust that our Officers will not have relaxed in their vigilance, and that he will have been effectually prevented from sailing. If he did not get away before these westerly winds set in, I presume that he could not get through the Maumusson passage. It is possible that he

---

[1] Keith apparently means that only the French in the immediate vicinity of the British ships showed an inclination to embrace the Royalist cause.

[2] Lady Keith's sisters—Cecilia (Mrs. Mostyn) and Susan Thrale (afterwards Mrs. Hoare). Their sympathies were evidently divided between the belligerent parties.

may attempt a smaller vessel from some other Port ; but travelling through France will now be a perilous undertaking for him. The force on the French coast seems sufficient ; but if there are any disposable ships at Plymouth which are ready for sea, and which you may think would be useful, and which are not under your orders or Sir John Duckworth's, you had better lay your hands upon them and send them to strengthen the squadron in the neighbourhood of Rochfort, or wherever you may think they may be most advantageously stationed. Lord Castlereagh was endeavouring through the intervention of Louis 18th's Government to get our ships introduced into Aix Roads without molestation from the batteries. If that measure has been accomplished and the *Saale* is still there with him on board, the business will soon be settled.

I expect to hear again from Paris to-morrow ; and I remain, my dear Lord, etc.,

MELVILLE.

Journal

July 17.

(Wrote) to Captain Maitland (secret) acquainting him that the French Government had placed two Frigates at the disposal of Buonaparte, and furnishing him with further directions the more effectually to ensure his capture.

To Lady Keith

July 17.

I found Nap was not off on the 8th, but on board a frigate at Rochfort, but which frigates,

two in number, are watched by Capt. Maitland in
Bellerophon and others.

July 18.

Little Nap was on Isle d'Aix on the 10th.   Sent
to ask permission to sail for America.[1]   Of course
was answered the Capt. had no authority, but
would send to me.   Matters begin to close fast.

Journal

July 20.

Wrote Rear-Admiral Sir Henry Hotham (secret
and confidential) . . . furnishing him with additional instructions the more effectually to secure
the person of Buonaparte.

Ordered the *Eurotas, Tenedos, Spey, Rover* and
Falmouth to join Sir H. Hotham in Basque Roads.

To Lady Keith

July 20.

We are still at a loss about Napoleon.   He was
said to be at Isle d'Aix on 11th.[2]   I am doing
my best to nab Nap ! . . . .

Journal

July 22, 11 P.M.

Captain Sartorius of the *Slaney* arrived with
a despatch from Captain Maitland of the *Bellerophon* stating that Buonaparte had proposed to
embark with him in that ship for conveyance to

[1] Keith had been apprised of the occurrence by despatch brought
to him on the 18th by the *Dwarf* from Sir H. Hotham and Captain
Maitland.

[2] He had already surrendered to Maitland on July 15.

England and that he had consented to receive
him. Captain Sartorius was immediately commanded to proceed to the Admiralty with the said
despatches.

July 24.

At noon the 1st Lieutenant of the *Bellerophon*
arrived from Torbay, bringing an account from
Captain Maitland of his arrival at that anchorage
with the *Bellerophon* and *Myrmidon,* having on
board Buonaparte and his suite.

To Lady Keith

24th July.

Bonny is in Torbay with 5 Generals and 60
persons in all ; but I am obliged to prohibit all
intercourse with the ship, as all Plymouth would
have been off to gape at him.

To Miss Elphinstone

24th (July).

Bony is in Torbay with 53 men and women :
5 are Generals. I permit no soul to go on board.
I am glad you made so good a journey and are
all so well.

There has been a most ridiculous altercation
between Gen. Browne and Duckworth about which
was to keep Buonaparte. The Gen¹ sent Colonel
Byres (?) to me to-day to say he had ordered
a guard to receive and conduct him to the Govt.
House. To this I replied, "He is in my care;
I am responsible, and shall give neither of you
any trouble till the Government send orders ".

He, the General, is more absurd than ever. Napoleon seems in good spirits and converses with the officers.

To-morrow I expect Lady K. and Georgie.

Melville to Keith

Private.

ADMIRALTY, 24th *July* 1815.

My dear Lord,

I am much obliged to you for remembering me in directing Captain Sartorius to come to Wimbledon ; he arrived there between three and four this morning, and we have since had a Cabinet on the business. I am afraid that the result will not come in the shape of an official letter from Lord Bathurst in time to send off by this post ; but I can state, for your private information, that in all probability the ex-Emperor will be sent to some foreign colony. In the mean time he will not be allowed to land, or to have any communication whatever with the shore, and we shall not apprize him immediately of his future destination. With a view to his personal accommodation, we must diminish the number of his suite in the *Bellerophon* ; but they also must be kept in strict seclusion. Sir John Duckworth and you will be able to judge whether, if there is any influx of small boats getting round the ship from curiosity, it may not be necessary to have guard boats to keep everything at a distance, except boats approaching with official communications or other necessary business, and the ship's own boats. I suppose he will usually walk on the quarter-deck only, where he will not be easily seen and gazed at from the water. We once thought of allowing him to remain in Torbay ; but as he may be here some weeks, and that anchorage is not very eligible at all times, and as moreover the strict surveillance which we require may be under your own eye or Sir John Duckworth's (who will see and take care that our orders are carefully attended to, and will take all proper measures for that purpose), I thought it on the whole better and more secure to trust to Plymouth Sound, with all its inconveniences of greater publicity, than to leave the ship in Torbay, or send her to any other port, where connivance from motives of indulging the importunity of all curiosity could not be so effectually prevented. The Aide-de-Camp in the *Slaney* will be sent back to the *Bellerophon*, there to remain, and he will be told that he must send this, and all other letters through you, as no others will be allowed to come on shore. I am afraid we shall find Buonaparte and his suite troublesome guests while they remain here ; but we have no cause to grumble on the whole— very much the reverse.

Believe me, etc.,

MELVILLE.

To Miss Elphinstone

25 July.

I wrote Lady K. to Exeter that she may not go to Torbay upon the chance of the influence of the name to get on board the *Bellerophon*. I also refused Mrs. Maitland permission to go, and Govt.

has approved of it. I did not like to go myself, first because I did not know how to address him, secondly because my visit might have been construed into insult or curiosity; therefore I left it to the Great Man to determine these weighty points. Yet I am not without curiosity, for I went to see *Aladdin's Lamp* at the theatre, and uncommonly well done it was, the scenery quite beautiful! I have not failed to thank the ci-devant Emperor on account of James,[1] and am answered he recollects the circumstance and feels the obligation of my early notice of his kindness on the occasion.

No orders are yet come, but in the course of the day I expect an express concerning (him). Half Cornwall and Devonshire are arrived, and many off to Torbay. I have refused many applications, among others little Mrs. Farnell, who was here with a Sir Richd. Vaughan and family.

I should think P. C. will like Weymouth as well as Cranborne.[2] The Boringdons are coming with an immense party : he has taken stables for 80 horses, I am told, at Plymton, etc.

In delivering himself up, he had not all the credit you suppose, having made every attempt to get off : and the French authorities had

[1] James Elphinstone (*supra*, p. 144 n.). The Elphinstones afterwards sent, as an expression of their gratitude, a set of ivory chessmen, engraved with the letter N and an imperial crown, to St. Helena. They were impounded by Sir Hudson Lowe and returned to Carberry Tower, where they still remain.

[2] Princess Charlotte of Wales, whose confidante Miss Elphinstone had been for several years, had recently refused to carry out her father's behest by marrying the Prince of Orange. She was in consequence banished by the Prince Regent at first to Cranborne Lodge in Windsor Forest, and afterwards to Weymouth.

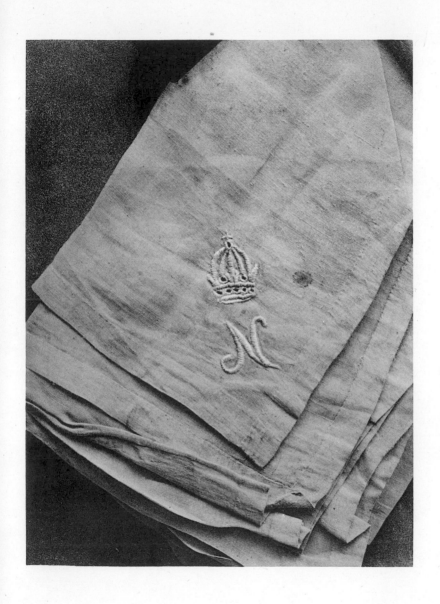

NAPOLEON'S POCKET HANDKERCHIEF
(Plymouth, 1815)

demanded him of the Governor of Isle d'Aix,[1] to enforce which I had ordered *Superb*,[2] *Swiftsure*, *Dragon*, . . . and *Bellerophon* to attack the Fort. Therefore the Governor told him he could not stay any longer.

Melville to Keith[3]

Confidential.

ADMIRALTY, 25th *July* 1815.

My dear Lord,

It would appear that the yards were manned when Bonaparte visited the *Superb* (which was an unnecessary visit), that he insists upon being treated with royal respect, that he invites Captain Maitland and other officers to dine with him, and in short, that if we do not interfere, the same follies in this respect arc likely to be committed as were exhibited last year by some officers in the Mediterranean. I have written the inclosed which may assist you in putting a stop to any thing of that kind, and which you can shew where it may be necessary.

I think we shall send Bonaparte to St. Helena, and that Sir George Cockburn's appointment as Commander-in-Chief on the Cape Station, which was suspended, will now go forward, and that he will convey this Prisoner to St. Helena and remain there for some time. We must take it under the King's Military authority, to which the Court of Directors, I believe, will not object.

[1] The Provisional Government had sent despatches to Bonnefoux, *Préfet Maritime* at Rochefort, ordering Napoleon to leave at once, either on the frigates or by some other means.

[2] Admiral Hotham's flagship.

[3] This and the succeeding letter from Lord Melville have already been published in Allardyce's *Memoir of Lord Keith*.

If Bonaparte or his suite are desirous of writing letters, they must be sent through you open, or addressed to some member of the Government. You had better transmit them all to the Admiralty, unless there is anything very confidential which you may prefer sending direct to me.

Believe me, my dear Lord, etc.,

MELVILLE.

Melville to Keith

ADMIRALTY, 25th *July* 1815.

My dear Lord,

On conversing with the Officer who came to England in the *Bellerophon* with the dispatches from Sir Henry Hotham and Captain Maitland, I think it would appear that Bonaparte had been allowed to assume a great deal more state, and even authority, and had been treated with more submissiveness, than belongs to his situation as a prisoner of war, or to his rank as a General Officer, which is all that can be allowed to him in this country. No British officer would treat his prisoner with inhumanity, and the recollection of the station which Bonaparte has so long held in Europe would naturally, and almost involuntarily, lead an officer to abstain from any line of conduct that could be construed into insult, and therefore to go rather beyond than to fall short of due respect ; but such indulgent feelings must be restrained within proper bounds, and I will be obliged to your Lordship to give such hint on this subject as may appear to you necessary.

Believe me, my dear Lord, etc.,

MELVILLE.

Journal

July 26.

At 4 P.M. the *Bellerophon* and *Slaney* arrived from Torbay with Buonaparte and his suite.

July 28.

At 11 A.M. had an interview with Buonaparte in consequence of a message that he sent to me by Captain Maitland.

To Miss Elphinstone

28 *July.*

I have seen General Buonaparte. He sent three times to desire I would come to him : " I am no more and can disturb nobody.[1] Cannot I live in England ? " We talked on many subjects—of Toulon, Egypt, East Indies, etc. I saw Madame Bertrand, a Dillon—speaks English perfectly. Madame Montaleaux [2] also is good looking, but not a good figure. Lady K(eith) went on board the *Eurotas* [3] at no great distance, but Nap kept in the cabin with me ; she did not see him.

He looks like a man in perfect health, thick calves, thin ankles, clear eyes and a thin mouth—like as possible the picture.

---

[1] Napoleon had said almost the same thing in 1814 on the way to Elba : " J'ai abdiqué : à present je suis un homme mort " (Capt. Ussher's account in *Napoleon's Last Voyages*, J. H. Rose), and also to Lord Ebrington at Elba in December 1814.

[2] *Sic.* Keith always found difficulty in spelling French names.

[3] The *Eurotas* and the *Liffey* had been placed on either side of the *Bellerophon*, in order to prevent any possibility of Napoleon's escape.

Melville to Keith [1]

Private.

ADMIRALTY, 28*th July* 1815.

My dear Lord,

Major-General Sir Henry Bunbury will convey this letter and another which I have addressed to you on the subject of Bonaparte's destination. As it will probably be more agreeable to you that some person should accompany you at the conference which it will be necessary for you to have with Bonaparte, and as it will also be convenient that, besides your written details, we should have a verbal report of such matters as you could not well introduce into your statement of what passed at the conference, Sir H. Bunbury [2] will attend you on board the *Bellerophon* if you see no objection to it. Bonaparte will probably ask many questions, and make many demands, on points which are not noticed in my other letter; in answer to all which you can only refer him to Government and undertake to convey his wishes.

If he desires to have Bertrand with him as one of his attendants, and Madame Bertrand and her family are also asked for, I scarcely think that we should be entitled to refuse it; but of course the matter must be referred to us.

The arrangements mentioned in your letters

---

[1] This and the letter from Melville which follows it have been printed in part in Allardyce's *Memoir of Lord Keith.*

[2] Son of H. W. Bunbury the caricaturist. He was at this time Under-Secretary of State for War.

of the 26th inst., respecting the *Bellerophon*, are perfectly proper. I hope that our instructions are as full as you desire.

Believe me, my dear Lord, etc.,

MELVILLE.

Private.

ADMIRALTY, *29th July* 1815.

My dear Lord,

I have little with which to trouble you to-day, except to acknowledge the receipt of your letters of the 27th inst. with the letter from Bonaparte to the Prince Regent. I have sent the latter to Lord Bathurst.[1]

The *Northumberland* was paid this morning at the Nore, and we understand by telegraph that they meant her to proceed so far this afternoon. She will probably be two days at Spithead, where the 53rd Regt. and a party of Artillery will embark in the *Bucephalus* and *Ceylon*, and if they are not sufficient the *Northumberland* will take the remainder. The *Havannah* Frigate, and six Brigs, which have been placed under Sir George Cockburn's orders, are to assemble at Plymouth.

I was not surprised that Bonaparte does not relish the idea of St. Helena, as I have understood before that he disliked it particularly. That circumstance does not alter my opinion as to its being the most eligible situation for him. I am glad, however, that he submits quietly to be un-emperored ; and I trust that all our Officers and

---

[1] Henry, 3rd Earl Bathurst (1762–1834), Secretary for War and the Colonies in Lord Liverpool's Administration.

M

men will agree so far with him and consider him only in his true light.

Believe me, my dear Lord, etc.,

MELVILLE.

To Miss Elphinstone

30th July.

Lady K. knew nothing of *General Buonaparte* being in England till she arrived at Exeter, when she found a note from me telling her of it ; but not to come to Torbay, for Maitland durst not admit her. She went on board the *Eurotas* and watched while I had my interview, but she was not very successful.

This day we are to announce his future destination, and I expect Sir H. Bunbury any moment : but this is for yourself only. In France there will be no quiet till he is removed and that vilanous army disbanded. I wish he was sent away, for I am plagued to death ; the women go near the ship and the guard boats have been desired to fire. Lady Duckworth and a party went with Mrs. Maitland so near as to speak. He came out and took off his hat to Mrs. Maitland. Gen. Browne in full uniform went also too near on board, but was driven away by the guard boats. I am not sure that he is annoyed so no one comes on board, but if I let people near him he would be abused grossly.

I am glad Adam[1] goes to the Princess, but I

---

[1] William Adam, M.P., of Blair Adam, chancellor to George, Prince of Wales, and afterwards Lord Chief Commissioner of the Jury Court of Scotland. He was nephew to the celebrated architects, Robert and James Adam, and had married a sister of Lord Keith's.

hope he will not write 'Papa'[1] all she says : they are all vain and like gossip, except William.[2]

Keith to Melville

VILLE DE PARIS IN HAMOAZE,
31st July 1815.

My Lord,

Accompanied by Major-General Sir Henry Bunbury I this morning went on board His Majesty's Ship *Bellerophon*, for the purpose of communicating to General Buonaparte the intentions of His Majesty's Government, as pointed out in your Lordship's letter of the 28th instant.

After common civilities had passed, I began to read to General Buonaparte the first paragraph of my instructions, and the remainder were successfully explained by Sir Henry Bunbury.

General Buonaparte in reply adverted to the state of his health, and expressed his doubts whether he could be compelled to quit England, repeating his wish for permission to live here as an individual.

He also observed that he had no power ; that he could do no harm ; that he would give his word of honour to hold no communication with France ; that he could have remained there with the Army ; that it was not an act of necessity, but of choice, which induced him to throw himself for protection into the hands of the English ; and that he now claimed that protection out of justice and humanity.

[1] The Regent.   [2] The Duke of Clarence, afterwards William IV.

These arguments were urged in various points of view, and very frequently repeated; and he also put the question individually both to Sir Henry Bunbury and myself, (a question to which we of course made no reply,) " what we should do under the same circumstances "—adding himself " Go to St. Helena—no!—no! I prefer death— I am determined not to go on board the *Northumberland.*"

Although he repeatedly solicited our good offices, he declined writing any observations upon the paper I left with him explaining the intentions of His Majesty's Government; adding at the same time that " he felt he was speaking to men of honour "—to which I replied that it was my duty to report precisely what he wished to be conveyed to my superiors.

I repeatedly proposed to retire, the General continuing to urge to the last the same style of argument.[1]

A conversation that passed at a second interview—when Sir Henry Bunbury was not present, your Lordship will find detailed in the enclosure.

I have the honour to be, &c.

KEITH

Admiral.

(*Enclosure.*)

After Sir Henry Bunbury and myself had quitted the Cabin and retired to the Quarter

[1] Compare Sir H. Bunbury's memorandum of the same conference, printed in the *Memoir of Lord Keith.* Allardyce gives Keith's enclosure but not his letter.

deck, General Buonaparte begged to see me again.

Upon re-entering the Cabin ; he asked me to advise him.

I replied, " I am an Officer and have discharged my duty. I have left the heads of my Instructions with you, in order that you may observe upon them if you consider it necessary." I added, " Sir, if you have anything more to urge, I must beg to call in Sir Henry Bunbury," to which he replied, " Oh no, it is unnecessary." He then said, " Can you, after what has passed, detain me until you hear from London ? " to which I answered, " that will depend upon the arrival of the other Admiral, of whose instructions I am ignorant."

He then said, " Is there any Tribunal to which I can apply ? " to which I replied :

" I am no lawyer, but I believe none. I am satisfied there is every disposition on the part of the British Government to render your situation as comfortable as is consistent with prudence."

He immediately took up the papers from the table and said with animation, " How so ; St. Helena ? " to which I observed, " Sir, it is surely preferable to being confined in a smaller space in England, or being sent to France, or perhaps to Russia."

" Russia ! Dieu garde ! " was his reply.

I then withdrew.

KEITH
Admiral.

31*st July* 1815.

Napoleon to Keith [1]

[*BELLEROPHON*.]   *July* 31, 1815.

Milord,

* I have carefully read the extract of the letter which you sent me. I have given you my views in detail. I am not a prisoner of war, but I am the guest of England. I came to this country on the *Bellerophon* man-of-war, after informing its Captain of the letter which I was sending to the Prince Regent, and obtaining from him an assurance that he had been given instructions to receive me on board and to take me with my suite to England, if I were to approach him with this object. A similar statement has since been made to me by Admiral Hotham.

From the moment that I came of my own free will on board the *Bellerophon*, I considered myself to be under the protection of the laws of your country. I would rather die than go to St. Helena, or be confined in some fortress. I desire to live in the interior of England, a free man, protected by and subject to its laws, and bound by any promises or arrangements which may be thought desirable.

I do not wish to keep up any correspondence with France nor to interfere in any political matters. My intention, since I abdicated, has always been to make my home in one or other country—the United States or England.

I trust, milord, that you and the Under Secretary of State will faithfully report all the

[1] The French original of this letter, which was sent by Keith to Melville, was recently acquired from Melville's descendants by the British Museum.

arguments I have adduced in order to make clear
to you the rights of my position. It is in the
honour of the Prince Regent and in the protection
of your country's laws, that I have trusted and
that I still continue to trust.* [1]

NAPOLEON.

To Miss Elphinstone

1st August.

I am miserable with all the idle people in
England coming to see this man. Here is among
others my niece Anne, with " dear friends " she
never saw before, arrived from Exmouth! Sir
J. Hippisley and Sir H. McLean and family—
people all the way from Birmingham—not a bed
in all the town. Windsor [2] makes up 50, so you
may guess my trouble and anxiety I wish him at
the —— or anywhere but here.

3rd August.

Bony is to have 15 with him, but I believe
not half the number will go with him, indeed no
one but Bertrand has offered—we have no white
cockades here! He was hot, agitated, verbose,
and repeatative in the extreme. I am worried to
death with idle folk coming, even from Glasgow,
to see him; there is no nation so foolish as we
are!

The Black boy [3] is arrived and on board, but I
take no charge of him hereafter, for I suppose I
shall come away soon and the ship (be) paid off.
Anne Elphinstone is gone to the Breakwater with

---

[1] Appendix No. 17, p. 323.
[2] The Windsor Hotel.   [3] A negro servant.

Lady K. and a party, Miss Georgina of the number.

What an escape Miss Thrale has had—her house struck with lightning, bell wires all broke, and her bedroom all black, chimney sent down!

I look for the *Northumberland* every day to take *Monsieur le Général* off my hands.

Journal

August 4.

At 11 A.M. embarked on board the *Tonnant* and ordered her, the *Bellerophon, Eurotas, Express,* and *Nimble* to weigh and stand out to sea. At sunset hoisted my flag on board the *Tonnant.*

To Lady Keith

Most Private.

TONNANT, *5th August.*

Cruizing for Sir Geo. Cockburn. Bony did not come out all day yesterday, and is sulky—sent for me yesterday twice, I answered (that) on disagreeable subjects criticism was unpleasant, I had no power, and to hear or discuss could only affect each others feelings.

What a mercy I left the house before the constable [1] came to it. He followed me to *Tonnant* : I left that ship and went to the *Eurotas,* he followed; I went out at the opposite side and rowed to sea. Neither of the Captains were in their ships (so much for wives!) After

---

[1] One Mackenrot, a messenger from the Court of King's Bench, who had attempted on August 4 to serve a writ of " habeas corpus " on Lord Keith in order to oblige him to produce Bonaparte as a witness in a trumped-up libel case between Sir Alexander Cochrane and Mackenrot.

a time I landed at Cawsand, but my friend followed. I therefore went out to the point and got on board the *Prometheus*, and remained till dark, when I had seen the man land at Cawsand. I should have been had up before the Justice ; and Bony under my wing till November next !

To Miss Elphinstone

OFF THE EDDYSTONE. 5 *August.*

The crowds of people and their very ill behaviour obliged me to put to sea with this Reptile to wait the arrival of Sir G. Cockburne. Writs of *Habeas Corpus* were also sent down to bring his person to the Court of Kings Bench ; therefore I am on a cruise, but not going to St. Helena, and I suspect very few of his present suite will attend him—even Bertrand begins to stagger.

I am in the *Tonnant*, the ship of Admiral Hallowell, but declined his company. I suppose I shall not be long at Plymouth after I return ; perhaps till a peace is signed, such as it is to be. You are not to expect much news from off the Start Point, so farewell.

5 (*August*) 8 P.M.

I wrote you to-day, and this is only to return your letters. I sincerely hope every article will be returned to its original place.[1] Conquest had no right over private property. Nap is very angry.

---

[1] This appears to be an allusion to the plan of the Allies to restore to their respective countries of origin the art treasures which Napoleon had brought to Paris.

To Lady Keith

TONNANT, OFF TORBAY.   6 *August.*

Northumberland is in sight and I hope the Admiral [1] has no occasion for going on to Plymouth ; in which case I shall stay out till he can return, but I fear I shall not be at the sale nor the play, if it is Monday. But all our troubles will soon be at an end now, and we may return to quiet again. I wish that was so in France—you see what enthusiasm at Bordeaux on the arrival of our ships. I believe as much of it as I can, and no more ! . . .

P.S. Cockburn is here and the job must be done.

Journal

August 6th.

A.M. Fresh breezes and cloudy weather at 8 ; the Start north 3 leagues. At 10, H.M.S. *Northumberland* joined, bearing the flag of Rear-Admiral Sir G. Cockburn. Ordered Captain Maitland by signal to prepare to remove General Buonaparte and his suite to the *Northumberland.*

P.M. Fresh breezes and squally weather. At 3 anchored in 20 fathoms with Berry Head N. by E., Start W.S.W., off shore 1 mile. *B(ellerophon)*, *N(imble)*, *E(urotas)*, and *N(orthumberland)* in company, having left the *Actæon* off the Start to direct ships coming from Plymouth. At 4 the *Ceylon* and *Bucephalus* joined. Sent my flag-lieutenant by land to Plymouth, with orders to hasten out the ships intended to accompany Rear-Admiral Sir G.

---

[1] Sir George Cockburn.

Cockburn. At 5 Count Bertrand came on board the *Tonnant*, with a list of persons whom Buonaparte wished to accompany him to St. Helena, when Sir G. Cockburn gave him, for the information of Buonaparte, an extract of such part of his instructions as he considered it necessary to be communicated to him. At 8.15 the *Express* joined from Plymouth. At 8.30, accompanied by Sir G. Cockburn, and my secretary Mr. Meek, I went on board the *Bellerophon* to visit Buonaparte, he having through Captain Maitland expressed an anxious wish to see me.[1]

Keith to Melville

Tonnant at Anchor under Berry Head,
7th August 1815, 6 P.M.

(*Extract*)

"At half-past eight o'clock in the evening,[2] accompanied by Sir George Cockburn and my Secretary Mr. Meek (the latter of whom I considered it necessary to take with me as a witness, in consequence of Sir George Cockburn being about to leave the Kingdom) I went on board the *Bellerophon*, and, after the customary civilities, upon entering the after cabin (where the General had remained since leaving Plymouth Sound on the 4th instant, without coming on deck or making his appearance at table) Buonaparte commenced the conversation by protesting against

---

[1] The extract which follows gives an account of this, Keith's third interview with Napoleon. It has already been published in Allardyce's *Memoir of Lord Keith.*

[2] Of August 6.

the measures adopted with regard to him by the
British Government, repeating in detail, and almost
verbatim, the language and reasoning contained
in his protest, to which he referred; observing that
he came freely on board the *Bellerophon* ; that he
was not a prisoner ; that he threw himself upon
the hospitality of the country upon which he
had made war for upwards of twenty years ; that
he sought an asylum there under the protection of
the laws ; that he embarked even at the instiga-
tion of Captain Maitland, who told him that he had
orders from his government to convey him to
England ; that as soon as he was on board the
Bellerophon, he was entitled to the protection of
the laws of the country ; that all Captain Maitland
had done was only a snare to entrap him ; that
he was entitled to all the privilege of an *Habeas
Corpus*, but was deprived of the means of obtaining it, and thereby prevented from frustrating
the measures now pursued against his rights and
liberty ; that with regard to the orders to consider
him only as General Buonaparte, the Government
acted with injustice and inconsistency, as they had
treated with him as First Consul, had received his
ambassador, and had sent an ambassador to him.
But, added he with a smile, that was a trifle—
that was nothing compared with their present
conduct towards him, which was a violation
of every principle of justice, humanity, and
generosity, and which he was morally certain,
although he was but indifferently informed of
matters in England, was not less contrary to the
wishes of the English people, than to those of
Europe in general.

"I then observed that the protest had been forwarded to Government the moment that it had been received, and that as both myself and Sir George Cockburn were officers in the execution of a duty prescribed to us by our superiors, we could only listen to the remarks he had made, but were not authorised to answer them. The General replied that that he was perfectly aware of ; but as we were the only persons permitted to approach him, he owed it to himself and to the world to protest before us, and he did it in the most earnest manner, against the measures pursued by our Government with regard to him ; adding that he trusted a faithful report would be made of all he had said.

"I then asked General Buonaparte if he had read the extract of Sir George Cockburn's Instructions which that officer had delivered to Count Bertrand for his information. He replied that he had not ; that the Count had not yet finished the translation ; but that it was a matter of no consequence whatever, as the British Government appeared to have taken its course of proceedings with respect to him, and seemed resolved on pursuing that course even to his death.

"Sir George Cockburn then enquired at what time he would be ready to remove to the *Northumberland*, and he replied, at any hour he pleased after breakfast, which was generally about ten o'clock. Some unimportant conversation then ensued as to St. Helena, the extent of Sir George Cockburn's command, etc., and presently afterwards I withdrew."

Journal

August 7.

A.M. Fresh breeze and hazy weather but very light [winds]. Completed the *Northumberland, Ceylon,* and *Bucephalus* with water, &c. At 8 Count Las Casse came on board to deliver a letter from Buonaparte.[1] The *Myrmidon* joined from Plymouth. At 9.30 Sir George Cockburn went on board the *Bellerophon* to take an inventory of Buonaparte's effects, previous to his removal to the *Northumberland.* The *Actæon* returned to Plymouth. At 11 went on board the *Bellerophon.*

P.M. At 1.30 in the *Tonnant's* barge conveyed Buonaparte, Count Bertrand and his wife, General Montholon and his wife, General Gourgaud and Count de Las Casse from the *Bellerophon* to the *Northumberland,* and there left them in charge of Rear-Admiral Sir G. Cockburn, when I returned to the *Tonnant.* At 6 weighed and made sail [from] *Northumberland. Bellerophon, Eurotas, Myrmidon, Nimble,* and *Express* in company. At 7.30 the *Dwarf* joined from Plymouth. At 8 Start W. by S., Berry Head North, distant off shore 7 miles.

To Lady Keith

TONNANT (PLYMOUTH, *August* 7).

I am this moment returned and the Gentleman is off in good spirits. Bertrand, Las Casses, Gorgaud, Monthaleran,[2] the 2 ladies, 4 *enfants*, 12

---

[1] This is printed in Allardyce's *Memoir*, p. 403.
[2] Montholon.

THE TRANSFER OF NAPOLEON FROM THE BELLEROPHON
TO THE NORTHUMBERLAND
(AUGUST 7, 1815)
From a painting by T. Luny

domestics. His Dr. would not go; I sent that of the *Bellerophon*,[1] who speaks Italian.

One boat ran down another, some were drowned, in like manner as happened here ; Anne Elph[instone] and 20 of her friends were alongside, although we were 20 miles off and the weather indifferent.[2]

Journal

August 8.

Captain Palliser of the *Eridanus* saw the *Northumberland* off the Dodman yesterday at 5 P.M., making all sail to the Westward.

August 12.

P.M. At 1 fired a royal salute in honour of the Prince Regent's birthday. At sunset shifted my flag to the *Ville de Paris*.

To Miss Elphinstone

[*VILLE DE PARIS.*] *Sunday 13th.*

Yesterday we held the birthday—a man party of eighteen — to-morrow the Ball on the like occasion. I have your note this morning and am sorry you have cause to complain ; still, you will get all right at Purbrook I trust soon. I expect every day to have directions about the remaining Frenchmen,[3] and then I am off.

---

[1] The doctor sent in place of Maingaud was the notorious O'Meara, who afterwards wrote *Napoléon en exil*. It is now known that the plan had been prearranged between O'Meara and Napoleon on the voyage from Rochefort.

[2] Printed in part in Allardyce's *Memoir*, but wrongly dated August 15th.

[3] Savary, Lallemand, and Planat, who, having been proscribed by Louis XVIII., were detained and afterwards interned at Malta.

All you see in the papers is nonsense about
Bony.   Sir H. Bunbury had no conversation with
him.[1]   He had no conversation with Nap, only
brought me a letter and took my answer.   Bathurst
never was in the ship.   Lyttelton,[2] Byng,[3] and
Lord Lowther[4] came with Cockburn and wanted
to go on board the *Bellerophon*, which I refused.
He was anxious no doubt about his fate, but
always temperate and civil ; even funny, and
jocose at times.   Asked my advice about law,
etc., etc.   Not pleased at being styled General.

" If not Emperor, I am First Consul.   You
made treaties with me as such."

" Yes, Sir, but when you crushed the Common-
wealth, you sank that title in Emperor."

He did say he would not quit England alive.
I laughed.

He said, " Would you go to St. Helena,
Admiral ?—Oh, no, *Plutôt la mort*.   I will not
leave this ship, you must take me by force."

" Surely you will not reduce an officer like
[me] to a measure so disagreeable."

" Oh no ! but you shall order me," and at
the door of the outer cabin he said :

" Admiral, I have given you my solemn protest in writing.   I now repeat I will not go out
of this ship but by force—you must order me."

" My barge is ready for your reception, and if
you choose to go in her, please to warn them and

---

[1] But cf. Bunbury's memo. of his conversation on July 31.

[2] ? William Henry Lyttelton, afterwards third Lord Lyttelton, at
this time a Whig member of Parliament.

[3] ? General Sir John Byng, afterwards Earl of Strafford.

[4] William Lowther, afterwards 2nd Earl of Lonsdale, at this time
in Parliament and a member of the Treasury Board.

the ladies. It depends on you, and I order you to go."

" Allons."

He went to the gangway, thanked Maitland and the officers, and then the men ; bowed to all, and went on to the boat. Bertrand and Madame, Montholon and Madame, Gourgaud and Las Casses I fetched and put beside him, but he said, " What ! do you take the trouble to come too ? Sit by me, we shall *cose*." [1]

He talked of St. Helena, laughed at the ladies being sea-sick, asked if that was the *Tonnant* of Aboukir ? If the *Bellerophon* was old ? Why I changed my name from Elphinstone, which he knew me by ever since Toulon ?

When on board the *Northumberland* he talked to all, and asked questions very quick, and said, " Let us look at the cabin," took me with him, said :

" This is very good, better than the *Bellerophon*, for my little green bed is in it."

We then came out on the deck, he began to talk to the land officers, and I took leave of him and Sir G. C[ockburn] and in an hour made the sig[nal] to weigh and part company—it was then dark.[2]

Journal

August 19.

Ordered my flag to be struck this evening at sunset.

---

[1] *Sic*, but *causer* is evidently intended.
[2] Printed in Allardyce's *Memoir*, but with numerous mistakes in transcription.

The surrender of Napoleon marked the end of Keith's activities. He was in his seventieth year, and thenceforward lived in retirement.

It was two years afterwards that his eldest daughter, Margaret, became the wife of Napoleon's ex aide-de-camp, who towards the close of the year 1815 had come to live in England. As may well be supposed, Keith evinced the strongest aversion to the marriage. He refused at first even to see the young couple, but soon relented towards his daughter. It was some years before he consented to meet his son-in-law. Flahault's tact and charm of manner, however, eventually triumphed over all obstacles, and he was at length admitted to the Admiral's home circle, if not to his affections.

" Bonny, the Reptile ", had by that time been laid to rest at St. Helena, and his one-time antagonist at sea survived him less than two years. He died at Tulliallan, the castle which he had recently built on his property near Kincardine-on-Forth, on March 10, 1823.

IX
ST. HELENA

LETTERS FROM LADY MALCOLM DURING
NAPOLEON'S CAPTIVITY

IN the last chapter we saw Napoleon on his way to St.
Helena, on board the *Northumberland*. On October 17,
1815, he landed on that island, where for the first six months
he was placed under Sir George Cockburn's charge. Cockburn fulfilled at the same time the functions of Admiral in
command of the Cape station, but in 1816 a double change
was made. Sir Hudson Lowe, whose quarrels with the ex-
Emperor were afterwards to become notorious, was sent out
from England as Governor of the Island and was given the
custody of Napoleon's person, while a little later Sir Pulteney
Malcolm was appointed to the chief naval command in
succession to Cockburn.

Admiral Malcolm had married a few years before,
Clementine, the eldest daughter of William Fullerton
Elphinstone, a brother of Lord Keith's. She accompanied
her husband, arriving at St. Helena on June 18, 1816, and
returning to England (when Admiral Plampin became naval
commander at the Cape) in July of the following year.

Everybody at St. Helena during Napoleon's captivity on
the Island would appear to have kept a diary or written a
book about their experiences, and the Malcolms were no
exception to the rule. Their Diary (for its Editor informs
us that it was the joint production of husband and wife)
was not published till 1899, when it appeared under the title
of *A Diary of St. Helena, 1816, 1817: The Journal of Lady
Malcolm* (A. D. Innes & Co., 1899).

Lady Malcolm's letters, which we are now printing for the
first time, are addressed to her first cousin, Miss Margaret
Elphinstone, and to her aunts, Hester Lady Keith and Miss
Mary Elphinstone. They cover, of course, much the same

ground as the diary, but throw a few interesting side-lights on the story of St. Helena.

The Malcolms remained on the island till September 22. They then went off for two months to Cape Town, but returned on November 23, and finally left for England on July 4, 1817. As will be seen, three of Lady Malcolm's letters were written during her first visit, one during the second, and one immediately after her return to England.

To Miss Margaret Mercer Elphinstone

BRIARS, *June 28th* (1816).

My dear Marg^t,

It is ten days since we arrived; I would not write to you before, because of Longwood. I heard such opposite accounts. Every story one person told me was altered by the next I happened to see, and contradicted by the third; so I waited till I had been there.

All communications are made through Bertrand;[1] the day after our arrival Sir H. Lowe wrote to him that he meant to bring the Admiral to introduce him, and the following day they went. Bonaparte received them very kindly, talked to Pulteney about English naval officers; what was the best sort of ships; asked if there was any particular news in Europe, and such like subjects. Then Pulteney asked leave to introduce some of his officers, who were also very well received.

The only carriages on the Island are the Governor's, drawn by six bullocks, and Bonaparte's. Riding is the best, and in some parts the

---

[1] In the original "Bertrande". It is curious that Lady Malcolm invariably misspelt the General's name.

only way of moving. I have been fortunate enough to get a good horse, and my first ride was to call on Mde. Bertrand. She is tall, thin, not handsome, but I daresay looks well when rouged and dressed ; she complains of ill health, but as she is in the way to increase her family, it is no wonder she feels sick. Bertrand is a soldier-like man with plain manners. Both of them appear in worse spirits than any of their party. Her manners are very pleasant. She makes no secret of her dislike to this place, and her wish to return to Europe for the education of their children. She is particularly anxious about her mother who by her last letters is in bad health. She speaks English perfectly. When they first arrived she went to Sir G. Cockburn's balls, but they have not gone out of late, and declined Sir Hudson's invitation to dinner. Sir G. & Ly. Bingham [1] and many of the Officers, often call on her in a morning. She used to dine every day at Longwood, but now only goes once a week. People say Bonaparte dislikes her and will not let her come oftener, but she told me it was the Emperor's great kindness in consideration of her being unwell.

The Governor sees all their letters, and though in our case I believe he would have dispensed with it, Pulteney thought it right to show him the one I had.[2] You will be surprised at what he

[1] General Sir George Bingham was the military commander on the Island.

[2] The context shows that this letter must have been from Flahault, and we can guess that it had reached Lady Malcolm through her cousin Margaret, who was to marry Flahault twelve months later. Flahault was a close friend of the Hollands, and was continually with them at Holland House at this time.

objected to in it : "*The Lady to whom you sent Iron ore eight months ago, begs you will ever rely on her attachment.*" You understood it to mean some French friend ; but it was Lady Holland, for Sir Hudson happened to be at Holland House when she received it from Bertrand. (Iron ore found at Elba.) There seems not much in the paragraph, were it not that Ly. Holland has written several letters to Bertrand (and I rather think I was told to Bonaparte also, but of that I am not quite certain). These letters she sent in parcels and in various clandestine ways. One was enclosed to a man of the Island whom she only knew by name and who of course carried it to the Governor. The purport of them was to encourage an idea that the *party* of which she affects to be the spokeswoman, feel a zealous interest for the inhabitants of Longwood. It is provoking that a woman who is a disgrace to the revered name she bears, should bring odium on a Party among which are ranked some of the first and best men of our country, and it is cruel to those she writes to (some letters are supposed to have reached them) because it is keeping alive a hope that can only end in disappointment.[1]

As Bonaparte has been sent here, that he shall be treated with all kindness, respect, and attention consistent with preventing his escape, is, I

---

[1] At Holland House this hope was expressed in the following inscription, dated 1817, which may still be seen beneath a bust of Napoleon (by Canova) in the garden of that historic residence. The lines are taken from Homer's *Odyssey*, Book i. 196 :

οὐ γάρ πω τέθνηκεν ἐπὶ χθονὶ δῖος Ὀδυσσεύς,
ἀλλ' ἔτι που ζωὸς κατερύκεται εὐρέϊ πόντῳ
νήσῳ ἐν ἀμφιρύτῃ, χαλεποὶ δέ μιν ἄνδρες ἔχουσιν.

imagine the opinion of all parties; I think I can venture to say it is Sir H. Lowe's. The chief difficulty seems to be the title of Emperor which he wishes to retain, and you know has been positively forbidden to be given to him. Sir Hudson, wishing to be as civil as possible, never names him at all; communications pass through Bertrand when he desires to make known at Longwood whatever he has to say. The Pole who came out to Bonaparte (I cannot recollect his name [1]) affirmed he had left his wife living with Lady Burdett, and that Sir Francis was to make a speech in Parliament against Bonaparte being kept here, in which all the opposition were to join. Wrong-headed as Sir F. is, one cannot suppose him wishing Europe again deluged with blood, and to suspect it of the more steady members of opposition, is too absurd to be believed by any except those foreigners ignorant of the characteristic of Englishmen, and willing to credit what they wish.

In consequence of this message from Lady Holland, Sir Hudson said he thought I had better not give the letter, but I might if I pleased. I, however, did as he advised, and merely told Madame Bertrand I had been asked to carry an open note, which I refused, not from it containing anything improper, but lest it had given rise to reports of my being the bearer of letters. I told

[1] This was Captain Piontkowski, a mysterious individual who was not allowed to accompany Napoleon to St. Helena in the first instance, but subsequently got leave to join him as " equerry ". Piontkowski later on tried to persuade a British officer, who was returning home, to take with him a copy of Montholon's " Remonstrance " against the ex-Emperor's captivity. He was at once sent back by Sir Hudson Lowe.

her all I knew of the writer, the reason you gave me for his not writing through the Secy. of State's Office, and all the rest of the note, Sir Hudson having said there was nothing else objectionable in it. By the bye Sir H. also observed that he did not see how it could hurt his mother [1] though he had written in the regular way, for he, Sir Hudson, had repeatedly sent letters from persons in France to Longwood.

I told Madame Bertrand of my wish to pay my respects then, and as she replied whenever I pleased, the Emperor had said he would always be happy to see the Admiral, Tuesday [2] was fixed. A house is building for the Bertrands, meantime they are living in a little place a mile on this side of Longwood.[3] Only Pulteney and I went ; we stopped there, and found Bonaparte had sent his carriage for Mde. B. and me—a German barouche drawn by six little Cape horses, the only ones that are reckoned safe in this country. They were driven by two men who used to drive him in Paris, and went at the gallop ; the road round a hill with a precipice on one side. At the gate the leaders took fright, but happily there were so many people standing they stopped them. We were received by all his people who took us into the dining-room, where Montholon, Las Cases, and Gourgaud were introduced to me. Las Cases, a little old man, I imagine very pleasant and entertaining. Montholon is like what we fancy " a French Count ". Gourgaud and Bertrand

---

[1] Madame de Souza.
[2] June 25, *vide* Lady Malcolm's account of this interview, *Diary*, pp. 17-25.   [3] This was the house known as Hutt's Gate.

are more soldier-like in their appearance. In a
very short time Bonaparte sent for us into the
drawing-room, which was darkened with green
venetian blinds. He met us near the door, bowed
to us all, and asked how we did. Having seen
Pulteney before, he addressed most of his conversation to me : said he heard I had been very
sick on the passage. Was it my first voyage ?
How did I amuse myself ?—and such sort of
questions. In about five minutes he asked us to
sit down, me on the sofa by him. He is said not
to pronounce French well ; I cannot judge of
that, but he does not speak distinctly, and I was
at a loss to understand some of his words ; which
on observing he desired Las Cases might come in,
when he recollected Madame Bertrand spoke
English. She, however, had opened the door and
Las Cases entered ; we continued to speak in
French with occasionally their assistance. On
asking me how I liked the Island, I replied that I
was a Scotch woman and therefore admired hills.
Then said he, " You know Ossian's poems ? " I
replied not in their original—for I was not a High-
lander, and could not speak Gaelic,—but perfectly
well in their translation, and assured him of their
authenticity ; that MacPhearson never made
them ; that I had met many people who knew
them in the original—which is all true. He said
he admired them very much, and on my observing I believed they were even more admired on
the Continent than in England, he replied, " It
was me made them the fashion ; I have even been
reproached with having my head filled with
Ossian's clouds ". Both the French translations,

he said, are bad, the Italian very fine.[1] The only time I observed him smile, was on his saying Fingal was an Irishman. I exclaimed I could not allow that, he lived in one of the Isles. " Of your Archipelago," he replied, "but you call it by another name." I think he is happy in his choice of questions. To Pulteney he spoke of Lord Hood, Admiral Cornwallis, and more particularly of Lord St. Vincent; to me of Lord Keith. He expressed his surprise at there being slaves on this Island — I thought with a satirical expression.

I daresay you have often heard a description of him. He is neither like any picture or anybody I ever saw. The profiles are like those of some of the pictures, but not the full face, which is rather too fat and very pale. His eyes light blue or grey, with a pleasant expression. His neck is very short and he holds his head forward when he sits. His figure is not unlike Mr. Adam's. I think his manner rather graceful than otherwise.

We were about half an hour in his company, then he bowed and rose, and we took our leave. In the dining-room we found cakes and wine. Madame de Montholon had a daughter the day we arrived, at the seventh month. I asked for her, and was told she would be glad to see me, accordingly Madame Bertrand went with me to her room. She was in bed with her infant. I was told she was very ugly, but in a becoming french nightcap she did not look so. She seemed

---

[1] Cf. the conversation on this subject with Capt. Ussher in 1814 (*Napoleon's Last Voyages*, p. 136). "Ossian" (Macpherson) was his favourite poet.

annoyed at the smallness of her child, I endeavoured to comfort her by telling her I had a
niece who had been much less (Mrs. C. Malcolm's
child). I was glad to hear she thought the doctor
who attended her as clever as those she had been
sent to in Paris, and she seems to be making a
good recovery.

Bonaparte has hitherto refused to see the
Commissioners.[1] Sir H. has found a house within
a mile of himself that the Austrian has agreed to
take, and it is putting in order for them. Balmain
is, I believe, to have a room in it, at least for a
time. What Montchenu is to do, he has not yet
determined. Houses are so scarce on the Island
our own soldiers are very ill off, particularly the
Officers with wives and families ; and everything
is so dear, it is next to impossible these Commissioners can live on their allowances. Everybody likes Balmain, clever, interesting, and
perfectly well bred ; he was really an acquisition
on the voyage. We liked the Marquis very well
too. He taught me French, and was very good-
humoured and agreed with every thing ; more
polite, with less civility than the Russ. Since
they have been here Balmain has conducted
himself with more good sense and propriety than
any of them. The Austrian is a Diplomatist, his
wife a pretty lively French girl. As acquaintances I like them very well all, but the Russ both

---

[1] The three Allied Commissioners (Baron Stürmer for Austria, the
Comte de Balmain for Russia, and the Marquis de Montchenu for France),
appointed in virtue of the Convention held at Paris in August 1815,
had come to St. Helena on the same boat as the Malcolms. Napoleon
refused to recognise them, or to see them otherwise than as private
individuals.

Pulteney and I think a superior man. What would make you tell us he was cracked ? [1]

Pray say to Aunt Mary and Ly Keith I will write them by the next opportunity, for I have had so much to write home, I am quite tired holding my pen. With Pulteney's kind regards, believe me ever, my dear Margaret

Your affect.

CLEM. MALCOLM.

To Hester, Lady Keith

BRIARS, *July 4th*, 1816.

My dear Lady Keith,

The only relic of Bonaparte I have yet been able to procure for Mrs. Mostyn, is a little of his hair which I enclose you ; it would be very precious were there not already in England as much as might make a fashionable wig ! This which I send, Mr. Balcombe [2] gave me, telling me the way he got it. It was one morning when Bonaparte lived in his house ; he arrived while he was dressing, so he said to Las Cases he was going to write to his mother and he wished much he could have some hair to send to the old lady. Las Cases replied he would ask it, so he went into the room and returned with some, of which this is a part. The writing paper your sister may think also deserving of a place in her Museum, it being the same in which Las Cases brought it

[1] Balmain was one of Miss Elphinstone's numerous suitors. Shortly before leaving England he had offered her his hand in writing. The letter is amongst the Bowood papers.

[2] The owner of "The Briars ", with whom Napoleon stayed when he first landed at St. Helena.

out of his room.   The hair on his head certainly
appeared to me like this specimen ; it is thin on
his forehead, and cropped, but not short, on the
neck.   His eyes are much lighter than I imagined.
I saw nothing in them ferocious, indeed the
expression of his countenance is pleasant, and if
his face was not too fat and too pale, I should
call it very handsome.   His manner too I think
graceful rather than the contrary.   He asked me
particularly for my relation Lord Keith ; if he
was still at Plymouth ; if he usually enjoyed good
health ; his age, and if he ever had the gout, a
disease he had heard sea officers are very subject
to.   He prefers speaking Italian to French, that
is not the only occasion when I have thought
how well it would suit you to have been in my
place. . . .

You would delight in the only conveyance,
horseback ; even my timidity prefers it to
climbing up the hills in the Governor's coach,
drawn by six bullocks at the rate of two miles
an hour.   Bonaparte has the only carriage drawn
by horses.   About Longwood is the most level
part of the Island ; he can drive a round of three
or four miles within his limits, on horseback he
can ride ten or twelve.   Whenever he likes to
ask for an English officer to attend him he can
come beyond them, but that he does not like.
The story of Capt. Poppleton [1] refusing to ride
with him was false, as also that of a sentinel
having fired at him.   When any of his suite

---

[1] Captain Poppleton was the British orderly officer whose duty it
was to attend Napoleon on his excursions.   Though Poppleton did not
refuse to ride with Napoleon, Napoleon evinced a strong distaste to ride
with Poppleton (Forsyth, *The Captivity of Napoleon*, ii. 179).

come beyond the bounds, they also have an officer with them. Bertrand rode here yesterday with a Dragoon officer. The French Commissioner happened to be with me at the time he arrived, which I was very glad of, for Montchenu knows a great many of Madame Bertrand's friends and relations as well as Bertrand's, and it was very tantalizing for them not to be able to see him to ask about them. Bonaparte refusing to see the Commissioners made the difficulty. Till he receives them he could not meet, except as they did here, by accident. I am sorry for the Bertrands, they seem so much more out of spirits than any of the rest of the party ; but they are all said to be a sad set, deceiving Bon^{te} and misrepresenting things to him on all occasions. I wrote so particularly of my interview with him, I do not repeat it.

Longwood stands high and it is often cold enough for a fire in the evenings,—a luxury I can never have the pleasure of wishing for here in the Valley. It is the middle of winter, and still so hot that I have no regrets my sweet boy was left in England. This is a pretty little cottage above a mile from the town, where a house is preparing for the Admiral. The difficulty of getting houses, and materials, and workmen to build them, is very great. They complain of the rain and damp at Longwood ; there is a camp near it, where our own people are only under canvas. I went to return Mrs. Younghusband's visit (the lady whose cruel correspondent put her silly letter into the newspapers) and found her living in a tent ; her bed, and her little daughter's, on the ground beside it, concealed by a sort of curtain, all their packages around. You never saw such a place, and though it might have been a degree better, the neatest person in the world could not have made it comfortable. A house is begun for them, but so many more people are on the Island than used to be, the numbers building makes them get on but slowly. I am told Bonaparte was extremely provoked at that letter; he said she had written what was not true, but concluded that it deserved contempt rather than anger. Provisions are almost as difficult to be got as houses. A cart load goes to Longwood every day; there are above 50 persons to be fed there. They complain the wine is bad, and how can it be otherwise, for if they get a week's supply at a time, the servants drink it all in three days. Bonaparte has a great appetite and the only time he remarked on what he got was the 14th following day of roast pig, he said, "Encore cochon de lait". It was however the fault of his own people, who took the turkeys and geese, and continued to send the pigs to his table! He must have a roast every day, but not a joint of meat, so it is difficult to find much variety. I am told he has an excellent cook, who wastes accordingly. There are no markets, so officers and people with small families can hardly procure fresh provisions. Five and six shillings is the common price of a lean fowl, an egg seven pence, so you may imagine the expense of Bonaparte's table. He is said to have observed, he costs more than he is worth.

Pulteney went to-day to introduce some of his

officers to him, he talked to him for two hours and half [1] on various parts of his life, and said he would give him some of the chapters of his history to read. They discussed the battle of Waterloo, which he said Wellington ought not to have fought, as according to all the rules of war he should have won it, because he calculated on Grouchy keeping the Prussians in check. Pulteney replied the Duke had felt confident the Prussians would join him in the afternoon and the result proved he was right. Then they talked on various other subjects, particularly the present state of Europe, which he considers very unsettled.

Pulteney joins in kind regards to all the family, and with my love to Georgy,[2] believe me, my dear Lady Keith, yours sincerely,

CLEM : MALCOLM.

To Hon. Mary Elphinstone

THE BRIARS, *July 25th*, (1816).

My dear Aunt,

. . . . When Bonaparte was here while Longwood house was preparing for him, only the drawing-room of the other house was built. In it he had a little bed in the corner, sofa, tables, books neatly arranged, and a tent pitched close to it, for a dining-room. Las Cases slept in one of the rooms above, the rest of his attendants were lodged in the Town, for Mr. Balcombe and his family were in this house. He used to have coffee before he was up in the morning, then breakfast

---

[1] This conversation is given *in extenso* in the *Diary*, pp. 25-35.

[2] Lady Keith's infant daughter, Georgina Elphinstone, afterwards Mrs. Villiers and Lady William Osborne.

in an arbour in the garden, which is at a little
distance behind the house; there he spent many
hours, reading, writing, and sometimes playing
at chess. There is a field in front of the house, a
grass walk between two rows of trees from a gate
at the bottom to the house door, to which there is
a porch with a seat. After it grew dusk he used
to sit in this seat, and walk up and down the walk
for an hour or two. He usually dined about
seven, and after dinner he used to join Mr. Balcombe's family and play at cards or any game.
People desirous of seeing him used sometimes to
come to Mr. Balcombe's in an evening, but he
did not like it. Bertrand told me that during his
wars, getting up for one hour or two to receive
accounts from his outposts about one in the
morning had given him a habit of getting up in
the night, and at Paris he used to rise and transact
business at that extraordinary hour. He perse-
veres in the custom, and reads for an hour or
more, which makes him late in a morning. That
accounts for the stories that have been told of
his being overheard walking about his room,
instead of sleeping. Bertrand also told me he
is very fond of Italian music—the slow and
melancholy kind—but it must be very good;
he has too correct an ear, and too fine taste to
endure bad, or French music, which he considers
execrable. He very often will not see people,
even when they go by his own appointment. We
are told he professes himself a physiognomist,
and took a liking to Pulteney's countenance.
However that may be, he received me with all the
attention and civility in his power, but I wrote so

minute an account of my introduction to my
Father, and also mentioned it in my letters to
Margaret & Ly Keith, that I daresay you have
already heard every particular of it. By Sir
George Cockburn I wrote you a note, and I also
sent you one from Teneriffe. I reserved my
letter to you for further particulars.

I have seen Mde. Bertrand several times, and
she has called here. I wished to have asked them
to dine, but the steepness of the roads makes it
almost impossible for a woman to move after
dark, unless she is a very bold horsewoman—not
Mde. Bertrand's case. Hers, as she tells me,
having been the gayest house in Paris, it is no
wonder she thinks this solitude frightful; they
now do not dine at Longwood above once a week.
I have lent her some novels to help to pass the
time. I wonder she does not try to teach her
three very fine children, if it was only for amusement, but she has no idea of that. Bertrand
teaches them the little they are taught; the Miss
Balcombes tell me he also dresses Madam, and
" does hair quite beautiful "; it seems an odd
employment for one of great Nap.'s Generals!
Poor man, he seems even more wretched than
Madame.

I have been again at Longwood visiting
Madame de Montholon after her recovery; she
is a lively Frenchwoman, but I like Madame
Bertrand better. We desired Las Cases to inform
Bonaparte we were there, in case he had been
inclined to see us; but he sent a message he had
not been well that morning and was very sorry he
was not dressed. I believe he often passes the

morning in his dressing-gown, and does not dress
(which after all is only in an old coat) till three
or four o'clock. When Pulteney had his long
conversation with him the day he went to introduce some of the officers of the *Newcastle*,
among other questions he asked him, What would
have been the best time for the English to have
made peace with him ? Bonaparte replied, When
Lord Lauderdale was at Paris, if Mr. Fox had
lived. Pulteney then asked if Mr. Fox's death
had made any difference in the terms proposed.
He answered, " No ". Then, said Pulteney, you
left Lord Lauderdale in Paris and went to make
war on the Prussians. Bonaparte laughed, and
said there was no time to be lost. Then he talked
of something else ; and Pulteney remarked, whenever he did not like what he said, or was not
prepared to answer him, he immediately changed
the subject. He has not yet seen the Commissioners. He said he would see them as private
individuals. That they did not choose ; and then
he desired to see a copy of the convention by
which they came here, and it was long before the
paper could be found. Stürmer (the Austrian)
has got a house near Plantation House. It was
in a ruinous state, but Sir Hudson assisted them
to make it habitable. It is called Rosemary
Hall, and was formerly the residence of the
Wranghams. He affects the diplomatist, and
Monchenu, like a true Frenchman, puts himself
foremost on all occasions. Balmain's spirits
seemed to sink at the sight of the Island, and he
is fanciful about his health ; but in all the little
difficulties that have occurred he has conducted

himself with more propriety and good sense than any of them. He is by much the superior man of the three. We have been several times at Plantation House.[1] They have dinner parties of between 20 and 30 two or three times a week. Lady Lowe is very pleasant, and Sir Hudson too sometimes, but he is very absent in company. He speaks little, and if not spoken to he often falls asleep. There is not much sociality on the Island; few or none of the inhabitants ever ask any one to dine.

I hope, my dear Aunt, you will continue to write to me, and with kind love to Lord and Lady Keith, and to Margaret,

Believe me ever your affectionate
CLEM. MALCOLM.

To Hon. Mary Elphinstone

ST. HELENA, Janry 26th (1817).

My dear Aunt,

Sir John Malcolm [2] sent me yours and Lady Keith's letters from the Cape. I regret Pulteney's duties did not permit our remaining there till his arrival, to have heard his histories; however the letters were a great treat. From No. 2 you would hear we returned here in November.[3] We found our house not in a very habitable state, but we have now got it tolerably comfortable. It is the best and coolest house in the town; nevertheless

---

[1] The Governor's (Sir Hudson Lowe's) residence.

[2] The Admiral's younger brother, who was then on his way to India, where he was to distinguish himself in the war against the Peshwa.

[3] The Malcolms were away at Cape Town from September to November 1816.

from one till four o'clock it is far too hot to be agreeable. But that is all the complaint I have to make of it, for in spite of the heat I never was in better health, and Pulteney too, except his eyes, and for weak sight certainly the climate is very unfavourable.

I did not write you by the *Orontes* [1] because Capt. Cochrane was to call and tell you all about us. There is not much news on the Island. Madame Bertrand and Mrs. Wynyard have both got sons, and with their infants are doing well. Bonaparte still confines himself to the house, and all his exercise is sometimes playing at billiards. I am told he has invented a new game, which he plays with his suite ; they have all the balls and push them about with their hands. I believe Pulteney is the last visitor who has seen him ; he had an interview of about three hours about a fortnight ago. [2] I trust the report that a successor to Pulteney is appointed will prove true. He will be very glad to see him arrive, and I shall be delighted, for I tire much to see my pretty darling again, and all my friends. I flatter myself I shall find them as well as when I last heard of them.

I am very glad of the improvement you tell me in Clemy Elphinstone's health. I wonder I have never heard from any of them! Surely they know all they need do with their letters is to put them into the post. This goes by the *Icarus*, which

[1] The *Orontes* (Capt. Cochrane) had left St. Helena for England in December 1816 with Captain Piontkowski and three of Napoleon's servants on board.

[2] A full account of this interview is given in Lady Malcolm's *Diary*, under January 11, 1817.

came out at the same time with Bonaparte; of course Captain and Mrs. Devon were well acquainted with his party. They are just returned from Longwood; they found Madame Bertrand wonderfully well. They did not see Bonaparte; both the Montholons and Bertrand said he was always in his dressing-gown in the mornings, and as they did not seem to wish them to visit him, Captain and Mrs. Devon did not press it.

My kind wishes to all the family party, and believe me,

Your affec.,

CLEM. MALCOLM.

To Madame de Flahault

UPPER HARLEY STREET, *Sep.* 3rd (1817).

My dear Margaret,

. . . I received your last letter so short a time before I was to leave St. Helena that I did not write in answer to it. Madame Bertrand was very glad to hear of Madame Lavalette, who is her relation. No doubt anything respecting Longwood must be interesting to M. de Flahault, and of course to you too.[1] Pulteney was there the day before we sailed, taking leave himself, and introducing his successor.[2] General Bonaparte had had a toothache and swelled face, which occasioned his delaying for a day to receive Lord

---

[1] Margaret Elphinstone had married the Comte de Flahault in June 1817.

[2] This was on July 3, when Sir P. Malcolm took leave of Napoleon and introduced Admiral Plampin, who succeeded him in the command at the Cape.

Amherst : [1] he, however, saw his Lordship on the 1st July, and had a *tête-à-tête* conversation with him for about an hour, after which the suite were admitted. When Pulteney saw him on the 3rd July he was quite well and conversed with his usual good spirits.[2]

My last visit was on the 19th June. Lady Lowe lent me her little carriage, a thing like a sedan chair on wheels, drawn by a pony, which shook me so much I was very unwell for several days after, so could not venture up the hills again on the eve of my voyage. Complimentary messages, however, passed between us, and General Bertrand and General Gourgaud came to see me on the morning of my departure (July 4th). On the 19th June we had a long interview with Bonaparte ; [3] it is impossible to imagine he does not at times give way to deep depression, and I used to fancy that might be the case when he sometimes declined seeing us, saying he was unwell. I have often heard of him angry, but I never heard of any one having seen him low. Every time after Pulteney, alone or with me, visited him, he talked and laughed—with a degree of spirit, that if I had not seen I could not have believed—on past events in which he was the chief actor, and on subjects so interesting to him, that but for the " je " and " moi " I could not have believed he was talking of himself. He still spends

[1] William Pitt, Earl Amherst (1773–1857), afterwards Governor-General of India. He was on his way home from a diplomatic mission in China.

[2] The *Diary*, however, states that the Admiral " had never seen him so much apparently indisposed ".

[3] *Diary*, pp. 146 ff.

the greater part of his time writing his history.
Escape, I think, he is perfectly aware is completely
impossible, but I doubt his having made up his
mind that amidst the changes that are continually occurring in the world, he may not some time
or other be allowed to quit St. Helena. Walking
is the only exercise he has taken for many months,
and not much of that. In my last visit he gave
me a beautiful coffee cup and saucer of French
china, and expressed his satisfaction at the
attention the Admiral and I had shown him and
the ladies with him, in coming to visit them
sometimes.

I understand it is generally believed a house
was sent out to him from this in frame. That is
not the case; he lives in what was the Lieutenant-
Governor's country house, with additions that
were put to it by Sir G. Cockburn. His compart-
ments consist of a billiard, a drawing, a dining-
room, and library, bedroom, dressing-room, bath
and servant's room. I cannot say they are all the
handsome large rooms they ought to be. At the
same time the good furniture which was sent out
gives them a look of comfort.

Count de Montholon has four apartments
joining Longwood House, which Madame has
arranged to look very neat. I never saw either
her or the Count but apparently in good spirits.
She used continually to complain to me of her
triste life (and to be sure, a more *triste* state
for a Parisian lady can hardly be imagined), but
mixed with so many enquiries about dress, laugh-
ing and chatting all the time ; I never could feel
for her as I did for Madame Bertrand. One of her

complaints was that Madame Bertrand had more visitors than her, which was true; for almost every passing stranger got a pass to go up to Count Bertrand's in the hope he might procure them an interview with Bonaparte, or if that could not be obtained, that at least they might have a glimpse of him walking in the garden. Madame Bertrand speaking English made them prefer visiting her. Besides there was a general belief that Madame de Montholon hated to see English people, from her dislike to the whole nation. Judging from the reception she always gave me, I have no reason to believe it was true. As she rode well, I recommended to her to ride often, both for health and amusement, but she said the Count was so much engaged writing or copying for *l'Empereur* he could not accompany her, and she did not like riding without him.

General Gourgaud has also a room in Longwood House; like the others, I believe, he writes or copies a good deal for Bonaparte. He rides on horseback most days, often to the camp at Deadwood, where he used to converse with the officers of the 53rd Regiment. When they had a review, or races, he always attended, but was the only one of the party who did so. Dr. O'Meara and Capt. Poppleton have each their room; the rest of the house of Longwood is occupied by the servants.

The Bertrands have a separate house across the garden, four rooms, and four over; it was built on purpose for them. I must confess they are the part of the Longwood party I am most sorry for. I believe Genl. Bertrand is sincerely attached to Bonaparte, and if his condemnation

in France had never taken place and he had the
power of returning there, or coming to this
country, still I think it would cost him a severe
struggle to resolve on leaving his master. At the
same time he has a great affection for his wife
and children. She is miserable at St. Helena,
which cannot be wondered at in a woman used to
society and formed to shine in it, uniting what is
agreeable in both English and French manners.
She pleases every one who visits her. The eldest
boy is of an age to go to school, the rest coming
on, and there they can get no education. The
Count is continually with Bonaparte. He does
teach them, as much as he has time for, but
unluckily she has no turn for instructing them;
so that on her and the children's account I think
he would perhaps come away; but until his condemnation is reversed where can he come to ? [1]
In talking of what they mean to do, she said
she would never consent to leave the Count.
I believe he would have been very glad to have
sent his oldest boy home with us to a school
in England, but she would not hear of it. Her
infant is a great amusement to her; she nurses
him herself. She is very ill off for female servants;
her aunt, Lady Jerningham, whom I have seen
since I arrived, is in hopes of being able to send
her out one or two, which will be a great comfort
to her.

The party are very fortunate in their physician,
Dr. O'Meara, who is an honourable and well-
informed man. They all like him, and have a

[1] Bertrand returned to France after Napoleon's death in 1821. He
was then restored to his former military rank.

good opinion of his professional skill. Also in Capt. Poppleton, with whom they all seemed to be on the best terms; he is the orderly officer. Bonaparte does not like his office, but I heard him mention Capt. Poppleton himself in terms of approbation. Hardly a day passes in which Bonaparte does not see Dr. O'Meara; often converses with him for hours, sometimes in French but more frequently in Italian. The Dr. speaks both languages perfectly.

I see no reason why their friends should not write to them or send them things, provided it is through the Secretary of State's office; but, even in kindness to them, in no other way should it ever be attempted, as sooner or later it is always found out and occasions irritation. Many people here imagine addressing to Sir Hudson Lowe's care is the same thing as sending officially; but Sir Hudson does not consider it so, nor does he like letters or things for them to be addressed to himself, though coming open through the Secretary's office he sees them all. The Bertrands begged me to thank various persons for writing to them and sending them books and toys for their children, which were very acceptable; adding they hoped to be excused doing it themselves, as except on matters of the greatest importance they never wrote to anybody. I confess I think their not writing is from a foolish pique. When our officers were prisoners in France, that their letters were obliged to pass open, did not hinder their writing to their friends when they had an opportunity, and the cases seem to me similar. I find people here so ill-informed respecting St. Helena;

I hardly know whether what I have written will be information or not to M. de Flahault, further than that we left the whole party in good health.

.   .   .   .

Believe me, my dear Marg^t,
Your affect. Cousin,
CLEM. MALCOLM.

Nearly four years had still to elapse before the Emperor was laid to rest under the weeping willows of his island prison. " Bonapartism " was then already on the wane—it was soon to be considered " extinct ".[1] The news of his death did not reach France till more than two months after the event, and a contemporary diarist has recorded his sense of disgust at the absence of emotion displayed in Paris when (on June 10, 1821) the newsboys ran down the streets crying : " Mort de Napoléon à St. Hélène—deux sous ".[2]

[1] James Gallatin, *Diary*, p. 259.
[2] *Ibid.* p. 186.

X

THE EMPRESS JOSEPHINE

AN APPRECIATION BY MADAME DE SOUZA

" J'ENVOIS une bague à ma fille. Elle me vient de la meilleure personne qui ait été au monde—l'Impératrice Joséphine. Je la prie de la porter, parce qu'il faut porter du Rose sur soi tout le temps de sa grossesse si l'on veut avoir un garçon."

These words are extracted from a letter written by Madame de Souza to her son Charles, a few months after the latter's marriage in 1817 to Lord Keith's daughter, Miss Margaret Mercer Elphinstone. We should perhaps add that any hopes founded on Josephine's ring were doomed to disappointment, for the Flahaults' first-born proved to be a girl, and was in course of time followed by four more daughters.

Née Adèle Filleul, Madame de Flahault had at the age of seventeen married the Comte (Charles François) de Flahault de la Billarderie, an elderly French nobleman of ancient lineage, who in the last years of King Louis XVI. succeeded the famous Buffon as *Intendant du Jardin Roi.* He later fell a victim to the revolutionary guillotine, and his young widow was left with an infant son to fight the battle of life alone and almost without resources. Some time before Charles François de Flahault met his end, his wife had fled with her child to London. Thence they moved to Germany, and it was not till the Directory was about to be replaced by the Consulate that they returned to Paris, after an absence of nearly seven years.

Madame de Flahault had supported herself whilst abroad largely by writing the novels through which she is now best remembered. Her first work, *Adèle de Sénange*—a romance in which the story of her own life is thinly disguised—was published in London in 1794, and enjoyed an immediate and unqualified success. Others followed it in due course, notably *Eugène de Rothelin*, which earned the encomiums of

MADAME DE FLAHAULT (SOUZA)
AND HER SON CHARLES
Painted by Madame La Bille Guiard in 1785

so competent a critic as Sainte-Beuve, and was considered by him to be her *chef-d'œuvre*.[1]

In 1802, three years after her return from emigration, Madame de Flahault married again. It was from her second husband, Don José Maria de Souza de Bothelho, that she received the name by which she was henceforth and more generally known.

It seems curious that in contemporary accounts Madame de Souza is scarcely mentioned in connection with the Empress Josephine. That their relations must at one time have been most intimate, is proved by the document we print below, but the evidence is reinforced by the allusions to the Empress which may be found in Madame de Souza's letters, as well as by the presence of several keepsakes (besides the rose ring already mentioned) which originated with Josephine and are now amongst the treasured possessions of Flahault's descendants.

The two women were in years almost contemporary, Madame de Souza having been born in 1761, Josephine in 1763. They married about the same time, and both their first husbands perished on the scaffold. We may well suppose that their friendship was one of long standing and that it went back to the years before the Revolution, when both ladies had been prominent in the gay society of Paris.

It is probable also that Josephine assisted the young widow's return from her emigration in 1799. Madame de Flahault had obtained (possibly through her old admirer, Talleyrand, then Minister for Foreign affairs) a passport for this purpose in 1797, but apparently made no use of it at the time. This was in the days of the Directory, but two years later Napoleon was about to become First Consul, and Josephine had become a power in the land. Nobody was in a better position to extend to Madame de Souza a helping hand, and (although we have no evidence of the fact) there can be little doubt that Josephine did so.

In the early months of 1800 Charles de Flahault wrote to Napoleon a remarkable letter which has been printed by Masson[2] and others. The boy was too young for military service, so his protector Talleyrand had installed him the year

---

[1] *Portraits de femmes : Madame de Souza*, Sainte-Beuve.

[2] *Le Général Comte de Flahault.*

P

before in the *Dépôt Général de la Marine*. This, however, did not suit young Flahault's ambitions, and in the letter in question he boldly asks the First Consul that he may be at once appointed his Aide-de-camp. He was not quite fifteen years old at the time! We may perhaps perceive in the wording of this document signs of composition more experienced than a schoolboy's, but in any case it is impossible to believe that, without friends at court, he would have dared to address the all-powerful First Consul directly, or that had he done so he would have received any reply. He did not, it is true, obtain the post he asked for, but it was at this moment, and evidently in response to his letter, that he was appointed to the "Canaris", or *Houssards volontaires*, a corps d'élite, whose privilege it was to guard the person of Napoleon. In all the circumstances, therefore, it may not be unfair to suspect that the famous letter was composed by his fond mother, and that she was in a position to ensure for it a favourable reception at the First Consul's court.

But however this may be, there can be no doubt that by the year 1800, if not before, Madame de Souza was on terms of intimacy, not only with Josephine, but with all the Bonaparte family. This is shown by a phrase from a letter (almost the only one written before 1815 which survives from Madame de Flahault's pen) written to her son in August, which we shall quote later on in another connection (*infra*, p. 219). It is also proved by the document which forms the subject-matter of this chapter. As will be seen, Madame de Souza recounts therein an incident which occurred when Napoleon became enamoured of Mademoiselle Georges, and we have it on the authority of the lady in question that this was towards the end of the year 1800.

As already stated, Madame de Flahault's second marriage took place in 1802. Thenceforth her relations with the Bonaparte family seem to have been less close than formerly. We are told that Monsieur de Souza fell out soon afterwards with Talleyrand about Portuguese affairs, and Talleyrand was still at this period all powerful in the government of France. Thus it came about that Souza's appointment as Portuguese ambassador in Paris was terminated in 1804. He was offered the Portuguese Embassy in Russia, but elected to remain as a private individual in Paris, where he spent the rest of his life.   He died in 1825, his wife eleven years later.

Under the circumstances above described Madame de Souza could scarcely expect to remain a privileged visitor at Malmaison.   Her letters, however, show that she continued to meet the Empress on public occasions and at the watering-places which both used to frequent from time to time, and that she never lost the love and veneration with which she regarded " la meilleure personne qui ait été au monde ".

Madame de Souza's note on the Bonapartes and Beauharnais was found—scrawled on two large sheets of paper without date or heading—amongst a mass of her letters, unfinished novels, and literary débris.   There is no indication as to when she may have written it, other than the handwriting, which would appear to be that of her later years.

The Empress Josephine and the Beauharnais Family

* Josephine was a Creole, and, like all Creole women, had a jealous disposition.   Her husband stimulated her jealousy, either by showing temper when she teased him, or by taking her into his confidence after the quarrel had been made up. She was, indeed, the only woman for whom he ever really cared.   At times he would surrender himself to her completely, confessing his infidelities ; at others he would be touched by her tears, or amused by her indignation.

He used to make her the most extraordinary revelations, allowing her to see through his mind as through a glass, and to discover all its workings.

When the jealous fit was on her she became uncontrollable, and if any one, whether it was her son or her daughter or her female friends, tried to reason with her, she believed them to be involved in a conspiracy against her.

I well remember an occasion when I had been attempting to make her see that as the year is divided by seasons, so life must fall into separate volumes. I pointed out that if her husband chose to have mistresses, she should resign herself to his caprices, so long as she retained his friendship. Then if he were only certain of finding in her company the most tender friendship, a spirit of sweet reasonableness and a genuine and constant interest in all that concerned him, he might even come back to her. I argued that in married life the object should be, not to look for complete happiness, which was not there, but to give one another such an amount of satisfaction as would make each wish to be in their own house rather than in somebody else's. I pointed out that once a woman was past her thirtieth year, she could only expect the second place in the affections of the man she loved ; but that at any age, and with any husband, she could retain this second place—provided she freely surrendered the first, and made up her mind to show her husband all those little attentions which go to make life pleasant.

I was waxing quite eloquent on this theme when she turned on me her dark eyes, flashing with passion, and said : " That would be a premature death, and worse than death itself ". She then turned her back on me and did not speak to me again for a week. But my advice went home.

When the Emperor returned he found her in a calm and gentle mood. This put him out of temper, for he had been expecting her to make a scene, and was astonished when she did not do so. He was suspicious by nature, and always uneasy when things did not turn out as he expected. He told her that he had just come from Mme Duchâtel.[1] She raised her eyes to heaven and said not a word. Then he tried to goad her, but without succeeding in making her show the slightest sign of anger. Still more at a loss, he began to talk of Mlle Georges to whom he had just then taken a fancy.[2] Josephine heaved a sigh but made no reply. By this time he was fairly puzzled and asked her if she no longer loved him. " I shall always be your best friend," she replied, " but I am uneasy about you, and your state of health makes me anxious. You may not care for me any longer, but surely you still care for yourself ? " She then began to cry, for she was genuinely distressed. He was now touched and bade her tell Mme Duchâtel that he would see her no more, while he gave warning to Mlle Georges, and for a few days proved himself the most devoted and assiduous of husbands. But in the enjoyment of this blissful moment, the Empress Josephine forgot both her age and her good resolutions. The Creole blood asserted itself once more, and with it the Creole jealousy. Thenceforward their life was made up of months of discord, with only rare moments of peace.

I am still convinced that if she could have been satisfied with his friendship, he would never

---

[1] The pretty young wife of an old conseiller d'État.

[2] It was Nivôse an IX. (1800–1) that Napoleon's liaison with Mlle. Georges first started. It lasted, according to her own account, about two years.

have divorced her; for he would have opened
his whole heart to her, while she would have
detected the intrigues of which she was the
object, and would have known how to counter
them.

Her position as Empress, constantly threatened as she was with a divorce, married to a man
much younger than herself, in the plenitude of his
fame and power, and surrounded on every side
by relations who hated her and put every kind
of temptation in the Emperor's way, was indeed
full of difficulty. If he had once begun to confide
in his own family about his love affairs, he might
have confided in them about more serious matters
also. It was Josephine herself who allowed him
to discover that he could get on without her. As
a general rule he followed the line of least resistance. When he was displeased with Josephine
he turned to his own family. After he had made
up the quarrel with his wife, he would strike at
the Beauharnais through the Bonapartes, whilst
he would wound the feelings of his brothers and
sisters by comparing them to their disadvantage
with Eugène and Hortense. Yet all the while he
was tender-hearted towards everybody, and ready
to do any one a good turn, but he could never
hide his ill-temper. Unfortunately for himself,
he never punished his enemies, although he frequently attacked them in such a way as to pro-
voke the bitterest resentment. The Bonapartes
were extremely jealous of the Beauharnais. They
detested the Empress Josephine, wherein they
were wholly wrong; first because she was really
an excellent woman, but apart from that, because,

PLATE USED BY NAPOLEON AT ST. HELENA, WITH
PORTRAIT OF THE EMPRESS JOSEPHINE
"Peint à la Manufacture Impériale de Sèvres par J. B. Isabey"

being continually threatened with a divorce she was naturally anxious to please, oblige, and win them over : she was in fact rather predisposed towards them than otherwise.* [1]

[1] Appendix No. 18, p. 324.

XI

LOUIS BONAPARTE

A Correspondence with Madame de Souza
(1800–1802)

We print in this section a fragment of what must have been
an extensive and intimate correspondence between Louis
Bonaparte and Madame de Flahault before her second
marriage with M. de Souza. The letters are few in number,
but in the light of the liaison which afterwards existed
between Charles de Flahault and Louis's wife, and of
Madame de Souza's encouragement thereof (*vide infra*, Part
XII.) they are of a somewhat suggestive character. Madame
de Flahault had a large correspondence, and her admirers
were not a few ; it is significant that, under such circumstances, the only letters which survive are those addressed
to her by Louis Bonaparte.

Madame de Flahault, as we have already seen (*supra*,
p. 209), returned from emigration in the early part of the year
1799, and was soon on a friendly footing with the family
of the First Consul. The first of Louis's letters shows that he
was already intimate with her in August 1800, and when we
discover from Flahault's *détails de service* that he had not long
before this been transferred from the *Houssards volontaires*
to the regiment (the Vme *Dragons*) of which Louis had
lately become colonel, it is difficult to resist the suspicion
that his mother was in the plot. The sequel shows that
Flahault at once became the friend and the protégé of his
new colonel, with whom we find him travelling in Prussia
towards the close of that year. It may be remembered that
this journey was undertaken by Louis ostensibly to improve
his military education, but in reality to escape the impor-
tunities of Napoleon and Josephine, who were already endeavouring, from motives of state, to inveigle him into a
marriage with Josephine's daughter Hortense.

Madame de Flahault left unturned no stone in her

endeavour to secure her son's advancement.[1] Here is an extract from a letter which, though without date, was evidently written to him when on his way to Berlin with Louis in October or November of 1800.

* " Do not cease to make yourself useful to Louis.[2] Let him see that you can give him the friendship of a man of education. Follin as your captain must come first, but you can win a place in Louis's heart so easily that he would be scarcely aware of it. Jérôme and Madame Bonaparte have both told me that he is very fond of you, and is always singing your praises. I am delighted to hear of it." * [3]

Louis and Charles de Flahault returned to France at the end of January 1801. Flahault then presumably went back to duty with his regiment, while Louis settled down for a time at Baillon, not far from Paris, where he had just bought a house. The marriage project was, however, soon revived, but Louis once more escaped the toils—this time by arranging for the transfer of the Vme Dragons to Spain, as part of the so-called army of observation under Leclerc. He joined his regiment on their way at Bordeaux, and went on with them to Burgos, whence on May 16 he sent the letter to Madame de Flahault which is printed below. It must have been about a month later that Charles wrote to his mother from Ciudad Rodrigo : * " The colonel continues to show me kindness—I am dining with him to-day. He occasionally puts me under arrest,—but it is all done in quite a friendly way ! " * [4]

In September Louis again returned to Paris, to succumb at last to the pressure of his brother and his sister-in-law as regards Hortense. The marriage was celebrated at the beginning of the following year (January 4, 1802). It will be observed (*infra*, p. 226) that Louis wrote to Madame de Flahault on January 3, and was apparently unaware that the ceremony was to take place the following day, while

---

[1] In August 1815, when Madame de Souza was placed under surveillance as one suspected of Bonapartism, she is reported as saying, " Hélas ! je n'ai jamais été que Flahaultiste " (*Letters of Harriet, Countess Granville*, i. 70).

[2] *Continuez à être aux petits soins avec Louis.*

[3] Madame de Flahault to Charles de Flahault (Bowood Papers).

[4] Charles de Flahault to Madame de Flahault (Bowood Papers).

he saw no prospect of paying Madame de Flahault a visit until after the marriage ! From the tone of this letter one may well believe him when he wrote in his Memoirs : * " Never was there so sad a ceremony, never can a married couple have felt a stronger presentiment of all the horrors attendant on a forced marriage between two persons quite unsuited to one another." *

The bridegroom remained only a few days with his bride, and on the 1st of March, pretexting military duty, went off to join his regiment, then quartered at Joigny.

It was here that Madame D'Arblay (Fanny Burney) met both Louis and Charles de Flahault. The first she described in her diary as " a young man of the most serious demeanour, a grave yet pleasing countenance, and the most reserved yet gentlest manners ".[1] Of Flahault she has much to say in an unpublished letter, written many years later to Lady Keith, at the time when Flahault was about to marry that lady's stepdaughter, Miss Elphinstone. Mme. D'Arblay here mentions Louis's devotion to Flahault, and tells Lady Keith that " he was never happy out of his sight ". She goes on to sing Flahault's praises, and it is evident that this young officer had won her heart by his good looks and agreeable manners. The conquest was completed by his singing for Madame D'Arblay's benefit " with a forcible and penetrating voice, God save Great George our King, with an expression of respectful devotion that came close to my heart and filled my eyes with tears of delight ".[2]

Louis is known to have come back to Paris for a few days in April. His visit, if hitherto unexplained, can now be accounted for by his letter of the 29th Germinal (*infra*, p. 228). It seems that Madame de Flahault was on this occasion the attraction, and that he never even saw his bride. He was soon back at Joigny, but departed again in May for Bagnères, to undergo one of the cures which henceforth were to occupy so much of his time. He returned in October, but only for a few days, for Hortense's confinement.

Historians are agreed that there was never any love between Louis and Hortense. There have been some

---

[1] *Diary and Letters of Madame D'Arblay*, iv. 173.

[2] Madame D'Arblay to Lady Keith, February 10, 1817 (Bowood Papers).

rather unconvincing attempts to suggest other women who may have had a prior claim on Louis's affections. Though Madame de Flahault has never been mentioned in this connection, it is difficult not to believe that he entertained something more than ordinary feelings for the woman to whom he could write as he did on the eve of his wedding day, and at whose request he came to Paris three months later. It will be observed that while neither of the two letters written at this time is signed, one opens with the initial letter of Madame de Flahault's Christian name, and the other has no beginning at all. The note of January 13, 1802, to Flahault is also not without significance. It would appear that Charles had found some difficulty in congratulating Louis on his marriage. Can it have been that the young subaltern had expected that his colonel would lead his mother, and not Hortense, to the altar ? Madame de Flahault was at this time in her forty-first year, and by all accounts she was still an attractive, if not a beautiful woman. We may note also she had been asked in marriage by Monsieur de Souza some three years before. Was it as a *pis-aller* that she accepted him in August 1802 ?

We are more familiar in history with Louis as the King of Holland than as the young colonel of a cavalry regiment. He is for the most part represented as a somewhat bad-tempered husband suffering from chronic ill-health, and as the recipient of caustic admonitions from his brother, on account of his failure to govern the kingdom committed to his charge on the lines which Napoleon desired. The letters which follow may serve to present him in a more attractive light—a man evidently capable of great affection, conscientious (perhaps even meticulous) in the care of his regiment, a reader of Sterne and a would-be writer of comedies. We can thus more easily understand how he made so favourable an impression on Fanny Burney at Joigny.

But all this was before his nature had been soured by ill-health and by his enforced union with a wife who professed to love him as little as he pretended to care for her. The estrangement between them was soon complete, but the love which Hortense could not give her husband, she was later, as we shall see, to bestow on one by whom it was fully reciprocated.

Louis Bonaparte to Madame de Flahault

PARIS.   1er *Fructidor l'an VIII.*
[18 *August* 1800.]

* I cannot accept, Madame, from your Charles, the beautiful Normandy mare—for of all vices selfishness is the one I dread and dislike the most. A dragoon needs a sound good-looking and reliable animal to carry him, and it is only fair that this one should not be appropriated by his colonel, who must of necessity have many horses. So you must not suggest it to me, or I might take your offer in the spirit of Sterne [1] and imagine that you had misjudged me. Finding myself viewed through eyes so beautiful and so indulgent as yours, must I not try, so far as in me lies, to be a better man! So I ask you to get your relative to buy for me the mare you spoke of, which " goes like the Devil ", and the other one, you mentioned to-day, which is already trained. It is important for me to have a horse of this sort, for I am going through a course of mineral waters which necessitates my taking things quietly.

I want to impart to you a project which, if I can manage it, I mean to carry into effect. We have been acting once a fortnight some plays at the Malmaison. We find it very hard to select them, and have been playing the pieces they give at the Français ; but although our audiences are not over critical, we feel ourselves somewhat eclipsed. Every one thinks that if we were to act something quite new we should avoid comparisons. I have therefore conceived the outline

---

[1] The allusion is not clear.

LOUIS BONAPARTE
From an etching by André Dutertre

of a comedy, and for some time past I have been cherishing the hope to see my work produced. I have been worried both by the subject and by the plot. My ambition is to give it a moral tone, whilst avoiding pedantry, and to display some originality—it may be too much to attempt, but the will to succeed always counts. I have found a subject and am only troubled by what remains, but for the whole of the next month I shall be in the position of a king who has shaken off the burden of sovereignty,[1] and I am resolved to take my time. I am in hopes that after a little rest, head and heart will work together for the execution of my great scheme. I have made up my mind that it shall be read only to you and the actors of the Malmaison. If you will promise me to listen to it, I will get to work at once, but pray don't tell any one of my secret. I am as yet only an author in anticipation; but after all hope is everything, especially when one reflects that so many clever men and institutions can hope no more, and that they have been crushed in the very act of forcing the gate of the Temple of memory. Pray excuse this outburst; perhaps it is a presage of success, for all the clever men of our day begin in this way.

Forgive, Madame, my scrawl [2] and my chatter. I implore you to remember only my dutiful admiration and my heartfelt gratitude.

LOUIS BONAPARTE.

[1] He had left his regiment, the Vme *Dragons*, and returned to Paris.

[2] *Mes pieds de mouche.* Louis was apparently well aware how difficult it was to read his handwriting. His letters, it is said, had always to be copied out before they were placed before the Emperor (Rocquain, *Napoléon Ier et le roi Louis*).

BURGOS, *le* 26 *Floréal an IX.*
[*May* 16, 1801.]

I have received, Madame, the letter which you have been good enough to write to me. If I could do so without using words constantly reiterated, I should once more try to express my feelings towards you, but I ask your leave to be silent. I would never believe that you could call my gratitude in question. Having filled me with pride by your friendship and your appreciation, you would surely not wish to rob me of the feeling that I must make myself worthy of them !

Your dragoon has for the last month held the rank of officer.[1] To his astonishment no doubt, I arranged that the squadron leader of whom he stood in such awe, should take him. I made him join a company whose captain is very strict, but the result proved quite contrary to my expectation ; for instead of being dominated by this officer, it was the novice who soon dominated the captain. I do not see more of your dragoon than of the other officers. When he misbehaves I scold him and punish him just like any one else ; I was treated thus at his age, and believing that it is for his good, I could not think of acting otherwise. But you may make your mind easy on this score, for I am bound to count as my first, and my most sacred duty, the welfare of the men who have been intrusted to my care. I shall never forget to keep an eye on my young friend, nor my duty to one who is your son. Though, Madame, I cannot be his mentor, I can contrive

---

[1] Charles de Flahault's *États de Service* show that he was promoted *Sous-Lieutenant* on March 25, 1801.

that he should, gradually and without too much hardship, familiarise himself with his profession— a hard one even for grown men, but much harder for a spoilt child like him.   I must beseech you to bear in mind that this is my affair and that I am under a double obligation in the matter.

As for money, you are giving him too much. Allow me to say that in his case you are doing exactly what is done by certain old nurses, who when children are unwell, stuff them with sweets which sooner or later make them really ill. Besides this I must add that it is inadvisable for a youth in his position, who has to associate with old soldiers, most of them bearing the scars of battle, to be set above them by the length of his purse.

Young Meulan [1] has wit and parts, but he makes a mistake in believing himself born to be an officer ; he should have suppressed these ambitions, especially from his comrades, who see in him only a raw recruit—if I may use the language of the barrack room.   He is in fact a very young soldier, has seen no fighting, rides indifferently, and holds himself so badly on parade that at reviews he is always picked out by the General.   He has no stability of character, and worse than all, he treats his comrades with unconcealed contempt.   He is always associating with the officers, and lives with them, which is contrary to all ideas of military discipline, and he has forced me to reprimand him—had I not done so the rest of the *sous-officiers* would have behaved likewise and discipline would be at an

---

[1] Théodore Comte de Meulan (1777–1833).   He afterwards served with distinction in the Napoleonic campaigns and became a General.

Q

end—for what is to stop them from following his example ? I cannot permit such things without being false to my duty and making myself generally disliked. I have published in regimental orders that " any one who tries to put himself above his comrades, instead of showing that he deserves promotion, shows that he does not deserve the rank he already holds "—this was with special reference to him. He should remember that your son has now been a dragoon for a year and that he has had the good sense to identify himself with his fellows. But M. de Meulan will settle down. He will learn his duties or will have to leave the regiment, and when we come back from Portugal he will have become a good officer ; but he will have to work. What I may say unofficially binds no one except Louis Bonaparte, but as commander of a regiment I can yield to no one in the strict execution of my duty. Any marked favouritism instead of . . .[1]

PARIS, 13 Nivôse an X.
[3 January 1802.]

A.[2]

It will be soon, but not just yet—probably the day after to-morrow.[3] I should have come to wish you a happy New Year, if I had not had a quantity of little things to attend to. I shall not be able to do myself the honour of seeing you till after to-morrow.

I am expecting my friend any minute. He comes from the regiment, and perhaps your son

[1] The end of this letter is missing.
[2] Madame de Flahault's Christian name was Adèle.
[3] *I.e.* his wedding, which in point of fact took place at 9 P.M. on the day following.

will take advantage of this to get a lift in his carriage.   I am so glad, both for your sake and his.

Pray accept my best thanks for all the evidences of your friendship. At the beginning of a new year, one bids farewell to a large part of one's past life, and one greets the first day of the future. In the past, as in the present, I have been delighted to see that you reciprocated my friendship, and it is a source of satisfaction to me to recall the admiration and devotion which, as you, Madame, well know, I have ever felt towards you.

To Charles de Flahault

PARIS, 23 *Nivôse an X.*
[13 *January* 1802.]

I was never offended by your silence, my dear Flahault ; this seemed to me to be merely a matter of thoughtlessness. But what hurt me was your writing that you could not think what you were to say to me, or how to begin ! [1] I feel for you true friendship, based upon your good qualities. Your faults are readily excused, I know all about them. I might stress them twice as much as they deserve, and they would still not be your most striking characteristic.

I am annoyed that Dommanizet [2] did not send you home at once. I was anxious that he should do so for reasons of my own. Situated as you are, the best argument is prompt obedience.

---

[1] It would seem that Louis had been expecting, but had not received, congratulations from Flahault on his recent marriage.

[2] Probably the officer commanding the Vme *Dragons* in Louis's absence.

Good-bye, my young friend ; though you are no longer 15,[1] I feel, and always shall feel, the same affection towards you.

Louis Bonaparte.

To Madame de Flahault

Mardi, 29 *g*[l].
[Paris, 19 *April* 1802.]

I am here, in fulfilment of the promise which in the kindness of your friendship you demanded of me. I have gladly resumed a life of solitude, and although Paris, with all its conflicting interests, contains some friends whom I love more than I am able to say, I shall be there all this week, a happy and busy man.

I will add no more. Why finish by paltry phrases which have been made cheap by constant use ? Is not the object of a letter to convey to the person one is addressing, one's true feelings towards her ? *[2]

The last letter is dated " Ce Mardi, 29 g[l] " but without the year. The Republican month of Germinal began on March 22, so the 29th Germinal would have been the 19th of April. But the 19th of April did not fall on a Tuesday till the year 1803, and this letter cannot have been written in that year. It is addressed to " Madame Flahault, Rue d'Anjou ", and Madame de Flahault had become Madame de Souza in August 1802. It is obviously written from Paris, while in April 1803 we know that Louis Napoleon was doing a cure at Montpellier. Moreover, it is on record that in April 1802, being then at Joigny with his regiment, he came up for a few days to Paris. There can therefore be little doubt that the letter was written in April 1802.

[1] Flahault was born on April 21, 1785. He was therefore now sixteen years of age.   [2] Appendix No. 19, pp. 326-330.

XII

QUEEN HORTENSE

(i.) "THE FROGS ASK FOR A KING"

WE print first in this section an account of the infantile
indiscretion of Napoleon Louis Charles Bonaparte, Queen
Hortense's eldest son, on the occasion of the installation of
his parents as King and Queen of Holland.

The story has been told before, but will bear repetition,
given as it evidently is by one who personally witnessed the
incident in question. Who that person may have been we
cannot say, but the story, as it seems, is related by one of
the ladies of Queen Hortense's entourage, and must have
been given to Flahault, amongst whose papers it was found.
The occurrence took place in 1806, but our account was
either written, or more likely copied, in 1813, as appears
from the watermark on the paper on which it is set down.

Napoleon Louis Charles died about a year after the
episode which is here related. It was generally said to have
been their common sorrow at this catastrophe which again
brought his parents for a time together, and led to the birth
of their third son, Louis Napoleon, in 1808.

* When the Emperor Napoleon determined to
place upon the throne of Holland his brother
Louis, he arranged that the request for their new
King should proceed from a deputation of the
States - General. It was then some time since
Holland had been conquered by France, and its
administration was conducted very much in
accordance with the Emperor's wishes. It is true
that there was still a *Grand Pensionnaire*, and
that the country was in name a Republic, but it
was completely subject to the power of France.

Thus it was an easy matter for Napoleon to
contrive that, while his ambitions were not too
apparent in the eyes of Europe, his rule should
be exercised through the medium of his brother
—a puppet monarch, from whom he expected
even more implicit obedience than from his own
prefects.

The Stadholders, who longed for a court, with
orders of nobility, and decorations, were pleased
to see their country become a Kingdom ; while
the Republican party, which had espoused the
cause of Republican France, had neither the
power nor the means to show any opposition.

All this is a matter of history. But in the
midst of great events there are often little inci-
dents which appeal specially to a woman's sense
of the ridiculous.

After Napoleon, in full panoply of state, had
listened to the request of the States-General,
he sent for the Prince and Princess Louis, who
were forthwith acclaimed as King and Queen of
Holland. The new Queen held by the hand
her son, a boy of five, who was now the heir-
apparent. He has since died, but was a charming
child, and had been very carefully educated. He
had an excellent memory, and every morning
used to learn by heart a piece of poetry, which
the Emperor often made him repeat. When
the presentation of the new King to the States-
General, and of the Deputies to the King, was at
an end, every one proceeded to assemble in the
drawing-room. The Emperor sat down, and in
order, I believe, to put the company at their ease,
he began to play with the child. While thus

engaged he said to him : " What have you learnt
to-day ? "—" A fable, mon oncle."—" Let me
hear it." In a shrill childish treble the boy
began *Les Grenouilles qui demandent un Roi.*
There was general consternation, followed by a
dead silence, and the child went on :

Les grenouilles se lassant
De l'état démocratique
Par leurs clameurs firent tant
Que Jupin les soumit au pouvoir monarchique, etc., etc.[1]

The new Queen, overwhelmed with confusion,
turned scarlet. Napoleon for a few moments
managed to keep his countenance, but in the
end he broke into one of those wild peals of
laughter which are impossible to control. That
night the incident was the only subject of conversation and the important change which had
taken place in the government of Holland was
completely forgotten. The French no doubt
showed their amusement too unreservedly, but
the Dutch were perhaps unnecessarily upset by
what had taken place, for it was after all purely
accidental—but was there ever so strange an
accident ! *[2]

(ii.) "Ma Cousine Henriette"

The documents which follow deal primarily with Queen
Hortense in association with Charles de Flahault and with
the birth and infancy of their son, Auguste de Morny.

These were matters on which at the time the closest
secrecy was maintained by all the parties concerned. It was

---

[1] *La Fontaine*, Book III. Fable 4.
[2] Appendix No. 20, p. 330.

"HENRIETTE"
(QUEEN HORTENSE)
From a miniature by Isabey

not until many years had elapsed that anything about them became known, while the early days of the Comte de Morny have remained wrapped in obscurity up to the present time.

It is scarcely to be expected that the Queen of Holland's letters would under such circumstances have been kept by her lover, and we have been unable to discover amongst the Flahault papers even a line in her own handwriting. We can, however, throw a good deal of fresh light from other sources upon this part of Queen Hortense's life.

We begin with the unpublished correspondence between Flahault and his mother. This, though unilateral (for we have, up to the year 1815, only the letters written by Flahault, and afterwards only those written by his mother—some five hundred in all), appears to be, so far as it goes, complete for the period with which we are dealing.

The Flahault-Souza letters are mainly interesting as containing a running commentary on the Napoleonic campaigns in which Flahault was constantly engaged until Waterloo; while the Souza-Flahault correspondence affords some vivacious sketches of society and politics in Paris during the years immediately succeeding the Second Restoration of the Bourbons. Both, however, include much intimate family matter, amongst which we should expect to find some allusion to the relations which are now known to have existed between Queen Hortense and Flahault, for it is clear that throughout life Flahault had no secrets from his mother.

The Queen of Holland, however, is scarcely ever mentioned in Flahault's letters by name, and on the few occasions in which she is so referred to, she is spoken of in the most formal manner, as if she were a mere acquaintance. It was some time before it became apparent that the letters were nevertheless replete with allusions both to her and to Morny, but that these (in common with any references to other persons highly placed with whom the Flahault family were concerned) are almost invariably cloaked behind false names. These names were of course well understood as between the correspondents, but were so ingeniously contrived as to put any one else completely off the scent. The ' code ' was so well conceived that it was calculated to deceive those who might read the letters (with a full knowledge of the facts) a century after they were written, as well as those who, without that knowledge, might have read them at the time. It was indeed a long time before their present editor was able to penetrate the disguises adopted.

In Flahault's earlier letters Hortense at first figures as *ma cousine Sophie*, after a time she becomes *Henriette de Capellis* — a good touch, since Flahault really had a cousin of that name, though she had married some years before her maiden name was adopted for Hortense. *Henriette* seems to have been considered a convenient pseudonym, for its use is continued by Flahault through the years preceding Waterloo, and by Madame de Souza afterwards.

In 1812 we first find Auguste de Morny (who had been born the previous October) as *Henri*—but this name and his sex was quickly dropped, and he is soon even better concealed as *ma nièce* or *ma petite filleule*, while sometimes he was more vaguely designated as *ma famille*. It was not till after Napoleon's fall in 1815 that Flahault begins to call him *Auguste*. Hortense had then left Paris, and Flahault was endeavouring to join her in Switzerland; it may have then seemed that the time was past for dissimulation. As *Auguste* the boy remains in Madame de Souza's later letters. We may note, however, that in 1817 when Flahault, having just married Miss Elphinstone, had acquired the habit of showing her his correspondence, Madame de Souza (with a due sense of delicacy) talks of the boy as *le protégé de papa*.

To complete the list of pseudonyms it should be explained that Flahault at times speaks of himself by his nickname *Néné*, at others by his second name *Auguste*. The Emperor Napoleon occasionally may be found as *ton oncle*, the Empress Josephine as *ta tante*. Talleyrand is *Monsieur Bégo*, and a certain Madame de Laval who was at this period one of Talleyrand's principal lady friends (and as such was not regarded with a kindly eye by Flahault's mother) is always referred to as *Madame de Roquépine*.

With this by way of introduction we will give some selections from the unpublished correspondence between Flahault and his mother. The pseudonyms are printed throughout in italics.

The first extracts are taken from letters written by

Flahault from Germany, where he was quartered in 1807-8. This is the period when Hortense figures as *ma cousine Sophie*, and we are allowed to see that she had already for some time been befriending Flahault in high places.

Flahault to Madame de Souza

BOGDANEN, 24 *June* 1807.

* Tell *Sophie* about me, offer her some of that amber which I sent you and let me have some news of her.

ELBING, *July* 1807.

If you could obtain *ta tante's* [1] interest in me through her daughter, it would be very useful to me. But it should not be done except in this way, for if *ton oncle* [2] knows that either you or I had anything to do with it, he would be against it. I shall be very glad of this, for one must keep in touch with one's family !

STOLPE, 3 *December* 1807.

Many, many messages to *ma chère cousine Sophie* if she is still in Paris. Will *her father* take her back to the country this winter or will she spend it in Paris ? [3] . . . I really cannot write to *Sophie*. I am too fond of her to write in such haste as I am compelled to do at this moment.

ANCLAM, 19 *January* 1808.

Sophie's letters are very kind, but the news that she is *enceinte* [4] hurts me more than I can

---

[1] The Empress Josephine.   [2] Napoleon.

[3] Hortense's husband, Louis Bonaparte, is here evidently intended, and the " country " means, no doubt, Holland.

[4] Queen Hortense gave birth to Louis Napoleon (afterwards Napoleon III.) on April 20, 1808.

say. I tell you this, but do not mention it to her, she is sufficiently unhappy as it is. Please write often to me about her, I feel very anxious, and I don't know why, but I am in dread of serious trouble . . . that *ta cousine* should be well is all I wish for. Nothing else counts, for I live only in my love for you and her. . . . I am getting a lot of grey hairs. I enclose half a dozen of them which I will ask you to send on to *Sophie,* that she may see the colour of her friend's hair ! . . . My aunt [1] only took an interest in my career because she did not want to leave to *Sophie* the credit of having been the only one to assist me in it. . . . *Sophie* could forget three years of unkindness if she knew that her friend was unhappy, but *she* would forget three years of felicity rather than run the risk of a little personal inconvenience.*

The next extract is from a letter which, though undated, we can place as written from East Prussia in March 1808. Madame de Souza had just finished her novel *Eugène de Rothelin,* and had sent her son an advance copy of the book. Charles is delighted with it, and writes to tell her that he has been able to recognise all the characters. He sees himself in the hero (*Eugène*) and *Sophie* in the heroine (*Athenaïs*). He takes exception, however, to the fact that (in the book) *Eugène* invites *Athenaïs* to tell him of all her troubles, while in similar circumstances he says *Sophie* had come to him and poured forth the story of her life, *d'elle - même et de son propre gré* ! We can gather from the context that this interesting declaration on Hortense's part took place in the early part of the year 1805, and thus it becomes apparent that her friendship with Flahault commenced at a very much earlier period than has generally been supposed.

[1] This would seem to be an allusion to a genuine aunt, Elizabeth de La Borde, Comtesse d'Angivillers, whose name occurs frequently in the letters of the preceding year. She died, however, in March 1808.

QUEEN HORTENSE'S MUSIC BOOK
Given to the Comte de Flahault

[*March* 1808.]

This characteristic action of *mon amie* not long before you went to Berlin,[1] touched me more than I can tell you ; tell *Sophie* that I shall never forget it. I am glad to think that *mon amie* is even superior to your heroine ! . . . What is this plan of which *Sophie* talks. It fills me with anxiety. How deeply I love her ! How happy all her little gifts have made me ! The aigrette . . . the little necklace . . . the songs[2] . . . the seal . . . the cross. . . .

Is it true that *M. Bégo*[3] and *le Goguenard*[4] are going off on a journey together ? I should be very sorry if this were so, and would rather not have anything to do with it. Tell this to *Sophie*.

Not long after this letter was written Flahault (as we must suppose, at Hortense's suggestion) was recalled from Germany. He proceeded at once to Spain, where he seems at first to have been without definite employment, but in July (through Hortense's agency again) he was appointed aide-de-camp to Berthier, Prince de Neuchâtel.

Henceforward we hear no more of *Sophie*, but (following perhaps an arrangement made with Madame de Souza on his way through Paris) *ma cousine* becomes *Henriette* or *Henriette de Capellis*. Now, as already mentioned, Henriette de Capellis had been the maiden name of one of Flahault's cousins (a grand-daughter of the Marquis de la Billarderie), The real Henriette had, however, married a Marquis de Cintré some four years earlier ; there can be no doubt, therefore, that we have here a fresh pseudonym for Hortense. In July of 1808 there appears to be yet another, for *ma tante*, whose 'position' was so 'alarming' at that time

[1] Madame de Souza's visit to Berlin took place in April 1805.

[2] Were these the " Romances " of our illustration ? The volume was certainly a present from Hortense, but there is no indication when it was given to Flahault.

[3] Talleyrand.   [4] Comte de Montrond.

and to whom Flahault sends a seal as a mark of affection, can surely by no possibility be any one but the Queen of Holland.

BURGOS, 13 *April* 1808.

Give me some news of *ma cousine Henriette de Capellis.* Has her marriage [1] taken place? How dear her happiness is to me. Tell me about her.

BURGOS, 16 *April* 1808.

Please give me some news of *ma cousine Henriette.* I am most anxious about her health. . . . When is she to be married? I think this event must be over by now. I should then know that she had recovered. Poor *Henriette*! She has not been very lucky so far, but God grant that she may be so in future.

BURGOS, 4 *May* 1808.

Tell *ma cousine* that I love her with all my heart, and that the note she has sent me has made me very happy.

[? BAYONNE] 9 *July* 1808.

I cannot understand what you mean when you speak of the alarming position of *ma tante.*[2] I was much afraid, after seeing a certain person here, that she would think she had a grievance against me. She was told stories and they succeeded. I beseech you to answer me, and to tell me what I ought to do, for I am much upset

[1] For " marriage ", it would seem, we must read " confinement ", which (as already stated) took place on April 20, 1808.

[2] The real aunt, Madame d'Angivillers, had died a few months before this letter was written. Flahault could, therefore, now use her name without risk of misunderstanding. The context of this extract, as well as of that which follows, shows that the person referred to can have been none other than Queen Hortense.

about it. It would be awful for me to know that she was wretched; if that were so, true happiness could never be mine.

BAYONNE, 21 *July* 1808.

I wrote not long ago to *ma tante*. . . . How good she has been! I have often judged her hardly, but if my mind has been unfair my heart has suffered for it.

How could she make up her mind to go and bury herself in the country, without even a home in Paris? Will she not come there any more? Poor woman, and after such a brilliant life! . . . . I could not wish to live without *ma tante* and you. Have a little seal made for *ma tante*. It must be well cut, with an aloes leaf and this motto round it, " Praemium aevi aurea dies " : " Un jour d'or est la récompense d'un siècle d'attente ".

The Prince de Neuchâtel has just told me that I am to be his aide-de-camp. I am proud to hold the post, and to owe it to her to whom I already owe so much.

The two facets of this seal are reproduced in our illustration. It is now in the possession of Lord Lansdowne, and until the discovery of the above letter had completely defied all attempts at explanation. On one side of the seal can be seen an emblem, which we now know to be a leaf of the Aloe — symbolical it must be supposed of a long period of waiting for the flower which this plant only produces at rare intervals. Above this is the Latin motto chosen by Flahault. Underneath there is another legend *Fuira-t'il jamais*, which may perhaps have reference to the reverse side. On this the sun (presumably concealed behind a mass of clouds) is invoked to show itself, by the words *Soleil je t'implore*. An anchor, the sign of constancy, can be dimly perceived in the centre of the picture. The second facet was clearly not in the original scheme. We must, therefore, conclude that it was added by the person to whom the seal was sent, and that the gift was thus returned to the donor. This would explain the fact that it remained eventually in Flahault's hands.

Though a definite separation between Hortense and Louis Bonaparte did not take place till the year 1809, their relations at the time this letter was written were already strained to breaking point. Louis was in Holland, and his queen had made up her mind to go there no more, and to " bury herself " in her château at St. Leu.

That Hortense must have been the person for whom this gift was intended there can, I think, in the light of the context, be no doubt.

*　　*　　*　　*　　*　　*

The single letter which follows, written from Schönbrunn in the year 1809, is interesting as showing how carefully Flahault's movements in Vienna must have been reported in Paris, and how jealously he was watched by Queen Hortense.

10 *September* 1809.

I found here a letter from *ma cousine* which has upset me, more especially as her suspicions are quite unmerited. These can make no difference to an affection as genuine as mine, but they really hurt me all the same. I go to Vienna no more. I was warmly welcomed there, but since it was wrong in her eyes, I shall not go there again. My only amusement there was making music. She knows how fond I am of music, but if to secure her peace of mind I must give up the most innocent pleasures, I will make the sacrifice. I am so anxious to make her happy that nothing will seem too difficult to secure that

SEAL GIVEN BY COMTE DE FLAHAULT
TO QUEEN HORTENSE

object. My own happiness must always depend on hers.

* * * * * *

We now come to the year of Auguste de Morny's birth. Flahault was taking the waters at Bourbonne in July and August, and his letters show that he went towards the end of that month to visit Hortense, who left Aix-les-Bains about the same time for Prégny. In the middle of September, in a letter to Madame de Boucheporn, Hortense announced her intention of setting forth on *un petit voyage pour voir mon frère*. According to the *Journal de Paris*, she returned to the capital on October 10. Masson inclines to the opinion that her confinement had then taken place, though Morny's birth was not notified till October 21.[1]

The extracts which follow are, as before, taken from Flahault's letters to his mother.

BOURBONNE, 19 *July* 1811.

I quite agree with you as to *le premier*—however difficult it may be. It would be delightful for me to have him in my home. . . . I enclose a letter for *Sally*,[2] ask her if she has any for me, and send them on to me

24 *July* 1811.

I am expecting to make a little journey and to leave this about the 15th or 20th of next month.

29 *July* 1811.

Here is a letter for *Sally*, please send it on to her for me.

3 *August* 1811.

You can write and tell me anything necessary, through *ma cousine* whom I shall see before long.

---

[1] *Napoléon et sa famille*, vii. 156 ff., and *infra*, p. 260.

[2] Sally was an English maid who had been for many years in Madame de Souza's service. She is, however, never mentioned except in Flahault's letters written from Bourbonne, and it would seem that here again we must read *Hortense*.

R

4 *August* 1811.

You do not tell me if you received my letters for *Sally* and if you pass them on to her. This poor girl and I have a correspondence which may not appear interesting to you ; it is so, however, to me.

REYNEL, 12 *August* 1811.

From the 22nd onwards you can impart to me anything you wish, through the same channel as you have been using for my own letters. My own health is fair, and it is only right that I should go and attend to hers.

If the Prince [1] were to ask you what I am doing and how I am, say to him : " He must be better, for he writes to me very seldom ! " That will put a stop to all questions.

I don't know at what moment in September I shall be in Paris. There was some talk of a tour in Holland—that would make things easier for me. . . .

BOURBONNE, 20 *August* 1811.

From the 23rd write to me at *ma cousine's*,[2] using the same address as you did for her. . . . Unless you see an exceptional chance please do not make any definite arrangement about the *châtelaine* [3] before I get back.

We will now give two extracts from *Le Portefeuille de la Comtesse d'Albany* (Pélissier, 1902). If we may judge by Madame de Souza's letters, the widow of the Young Pre-

---

[1] Berthier, Prince de Neuchâtel, to whom Flahault was acting all this time as aide-de-camp.

[2] *I.e.* at Prégny.

[3] Under this term the nurse or housekeeper who was to look after Hortense's baby was no doubt understood.

tender was one of her dearest friends; Madame d'Albany was not, however, allowed to share Queen Hortense's secret.

Madame de Souza to Comtesse d'Albany

PARIS, 25 *August* 1811.

Néné is at Bourbonne.[1] He has become mad about reading. . . . He is alone at the waters and reads all the day long.

PARIS, 7 *November*, 1811.

Votre penchant[2] has been very unwell, but I hope that it has been a case of evil out of which good may come. It seems that the poison has left her chest and taken the form of a lumbago, which made her scream with pain. But no one dies of the lumbago, and since she has had it, she has ceased to cough. All the same she is terribly thin. May God keep her, for she is an angel !

* * * * * *

There follows the Russian campaign of 1812, at the outset of which Auguste de Morny was about six months old. We now find him under various disguises—*Henri, ma filleule, ma petite nièce*, etc.

Flahault's letters of September 19 and 21 (from Moscow) show that some one had once more been trying to make mischief between him and Hortense by suggesting that his affections were elsewhere engaged. The rival in this case was no doubt the beautiful Comtesse Potocka, who, as she herself

[1] This was misleading (and no doubt intentionally so), since *Néné* (Charles de Flahault) was at that moment with, or on his way to Hortense at Prégny.

[2] Hortense. She reappeared, we are told, in society in the month of November, and some explanation had to be given as to her state of health.

tells us in her *Mémoires*,[1] had fallen in love with Flahault some years before, and had seen a good deal of him in Paris in the year 1810.   He met her again this year on his way through Warsaw, when he wrote to his mother that he had been received *avec une bonne et franche amitié*, adding *vous en auriez été parfaitement contente je vous assure*.   Now Madame Potocka makes no mention whatever of this meeting in the *Mémoires* above mentioned, a fact which implicitly corroborates Flahault's statement (*infra*) that he resisted all her blandishments on the occasion in question.

The frequent mention of one Bertrand will be observed in these as well as in subsequent letters.   This was the Abbé Bertrand, an old friend of the Flahault-Souza family, who from being an under master in Madame Campan's famous academy, had become tutor to Hortense's children—though, in order to divert suspicion, Flahault sometimes calls him *Bertrand, mon valet de chambre*.   Flahault's letters to Hortense were never sent direct, but generally through two removes—Madame de Souza acted as the first, and Bertrand was frequently the second.

Flahault to Madame de Souza

MAYENCE, 8 *May* 1812.

Be sure and kiss *Henri* for me.   Many tender messages to *ma cousine*.   I feel that, were ill luck to come my way, her affection would somehow keep it from me.   Embrace her for me, and tell her that I never cease thinking of her.

DRESDEN, 27 *May*, 1812.

Be sure and kiss *ma filleule*.

KÖNIGSBERG, 15 *June*, 1812.

All that you tell me of *ma petite nièce* makes me very happy.   I can assure you that it is not for

[1] *Mémoires de la Comtesse Potocka*, Casimir Stryenski, pp. 105, 112, 289.

nothing that I am so strict.   How could I refuse
you a pleasure, if I did not think it necessary to do
so ?   I can assure you that it would delight me
to permit it, but one must sometimes sacrifice
oneself.[1] . . . Here is a letter, which please pass
on to *Bertrand,* my *valet de chambre.*

VIASMA, 30 *August* 1812.

I am charmed with your account of my *petite
nièce.*   I should much like the very thing which
you would like, but it seems to me that we must
wait a bit longer.

Moscow, 19 *September* 1812.

I hope that *Henriette's* unhappiness has not
continued.   She surely cannot believe that
Auguste [2] could do anything which would distress
her.   I own that I am at a loss how the lady
in question [3] could ever have spoken of *Auguste's*
attachment to her.   Had it been true he would
have paid her a visit.   This new notion has probably entered her head because *Auguste* would not
go off to the country with her, and would not pay
her a visit.   I heard something about it since I left
Paris from one of her old friends, and was greatly
astonished.   I am perfectly certain that *Auguste*
loves nobody in the world except *sa femme,* and
will never love any one but her. . . . Here is a
letter from *Auguste* to *Henriette.*

Moscow, 21 *September* 1812.

I hope *Henriette* is no longer upset.   It can only
be a question of old letters from *Auguste,* and there

---

[1] It seems that Madame de Souza was already trying to get Auguste
under her own roof.

[2] *I.e.* the writer, Charles *Auguste* de Flahault.

[3] The Comtesse Potocka.

should not be even these. It is a trick on the part of the gentleman or of the lady, or perhaps of both, to see what may come. I am not anxious about *Auguste* and *Henriette*. They will always love each other.

Moscow, 4 October 1812.

How is it that you have given me no news of *ma cousine*? I am anxious about her. . . . Thank you for what you tell me of her *petite fille*. . . . My interests are confined to a few persons— three or four, including yourself.[1] These satisfy my affections.

Desne, 20 October 1812.

I am not writing to *Bertrand*, and shall probably not write to him for some days. You must show him my letters.

Königsberg, 20 December 1812.

I have only time to send my love to you and to the family—our good friend *Bertrand* is of course included in this designation. I have received from him a letter dated the 9th which has delighted me.

Königsberg, 27 December 1812.

You will not be astonished at the brevity of my letters, nor at the fact that they contain no enclosures for Bertrand.

Posen, 20 January 1813.

Shall I not find your *petite filleule* with Madeleine?[2] When do you think of installing her there? It seems to me that it would be

---

1 *I.e.* Monsieur and Madame de Souza, Hortense and Auguste de Morny.

2 Probably the *châtelaine* mentioned above (p. 242).

well to do so before my return—if I am ever to get home. We must be very careful with, but show no mercy to, the " fury ".[1] Pray remember the importance of breaking off all relations and communications with her. I hope you will let this impress itself on your mind, and not give way to the impulses of your good nature.*

* * * * * *

In 1813 Flahault, after a few months spent in Paris, is once more off to the wars. Almost every letter contains some reference to *ma cousine, la famille,* or *Bertrand.* We give a few typical extracts.

NEUMARCK, 13*th June* 1813.

What is the picture which *Madame Lundi* [2] has given me ? How grateful I am for her thought of me ! How kind she is ! Tell her please, all accustomed as I am to her goodness, how deeply I am touched.

NEUMARCK, 3*rd July* 1813.

Has *ma cousine* been to spend a few days with you ? Give me some news of her and embrace her for me. We are sufficiently nearly related for this to be permitted, though she can never be as near to me in relationship as she is in affection.

NEUMARCK, 18*th August* 1813.

Here is a letter for *ma cousine Henriette*, which I will ask you to send to *Bertrand* for her.

[1] *La furibonde.* She is several times mentioned, and was evidently a person in the secret of Auguste's birth.

[2] This is a new name for Queen Hortense. She is referred to as *la dame du Lundi* by Madame de Souza in her letters to the Comtesse d'Albany (*Portefeuille de la Comtesse d'Albany*, pp. 143, 146).

DRESDEN, *27th September* 1813.

Thank *ma cousine* for her seal and her motto. I shall put the word " par " instead of " pour ", and make the motto my own.[1] My well-being is not affected by anything which does not touch my family, they are everything to me. In their midst I defy misfortune, but away from them nothing can ever make me happy.

GOTHA, *23rd October* 1813.

You must give this good news [2] to *ma cousine*. She will be glad to know that my services have enabled me to recover the title which my father used to bear.

*   *   *   *   *   *

Our next extracts are from the letters written by Flahault at Fontainebleau during the fortnight which preceded Napoleon's departure to Elba.[3] Paris had capitulated to the Allies on March 30, and the Emperor, who had arrived at Fontainebleau too late to save his capital, was persuaded on April 4 to abdicate the throne in favour of his family. This conditional abdication was not accepted, and a week later (April 12) he was forced to abdicate without conditions. On the 20th he set out for Elba.

Flahault was with him during the whole of this time. His anxieties may well be imagined, not only on Napoleon's account, but on that of Hortense whose future lot was at the moment quite as uncertain as his own. He was ready, as we shall see, to marry her if she would but divorce her husband, and this we are told she had one moment almost

---

[1] We are unable to explain this allusion, for the seal in question is no longer extant.

[2] Flahault had been promoted *Général de Division* and made *Comte de l'Empire*.

[3] See also *supra*, pp. 67-72.

made up her mind to do.[1] Soon after the Allies had entered
Paris, Hortense quitted the capital with her children, and
joined the Empress Josephine at Navarre, whence a few
days later they all moved to Malmaison. It was while
they were there that they received a visit from the Russian
Emperor Alexander, and both mother and daughter were
soon established on the friendliest terms with that monarch.
Meanwhile a comfortable *dotation* of 400,000 francs per
annum had been assigned to Hortense by Napoleon. This
presumably would have been endangered had she formally
severed her connection with the house of Bonaparte. Her
position under the Bourbons was at all events doubly
secured, and though pressed to change it by her husband
as well as by her lover, she remained in name the wife of
Louis Bonaparte till the end of the chapter.

FONTAINEBLEAU, *7th April* 1814.

I send you a letter for *Henriette*. Try to
get it through to her. I hope that she may be
left in peace and happiness. For my part, so
far as in me may lie, I will do my very best to
make her so. . . . Kiss *ma passion* for me. . . .
Send this letter to *Henriette*, wrapped up in some
silk, or in any way you can, but try and get it to
her.

[15 *April* 1814.]

I do not think *Henriette* will be allowed to keep
her children with her. This would not be in
accordance with the canons of high policy, and
they are not likely to be waived in their favour.
If it rests with me to console her, I shall be very
glad to secure my own happiness, by making
hers. My whole life belongs to her, and with
her I would be the happiest of mortals. It is
probably best that at this juncture I should not

[1] Masson, *Napoléon et sa famille*, x. 119 ff.

be near her. I am sorry she was not able to arrange a divorce. That would have made everything simple, if it had been agreed to. Why don't you tell me more details about her ? There would certainly be consent so far as her brother [1] is concerned—but what does it signify whether they consent or refuse ? Neither the one nor the other means anything any longer. If it is fated that I am to go, I shall not in any case go beyond the frontier. You cannot conceive, my dear mother, what an agony it is staying here. But it must come to an end, and if in the event I am to pass my whole life between you and *Henriette*, I can only thank heaven ; I shall be the happiest of men. You know well that, in the matter of her children, I could scarcely have been of any use to Henriette so far as *l'ami de Néné* [2] is concerned. You know that it is difficult to touch him. Send this letter to *Henriette*,[3] if a good opportunity should present itself.

[? 16-19 *April* 1814.]

When I have performed this last duty I shall come back to you—if the Russians have relieved us of their odious presence—without shame and without regret ; ready, if *Henriette* will only say the word, for a life of perfect felicity. Did you send her my letter ? [4] Write to her, impress upon her by any means you can, that she must make

[1] Prince Eugène.

[2] *Néné* was Charles de Flahault's 'petit nom'. *L'ami de Néné* is of course Auguste de Morny, whose position was not likely to be affected in the same way as that of his half-brother by the change of regime in France.

[3] At Malmaison.   [4] Of April 15.

her arrangements with her own people, that her
husband's family need not concern her. The
basis of her action must be the separation which
already existed between them. Let her stick to
her own people. They are beloved and respected
—nobody has a word to say against them, while
from the others she must expect every kind of
trouble. In a word, my dear mother, a home
in the country with her and with you, would be
happiness unalloyed.[1]

*   *   *   *   *   *

Though Hortense was treated with the utmost consideration after Napoleon's first abdication in 1814, the Allies showed
no inclination to give her a similar chance the following year.
On July 17 she was ordered by Von Muffling, the Prussian
General in command of the allied troops, to leave Paris at a
few hours' notice. She made her way not without difficulty
first to Geneva and then to Aix in Savoy, where she remained
for some months.

Flahault, after Napoleon's departure for Rochfort, had
been given the command of the 9th Cavalry Division in the
so-called Army of the Loire, but we soon find him talking of
resignation, and before the end of July he obtained a *congé*
for six months, and returned to Paris. Thence he followed
Hortense to Aix, but was only allowed to stay with her for
two days (Aug. 13 to 15). He then moved on to Lyons,
where he remained for some weeks under police surveillance,
pending the arrival of the passports which he had demanded
from Paris. It was while he was there, and she at Aix, that
the unfortunate occurrence referred to below (first extract of
Oct. 1815, *infra*) took place. This would seem to have had
a really decisive effect on Flahault's life, for though Hortense
(as we shall see) bore no malice, and remained throughout
her life on friendly terms both with Flahault and his family,
she was never quite the same to him afterwards, and it was
thus that when he got to England he turned his attentions
elsewhere.

[1] See Appendix, p. 307.

LIGNIÈRES, 19 *July* 1815.

Charles [1] has handed me your letter. I had hoped for more particulars, I wanted them, but he gave me very few. He told me that the feeling towards *ma cousine* was very bad. This does not surprise me. Those who have no gratitude, and they are in the majority, are sure to be against her because of all the services she has rendered.

Madame de Souza to Flahault [2]

PARIS, 16 *August* 1815.

I have received two letters from *Henriette*, which are very strange, and all through *Vincent's* [3] gossip. I am quite sure that they want to set her against us. *Papa* is convinced of it also.

Flahault to Madame de Souza

LYON, 18 *September* 1815.

I am astonished at *Auguste's* thinness. Has he no appetite ? Can he be ill ?—surely this is a matter which *his mother* must see to ! . . . I am impatiently awaiting *Vincent's* letters.

LYON [*October* 1815].

I am very unhappy at the turn things have taken with *ma cousine*. Several old letters came

[1] De la Bédoyère. He had left Paris on July 12, and returned there (to be arrested and condemned to death) on July 25 (*Georgine de Chastellux et Charles de la Bédoyère*, Paris, 1824).

[2] Addressed to *Monsieur Valentin, chez M. de Jean, aux Sécherons*, Hortense had spent a few days here, before she was ordered back to Aix (Masson, *Napoléon et sa famille*, xii. 97).

[3] Vincent Rousseau, Queen Hortense's foster-brother, who accompanied her as her servant during her wanderings.

for me to Aix; she had them sent on to her and opened them—Amongst them was a letter from Mademoiselle M.[1] which upset her terribly and threw her into a nervous fever. Since then she has been very unwell, though she is now better. As you know, I love her so much that I have been even more distressed than her. I can neither eat nor sleep. How I long to be with her again! I can only do so with the passports for which I have asked you, and if I do not get them I would run any risk rather than not rejoin her.

LYON [*October* 1815].

Ma cousine is better, but you are mistaken— there are some natures to which reconciliation is impossible. One may make things up, but it is never the same again. I cannot leave this place without these passports. I await them impatiently. I should much like to have one for England. Would this not be possible?

LYON [*October* 1815].

Ma cousine is better. What can you be thinking of when you tell me to forgive? It is I who am asking constantly for forgiveness. But as for any idea of happiness, that is at an end. The impression has been made and cannot be effaced.

LYON, 21 [*October* 1815].

Ma cousine is better, but as I have told you our happiness is destroyed. A thousand kisses to *Auguste*.

[1] Mademoiselle Mars, with whom Flahault is known to have been on friendly terms.

FRANKFURT, 21 *November* 1815.

To-morrow I set forth across Prussia and Holland, to embark at Rotterdam. If I reach England safe and sound, I shall throw myself into the first arm-chair which I may find, and never stir from it again. Try and make *Henriette* decide for England.

*   *   *   *   *   *

We now come to the letters written by Madame de Souza (still in Paris) to her son in England, amongst which one or two from Flahault to Madame de Souza will also be found. There seems from the first to have been an *arrière pensée* in the minds both of Monsieur and of Madame de Souza that (in spite of Hortense and the little Auguste) Charles might make a brilliant marriage in England ; the notion is at all events ventilated by Madame de Souza, before Flahault had even set foot on British territory ! (See extract Nov. 1, 1815, *infra*.)

Flahault met Miss Margaret Mercer Elphinstone (probably at the Duke of Bedford's at Woburn Abbey) very soon after his arrival in England. Almost immediately there were reports that they were to be married, while it is evident that Flahault was anxious to go over and make his peace with Hortense before allowing matters to proceed further. Circumstances and his mother both conspired to make this meeting impossible. Hortense (who had perhaps heard something from England) would appear to have become more and more distant, and Miss Elphinstone more and more determined to triumph over the obstacles which politics, race, and religion set in the way of her union with Charles de Flahault. They were married—in defiance of the old Admiral, her father—at St. Andrew's Church, Edinburgh, on June 19, 1817.

Madame de Souza to Flahault

1 *November* 1815.

If you could manage to get presented to the Prince Regent, and if you made a good impression on him (which might be easily managed at the outset) perhaps you could get leave from him for *Henriette* to come to England. It is anyhow certain that she would be better there than in the awful hole [1] in which she is now obliged to crave permission to live.

21 *November* 1815.

Papa [2] made me a long oration yesterday, explaining what a shocking thing it would be to make *Henriette* unhappy. He began in a loud tone, but gradually lowering his voice, he ended by mumbling between his teeth, " unless he should happen to make a brilliant marriage ". For my part I am not so foreseeing as you. I walk backwards towards the future which I am afraid to face, and my own dear little *Henriette* has so large a place in my heart, that I should not hesitate to sacrifice any prospective ease, if I thought it might cause her a moment's unhappiness.

15 *December* 1815.

I have handed to Mme de Préville the two letters for your *cousine*, since you gave me no orders as to how they should be sent. She has no doubt despatched them to the address of a third party. Your poor *cousine* is on the move,

---

[1] *I.e.* Aix in Savoy. Hortense spent nearly four months there in the autumn of 1815. She was eventually permitted to move to Constance and finally settled at Arenenberg (*Napoléon et sa famille,* xi. 84-111). [2] *I.e.* M. de Souza.

which is apparently the reason why she does not write.

25 *December* 1815.

Your *cousine* has arrived at Constance, and seems to like the place. I have had no more letters from her. Louise has written to Lascours. I come out rather badly in her report! When they are pleased with *Auguste*, they think only of him, but when he has behaved badly they are angry with me.[1] Well, patience is the word! . . . *Auguste le petit* continues to be the delight of *Papa*, you have no idea what a little character he has already become.

1*st January*, 1816.

Auguste asked me yesterday when you would come back. I have written to *Henriette* that as soon as the book[2] was printed, we would go and find her, if we could be sure of establishing ourselves in that country.

11*th January*, 1816.

Auguste is established here for a fortnight.

18*th January*, 1816.

You might tell me her Christian names[3] so that I may mention in my prayers ! !

Flahault to Madame de Souza

LONDON, 2 *February* 1816.

"Mon mariage est un nonsense."

---

[1] *Auguste* (*le grand*), *i.e.* Charles de Flahault, as we have seen, was out of favour with Queen Hortense, and *Louise* (Cochelet), her *lectrice* and companion, had evidently been saying disagreeable things about his mother. M. de Lascours was an old friend of Mlle Cochelet. (See her *Mémoires sur la Reine Hortense*, iv. 314.)

[2] *The Lusiads of Camöens*, a new edition of which was absorbing all M. de Souza's energies at this time.   [3] *I.e.* of Miss Elphinstone.

19th February 1816.

I asked Paul [1] yesterday for the means of going to see *Henriette.* He told me that it could not be done for a month. Well what cannot be prevented must be endured !

Madame de Souza to Flahault

22nd February 1816.

I spend my life almost alone ; you can guess therefore how necessary for me it is to have *Auguste,* and how dear he is to me. When you come back we can send him to school. Until that time, as *Papa* truly says, the harm if any has been done, and there remains only the consolation of having near me a little being who loves me and whom I love.

3rd March 1816.

Here your marriage is the only subject of conversation. The *purs* are distressed—a friend of Princess Charlotte's ! That is something to stir up the whole wasp's nest.[2]

13th March 1816.

Vincent has still the same notions : his relatives will let him have his child from July to October. I must warn you that your horses will be con-

---

[1] Paul Antoine Esterhazy (1786–1866), Austrian diplomat. He was ambassador in London from 1830 to 1838, and would appear to have held a minor appointment in the Austrian Embassy in London at this time.

[2] The extreme Royalists in France were, of course, annoyed at the rumoured engagement of a pronounced Bonapartist with the friend of Princess Charlotte of Wales.

S

siderably the worse.[1] . . . Tété regrets *Auguste* very much. . . .

1st April 1816.

You talk of starting. I know that *Henriette* is going to the Baden waters and I am most anxious that you should not rejoin her before she has returned once more to her life of solitude. Your arrival here would make a stir, would be awkward for her in her family, and would in all probability cause us to be watched and perhaps sent away from here. . . . If you are not thinking of seeing her brother over there, could you not delay until after the season ? It is in these sort of places that idlers will invent a thousand stories, and with all their ' buts ' and ' ifs ' will make things quite disagreeable for her ; they may shut the doors of your own country against you, and possibly drive us from it. If it is a case of business, well and good. But if it is (only) to see her, wait till she has returned ; for then few will know, and fewer still will talk of your visit.

Flahault to Madame de Souza

LONDON, *2nd April* 1816.

Allow me to speak to you, not of your old friends, but of *your little friend*. In spite of all you tell me as to the pleasure which this love for children gives you, there are so many drawbacks that I must ask you for this once not to give way to it as you are doing.

---

[1] Vincent Rousseau had apparently suggested that Auguste de Morny should pay a visit to his mother at Constance. It did not, however, take place.

First of all it may mean much unpleasantness for me. Every one does not know how near is the relationship and the interest which unites you to him, and constructions might be drawn or invented which spiteful people would be only too glad to spread abroad.[1]

Madame de Souza to Flahault

2nd Mai 1816.

Prepare your future in England and afterwards go over there [2] and secure your release. How I love Paul [3] for having refused you that passport. Besides, I believe that your arrival would upset the brother [4] and especially the eldest sister-in-law,[5] who are all well disposed towards her ; and there is no object in presenting to people who would like to be neutral, an opportunity of finding fault.

9th September 1816.

Benjamin [6] says that the affections of a certain young lady have once more warmed towards you. . . . *Papa* disapproves of the marriage and I am delighted that you are going to see *Henriette* again, for though she does not write to me, I love her with my whole soul.

---

[1] This letter was written in answer to Madame de Souza's of February 22 (*supra*). Flahault's arguments were completely ineffectual, for Auguste remained an inmate of her house until he was sent to school.

[2] *I.e.* to Constance.

[3] Esterhazy.   [4] Eugène Beauharnais.

[5] Elisa Bonaparte, who had married the Corsican, Baciocchi. She afterwards became Princess de Lucques and Piombino and Grand Duchess of Tuscany.

[6] Probably Benjamin Constant, who returned to France after the dissolution of the *Chambre Introuvable* in September 1816.

30th September 1816.

Henriette's silence worries and distresses me. She is wretched enough in all the circumstances ; perhaps she makes things worse by her suspicion —but her position explains everything. Write to her as regularly as if she always answered you. . . . I do not believe, moreover, that those about her are your friends.

24th February 1817.

The English who come over here assure me that *Auguste* is going to be married. Is there anything in this fresh rumour, for it is a common report ? . . . You may be certain that *Vincent* is preparing some worries for us—I have sure proof of it. What will *la dame du chocolat*[1] say ?

17 April 1817.

For her peace of mind as well as for yours I trust that, if the marriage is to take place, it will be as soon as possible.

17th July 1817.

Le protégé de Papa[2] has been rather unwell with a heavy cold, but he is now all right again.*

(iii.) JEAN DE MORNY

We must now go back to October 21, 1811, when one Claude Martin Gardien, *médecin accoucheur*, of No. 137 Rue Montmartre, presented himself at the Town Hall of the 2me *arrondissement* in Paris, and there certified that Louise

---

[1] An earlier letter tells us that Madame de Souza had been ransacking Paris for a special form of chocolate, which was evidently destined for her son's fiancée. Miss Elphinstone was married to ' Auguste ' (Charles de Flahault) on June 19, 1817. [2] *I.e.* Auguste de Morny.

Émilie Coralie Fleury, the wife of Auguste Jean Hyacinthe de Morny, a landowner of St. Dominique, had given birth to a son, Charles Auguste Louis Joseph, at his house on that day.

His statement was duly corroborated by two witnesses, one a bootmaker, the other a tailor. Such was the supposed origin of the future Duc de Morny.

We have already had a good deal to say about the real parents of Auguste de Morny—we may now try to throw some light on the couple who impersonated them on this interesting occasion. All sorts of theories have been advanced concerning them, and it has even been suggested that they had no existence in fact.

The document which follows, now printed for the first time, will serve to dispel this and some other illusions.

It was found amongst Flahault's papers, and is written on *papier timbré* of the First Empire. There can be no doubt that it is the original will made by Jean de Morny in November 1812.

The Will of Jean de Morny

This is my Will.

* I, the undersigned, Auguste Jean Hyacinthe de Morny, landowner at St. Dominique, being desirous of making provision for the contingency that my wife, Louise Émilie Coralie Fleury, who left eight months ago for Philadelphia (in order to recover the remnants of the fortune I had lost by the disasters which had taken place in that colony) and from whom I have heard nothing since her departure. . . .[1] In the event of her returning with any realised assets, I advise her to invest them in France, as safely as may be, to reserve the income for herself, and to devise the

[1] *Sic.* The sentence, as will be seen, is unfinished. De Morny père seems to have had some difficulty in framing a legal document.

principal to our son, Charles Auguste Louis
Joseph, born on the twenty-first of October,
eighteen hundred and eleven, at Paris.   I implore
her—in order that I may make my mind easy as
to this investment—to take no action without
the advice of Monsieur don Joseph Marie de Souza,
on whom our very existence has depended since
we were overtaken by misfortune.

Should it happen that my wife were to die,
having lost all my relations at the time of the
disasters at St. Dominique, I select as guardian
for my son Monsieur de Souza, whom I have
already mentioned.   Should he leave France, or
should he die, I choose as my son's guardian,
Monsieur de Souza's wife, Madame Adelaïde Marie
Émilie Filleul (widow by her first marriage, of
Monsieur de Flahault), to whose succour we have
been so often indebted.   Should he be predeceased by Madame de Souza, or otherwise
prevented, I choose as guardian for my son
Monsieur Auguste Charles Joseph de Flahault, at
present aide-de-camp to His Imperial Highness,
Monseigneur the Prince de Neuchâtel.

I trust that all the persons above mentioned
will not refuse to render me this last service and
to give to my son, should he become an orphan, all
the care and the assistance due to his age and to
our former position, and meanwhile, until my wife
returns, I give them full authority and powers as
regards my son.

At this last moment I enjoin on my son to
show by obedience and gratitude that he acknowledges how much I am, and how much he will be,
indebted to Monsieur and to Madame de Souza,

and I pray God to reward them for their goodness and their kind actions. I revoke any other dispositions which I have made before this present will, to which alone as containing my last wishes, I adhere.

Made at Paris this thirteenth of November eighteen hundred and twelve.

AUGUSTE JEAN HYACINTHE DE MORNY.* [1]

We can thus guess the circumstances under which the Mornys came to give their services for the important impersonation which took place on October 21. It is curious to find that the old Portuguese diplomat, Monsieur de Souza (*ce bon papa*, as his wife used always to call him), though related neither by blood nor by nationality to Charles de Flahault, was nevertheless deep in the plot.

It will be observed that Louise Émilie Coralie had (rather obligingly) left for San Domingo a few months after her supposed confinement, and that nothing had since been heard of her. We may perhaps infer that, more obligingly still, she died there, as did so many of the French colonists at that time, of the yellow fever. But what of the father, who is known to have lived for two years after Auguste's birth ? We believe that we have found traces of him (though only once under his own name) in Flahault's letters to his mother, from which a few more selections follow :

October 8, 1812.

* Do not see the *gros père* again. It would be a mistake, and no good could come of it for you.*

There are several more short references to *le gros père* —always by way of warning to Madame de Souza against him, and generally in conjunction with inquiries about *ma petite nièce*—in Flahault's letters of the time. Here are some further extracts written from Germany during the 1813 campaign :

[1] Appendix No. 21, p. 332.

13 *June* 1813.

* As to Morny there is still nothing to be done. I like your reproaches and the faults you find in this man, who performed a temporary service for me! The fact that he would not come with me does not show that he was not perfect, but rather that I was not sufficiently so for him.

19 *June* 1813.

Those hundred and ten francs are quite enough for the *gros père*. It is more than he deserves and I doubt its doing him any good.

28 *June* 1813.

I have not much faith in the legacy[1] of the *gros père*.

30 *June* 1813.

I am very glad that *the person* has inherited something, for I think that it is best to leave everything *in statu quo*. Besides I do not trust the *gros père*, who has quite got round you.

1 *July* 1813.

I hope you do not mention to our *gros ami* all the unkind things I say of him. I should be sorry if he knew of them, and it might make trouble for me . . . it is for your ears only. I have my reasons for telling you that, and for believing that our *gros ami* knows that I find fault with him. . . .

Now don't mention all this gossip to him : This matter should be allowed to drop, and the best plan is to say absolutely nothing.

---

[1] *Reliques.* Does he mean the legacy mentioned in the will ?

ERFURT, 22 *October* 1813.

Please tell *ma famille* about me. I thank the
heaven which has preserved me for them. But
do not say any kind things to our *gros ami* with
whom I am not at all pleased.*

So it would seem that Jean Hyacinthe de Morny—after
the manner of those who become possessed of important
secrets—was inclined to be importunate ; that Madame de
Souza was too kind to him, but that her son kept him at
arm's length, though he had gone so far as to invite him to
accompany him on the campaign of 1813.

Morny died in 1814, his death being officially recorded as
having taken place on April 5 at the Hospice of Versailles.[1]
There can be no doubt about his identity, for the full name,
" Auguste Jean Hyacinthe Demorny, né à Saint-Dominique "
is given—but he is described as "officier au service de Prusse".
It will be remembered that the Allies had occupied Paris five
days before.   Can it be that Auguste's putative father had
entered the service of the enemy ?

(iv.) A LETTER TO MADAME DE SOUZA

We have already explained that our family papers contain
no word in the handwriting of Queen Hortense, and the
letter which follows is taken from a copy made by Flahault.
It has neither ' head ' nor ' tail ', but from its contents
there can be no doubt that it was from the Duchesse de
St. Leu (as Queen Hortense was then known) and that it was
addressed to Madame de Souza.   At the time when it was
written (1825) Flahault was a good deal in Paris with his
mother, though Madame de Flahault still remained in
England.   The copy was no doubt sent to her by her
husband.

It shows that the intimate relations which had formerly
existed between *Henriette* and Mme. de Souza had been

[1] Masson, *Napoléon et sa famille*, vii. 159.

kept up after Flahault's marriage. It is curious to see that even then their letters were not trusted to the post, but were sent through their mutual friend Gabriel Delessert, the banker who managed Hortense's affairs both before and after her departure from France.

Madame de Souza, as her unpublished letters show, was driven almost to desperation by the non-arrival of a legitimate grandson in her family. One may perhaps wonder whether (given all the circumstances) there may not have been a spice of malice in the condolences offered to her by the mother of the grandson who had to remain unrecognised.

Duchesse de St. Leu to Madame de Souza

ARENENBERG, 20 *September* 1825.

* I wrote by Gabriel to tell you how deeply I felt for you in your bereavement [1] and I have received no answer from you. Knowing my feelings, you might surely have written to tell me something about yourself, and particularly of your health and your circumstances. It is not kind of you ; for though I have heard of you from others, I am not satisfied.

I am going to undertake a long journey at the end of October. I trust that next year, should you find yourself in need of the waters, we may meet. Write to me by Gabriel, and believe me when I say that it will be a great pleasure to see you once more. We are both of us growing quite old, and we both live lonely lives ; but one may meet in thought and by correspondence, and although it is always to be expected that letters may be seen by prying eyes, this does not matter. It is natural to speak of one's belongings, and when

---

[1] M. de Souza had died in June 1825.

there is nothing evil to conceal, one need not mind, or rob one's life of this pleasure.

Good-bye ; I embrace you with the tenderest affection. I have had so many visits this year, that I feel a desire to be alone for a time. It is hard to accustom oneself to living out of the world, and harder still to become resigned to a life of solitude, without the conversation or the sympathy of any of one's friends. But this has been my fate and I have had to make the best of it.

I was much distressed to learn that there were only girls in your family [1]—this is indeed hard. I have never heard how the grandfather [2] disposed of his fortune, or whether there would have been any chance of its being inherited by a son. But it must be embarrassing to have such a lot of girls, and it is sad to think that such is the case.

Good-bye. A thousand tender messages to you and to your child. * [3]

(v.) A Visit from Madame de Flahault

Frédéric Loliée in his *Frère d'Empereur* (p. 57) tells us that in July 1829 Flahault, accompanied by Auguste, paid a visit to Queen Hortense at Aix-la-Chapelle. They proceeded thence to Scotland, on a round of visits, during the course of which Morny made many friends and shot his first grouse. Madame de Flahault had meanwhile gone herself to Aix for the waters. The extract which follows is taken from one of Flahault's letters to her.

---

[1] Flahault's fifth successive daughter had been born not long before this was written.

[2] Lord Keith, who had died in 1823.

[3] Appendix No. 22, p. 333.

August 1829.

I have a letter from the Duchesse de St. Leu, extremely kind and expressing all the pleasure it would give her to see you, if you would go and pay her a visit. I really do not see why you should not do so, especially if you go to Ems ; and if you do not, nothing is so easy as to go up the Rhine to Mayence and from thence to Constance.

Montrond gave her letter to Gabriel. He had seen a great deal of her during his stay with Madame Dommergue (?), and is come back enchanted with her good and simple manners. He writes to me that she is " plutôt élevée que déchue."

We do not know whether the suggested visit took place, but there can be no doubt that the Duchesse de St. Leu and Madame de Flahault had for each other feelings of the greatest regard. The portrait in water-colour by Isabey which forms the subject of our illustration, was a gift from the ex-Queen and always hung in Madame de Flahault's bedroom. This and the portrait of her husband by Gérard (p. 16) were destined by Madame de Flahault for Morny. Owing to his predecease they were left to Madame de Lavalette, from whom they passed respectively to Lady Emily Digby and Lord Fitzmaurice.

Montrond was not alone in his praises of the ex-Queen. Metternich, the great Chancellor, has left it on record that of all the women he ever knew Hortense was "la femme la mieux élevée. . . . Incomparable en ce qui concerne l'amabilité, la prévenance, et l'élégance des manières."[1]

As time went on Auguste de Morny almost took the place in the Flahault family circle of the son who never came. He was constantly with them in Paris, Scotland, and London. His later career is well known. The somewhat notorious

[1] Princess Pauline Metternich, *Souvenirs d'enfance*, p. 36.

LA DUCHESSE DE ST. LEU
(QUEEN HORTENSE)
From a water-colour drawing by Isabey

liaison with Madame le Hon, the " ambassadress of the golden
hair " (whose daughter afterwards married a Polish prince),
the financial speculations, the organisation of the *Coup d'État*,
and the important part he played under the Second Empire,
have all passed into history.

Morny was something of a cynic. He might well have
been responsible for the *mot* which is attributed to him :
" Je dis à mon frère ' Sire,' à mon père ' Monsieur le Comte '
et à ma fille ' Madame '—et tout cela est naturel ".

XIII

THE NAPOLEONIC CORRESPONDENCE

(i.) The First Commission for its Publication

* Napcleon by the grace of God, and by the will of the people, Emperor of the French. To all whom it may concern, greeting.

We have decreed and do hereby decree as follows: Monsieur le Comte de Flahault, Divisional General and Senator, is nominated a member of the Commission, appointed by our decree of the seventh September 1854, to collect, co-ordinate, and publish the Correspondence of our august predecessor Napoleon the First, in so far as it relates to matters of public interest.

Given at Boulogne. 30 September, 1854.

Napoleon.*

The Napoleonic tradition played no inconsiderable part in the events which brought Louis Napoleon to the Tuileries, and it was doubtless with a strong sense of all he owed to Napoleon I. that Napoleon III. determined to do honour to his " august predecessor " by the publication of his correspondence. The document quoted above, which is amongst the papers at Bowood, constituted Flahault one of the original members of the Commission appointed for this purpose, and during the fifteen years which followed it became responsible for the printing and publication of thirty-two large volumes of letters and papers, emanating directly or indirectly from the great Emperor.[1]

It has always been a question how much this Correspondence was ' edited ', and to what extent important letters were deliberately suppressed by the Commissioners. Léon Lecestre, in his *Lettres inédites de Napoléon*, has pointed out

[1] *Correspondance de Napoléon Ier. Publiée par ordre de l'Empereur Napoléon III.*

that, while only 20,000 documents were printed, it is known that more than 60,000 were available for publication. Of these it is probable that the vast majority were excluded, not with any desire to conceal, but because they were duplicates or otherwise wanting in interest. Commenced as a ' monument ' to the great Napoleon, the work very soon threatened to become monumental in another sense. Thus considerations of space prompted the omission of papers which would have still further swelled the publication.

The correspondence which follows may help to throw fresh light on the allegation that papers were deliberately excluded for the purpose of suppressing the truth. It establishes the fact that expurgation had not been the practice, at all events at the outset. It shows, however, that doubts began to arise in the minds of some of the original Commissioners (and notably in Flahault's), as to whether expurgation was not desirable, and that the second Commission was appointed largely because the first had failed to reject documents which were damaging to the ' Great Man '.

Flahault's correspondence with his wife makes it clear that from the beginning there were differences of opinion amongst the Commissioners. In an undated letter which must have been written in 1855 or 1856 he tells her that " To-day is our great battle. . . . We have fought on the Commission for the Emperor's rights, but I am sorry to say have been opposed by the Emperor's agents ". It was not, however, till some years later that criticism from outside began to assert itself.

The draft of the letter which follows was quite recently discovered amongst the pages of Flahault's copy of the Correspondence. It had no doubt reposed there for sixty years or more. It has neither a date nor the surname of the person to whom it was sent, but from the fact that his Christian name was *Léon*, it may be safely surmised that this was Léon Marquis de Laborde, who from 1857 onwards held the position of *Directeur Général des Archives de l'Empire*.[1] He was not a member of the Commission, but from the circumstances of his office would have naturally been closely concerned in their work.

[1] His son, Comte Alexandre de Laborde, is *Membre de l'Institut*, and a member of the Roxburghe Club.

T

The numbers of the papers to which Flahault refers are to be found in the XIIth volume of the Correspondence. The letter must therefore have been written before that volume was published in 1862.

Flahault to Laborde

[? 1862.]

* My dear L.,

I am entirely of your way of thinking, as regards the inconvenience, as well as the danger, which would result from a continuation of the system adopted by the Commission for the publication of the Emperor's correspondence.

I take first the principle which seems to have been followed of printing all letters and papers, however unimportant, provided they originated directly or indirectly from the Emperor. If we continue on these lines we shall end by producing a work both immensely long and terribly dull ; nobody will want to have it, and it will find a home only in the public libraries which may receive copies from the Emperor. I have not seen a single proof sheet in which there are not several letters which I should like to suppress, though I should make a point of keeping enough to show that nothing ever escaped the Great Man's untiring attention.

I now come to the danger which might be incurred by the printing of such documents as the one (10060) you sent me, and I have no hesitation in saying that its publication would do grievous wrong to the memory of him to whom it was the Emperor's intention to set up a monument. A policy such as that advocated [1] would justify the

---

[1] *I.e.* in the peccant document No. 10060.

measures (hitherto condemned by every honourable and fair-minded person) which were taken against him in 1814 and 1815. I have not received document No. 10138, and can therefore express no opinion with regard to it.

With what object did the Emperor Napoleon III. order this publication and set up this Commission ? Can he have intended that everything which came from his uncle should be printed indiscriminately ? If so it would be the first time that such a course has been taken by the heir and successor of a man of note. It is, however, surely clear that this was not his intention, but that he believed that the Commission, composed as it was of intelligent men devoted to the Imperial idea, would not allow the printing of documents which were never intended for publication, and which were written or dictated on occasions when even a genius as powerful, as strong, and as high-minded as his, may for the moment have lost self mastery.

I do not claim to exercise any more influence than my colleagues, either as regards the value of the work or as to matters in which the published correspondence of Napoleon the First may touch the interests of the Emperor Napoleon the Third or those of France; I am sure indeed that these interests are as precious to them as they are to me. But I have had the honour to be aide-de-camp to the Emperor Napoleon I., and am imbued with the deepest respect for his memory ; while His Majesty the Emperor, after being consulted on the matter, has declared that the Commission is to have the last word. Should it happen, therefore,

that they were to authorise the printing of a
confidential document—written perhaps under
the stress of irritation, not intended for publication, and of a nature calculated to wrong the
memory of the great man from whom it originated
—I should feel bound to ask the Emperor to
permit me to resign my seat on the Commission,
great as I feel is the honour of being included
amongst its members.

You know, my dear Léon, the regard in which I
have always held you.* [1]

The interest of the above letter lies in its reference to the
documents numbered 10060 and 10138. In the first of
these it would seem that Napoleon had expressed his ambitious intentions in so unguarded a manner as to justify
all the steps which were taken by the Allies (and notably by
England) to compass his downfall. One may appreciate
Flahault's naïve statement that " all honourable and fair-
minded persons "—who of course had no knowledge of this
incriminating document—had hitherto considered these steps
unduly severe. The second document, which Flahault had
not seen, presumably contained matter equally damaging to
Napoleon.

Now in the Correspondence as published (vol. xii.) we find
that No. 10060 is a short note to Regnier with regard to the
doings of the criminal court at Marseilles, while No. 10138,
addressed to Eugène Beauharnais, deals with nothing more important than the cession by Pauline Borghese of the province
of Guastalla to Italy; in neither of these is the Emperor's
good name in any way concerned. It follows, therefore,
that the documents which originally bore these numbers
were eliminated, and that the attempt to bolster up Napoleon's
credit at the expense of truthful history must have commenced at this point.

It might have been expected that this would have been
counted unto the Commissioners for righteousness by the

[1] Appendix No. 23, p. 334.

'Great Man's' nephew, but curiously enough this does not appear to have been the case, for they were very soon afterwards sent about their business, to be replaced by a new set of men, more amenable to the Imperial necessities of the situation. The manner in which the change was effected will appear in the letters which follow.

Vaillant to Flahault

PALAIS DES TUILERIES, 27 *November* 1863.

* Monsieur le comte et cher collègue,

H.M. The Emperor has just decided that the Commission appointed for the publication of the correspondence of Napoleon Ist is to cease its labours. I take from the letter in which His Majesty has been good enough to convey to me this decision, an extract which will explain to you the Emperor's intentions as regards the continuation of the great Napoleonic work with which we were intrusted. This runs as follows :

> " Thank the members of the Commission on my behalf, and tell them that in thus putting an end to their labours, my object is to try and expedite the work and to base the scheme of publication on new lines."

If you approve, we will reassemble on Tuesday next for a final meeting, and to bid each other farewell.

Pray, Monsieur le comte, accept this assurance of my devotion towards you.

VAILLANT,
Marshal of France and President
of the Commission.

Flahault to the Emperor Napoleon

[*November* 1863.]

Sire,

The Commission, of which I had the honour to be a member, and to whose labours Your Majesty has just put an end, has applied to the task which you entrusted to it, the best energies at its disposal. For it to have achieved success one thing only was lacking—the guidance which Your Majesty alone was in a position to afford. As I have often made bold to tell you, Sire, they should have learnt from you that, instead of accepting with a sort of blind devotion every document which appeared to emanate from the Great Man, they should have published only such as might serve, if it were possible, to enhance his renown; in other words, documents which he, if he could have been consulted in person, would have himself published.

Pardon me, Sire, for the liberty I am taking in writing at this juncture, but I alone am now left of those who were near the person of the Great Man, and his memory is my most cherished recollection. I thought therefore that you would permit me to put before you these few observations ; they might, should you think fit to convey them to my successors, be of use in future.

I am, Sire,

With the deepest respect,

Your Majesty's

most obedient servant and faithful subject

FLAHAULT.

Emperor Napoleon to Flahault

COMPIÈGNE, 3 *December* 1863.

My dear Comte de Flahault,

I stopped the publication of the Emperor's letters because I had perceived that letters had been published which would have been better suppressed. Prince Napoleon has lately pointed out to me several cases which I could not overlook, and he has sent me the report which I am enclosing.[1] Please read this carefully and tell me what you think. It seems to me a serious matter to commence the publication afresh, as my cousin suggests.

I have put down in pencil the names of those who might be included in the (new) Commission. I hope that you will see your way to serve on it again, for Prince Napoleon gladly recognises that in this connection you alone have shown an enlightened judgment, based on a true devotion to the Emperor's memory. I am glad to take this opportunity of assuring you once again of my sincere friendship.

NAPOLÉON.

Flahault's Comments on Prince Napoleon's Report

[*December* 1863.]

I fully agree with the views which are expressed with regard to this in the report. *The object of the publication.*

It seems to me that the opinions expressed as to some of the members of the Commission in *The form of the publication.*

---

[1] We have no copy of this Report.

this part of the report have been somewhat hastily formed. I must say that I have never observed that any of them have tried to misrepresent or to put aside any document which it was proposed to publish. If they deserve any blame it would be because they have been too indiscriminate in their acceptance of every thing which came from the Emperor, and too ready to incorporate in the collection papers which would have been better left out.

Alterations suggested in the publication : the contents under four principal heads. In my opinion the plan proposed would be a very bad one, and would detract from the chief characteristic of the work. Is not this characteristic, that it deals with so many diverse matters at one and the same time—with questions of general policy, of war, of army administration, of the interior administration of France, questions of philosophy, of morals, of family ties and affections, and concerning every kind of institution ? I might cite the letter about the institute founded at Écouen for the education of the daughters of members of the *Legion d'honneur* [1]—a masterpiece of careful and intelligent prevision, in which every detail has been thought out and considered.

I must repeat then that, apart from the genius and cleverness with which these matters are dealt with, the salient fact is that they occupied his attention day by day and hour by hour, and (even if there were no difficulty in the proposed system of classification) this aspect would be lost, if a system such as that proposed were adopted. Instead of a picture embracing every

---

[1] This was *La Maison Impériale d'Écouen.* Hortense was made its *Princesse protectrice* in 1807.

aspect of the Emperor's daily life, there would merely be four collections of historical papers, useful only for a historical survey of his reign.

There would be another awkward result ; if this plan were followed, it would necessitate the destruction of all the work done up to now. All the Sovereigns, all the libraries, every one in fact who has got them, would have to be asked to give up the copies which they have received. There would be good reason to fear that this would give the impression that the suppressed work had erred on the side of frankness, and that it was intended in the future to exercise more reserve. This could scarcely fail to destroy confidence in and to discredit the new Commission of Publication.

The Emperor has allowed me to express my views, and I have the honour to submit them with absolute frankness. I would ask to be allowed to await his decision before accepting the proposal, for which I am deeply grateful, that I should be included in the new Commission.

Vaillant to Flahault

PARIS, 13 *January* 1864.

Monsieur le comte et cher collègue,

Before signing the decree for the reconstitution of the Commission which has been ordered to carry on the publication of the correspondence of Napoleon the 1st, "they" wish to know[1] if you would consent to be one of its members ? It will be presided over by H.I.H. Prince Napoleon.

[1] *On désire savoir.*

Count Walewski will no doubt be amongst those designated to serve on it. The Prince has asked for his nomination. His Highness has told me that General Troppard will probably also be a member. Monsieur de Laborde has seen the Prince and is sure to accept if he be chosen; I have, however, asked leave to retire.

Be so good as to reply as soon as possible: "they" have made a point of my asking you this. I must not forget to tell you that the method of publication will go on as before; the idea of classification by subjects has now been given up.[1] I think the only difference will be that they will go faster, and that the inclusion or the rejection of papers will be made in a spirit, I will not say better intentioned, but perhaps more enlightened, than that which guided the former Commission.

Believe me to be always, as I have been for so many years, your most devoted servant,

MARSHAL VAILLANT.

Flahault to Morny

SAVERNAKE, 15 *January* 1864.

My dear Auguste,

I have received the letter of which I enclose copy, from Marshal Vaillant, and I do not feel sure what he means by "they". It is clear that the decree must be signed by the Emperor, but

---

[1] The new Commission issued their first volume (No. XIII.) in 1865. The only change in form appears to be the substitution of a *Table analytique* (or index) for the *Table synoptique* (or list of contents) which had hitherto been placed at the end of each volume.

nevertheless I should be surprised if it were he who is thus referred to. I shall await your reply before giving mine.

It would be with very genuine regret that I should find myself so situated as to be unable to accept the duties which the Emperor offers me, but the addition of Count Walewski to the Commission, makes me wish not to be a member myself. Tell me what you think about it, should you get an opportunity of mentioning it to the Emperor. Send your answer to London, where we shall be on Saturday.

P.S. Do not make use of Vaillant's letter with the Emperor, for I do not want to run the risk of doing anything which he might not like.

Morny to Flahault

Tuesday, 18 [*January* 1864].

My dear friend,

I received your letter yesterday, but only managed to see the Emperor this morning. Yes, it is he who will sign the decree, and he was much amused at Vaillant's " they ". He is awaiting your reply. I told him that if Walewski was to be a member of the Commission, you would refuse. " That is precisely the reason why I want M. de Flahault's answer ; for if M. de Flahault accepts, I should of course not appoint Walewski, whose nomination is desired by Napoleon."

If you wish to know what I feel about it, it is this ; that the Emperor would rather you should accept, and would not be sorry to keep Walewski out. You might if you liked in your letter, make your acceptance conditional so that, if Prince Napoleon should try and play you a trick, you would have made your conditions in advance. As far as the Emperor is concerned it is all right. I hope you will accept this, as well as the Legion of Honour. The Emperor said to me this morning, " I have told Rouher to offer Monsieur de Flahault the Legion of Honour. I should be very glad if he would accept it."

I embrace you.

MORNY.

Flahault to Vaillant

LONDON, 19 January 1864.

Monsieur le Maréchal et cher collègue,

I was in the country when I received the letter which you did me the honour to write on the 13th instant, and I was not quite clear in my mind as to the person intended by your " they "—who, as you informed me, wished to know if I would accept membership of the Commission ordered to continue the publication of the correspondence of Napoleon the 1st.

This publication is to me a matter of the deepest concern. Everything which is calculated to enhance the renown of the Great Man, whom I had the honour to serve in a personal capacity, touches me very closely, and I am unwilling to miss any opportunity of contributing, however feebly, towards this object. My inclinations, therefore, are towards acceptance; but since you have been good enough to tell me beforehand that Count Walewski will be amongst these designated, and that it is the Prince's wish that

his name should be included in the Commission, I
will not attempt to hide from you that it would
be extremely distasteful to me to find myself
associated with him, and I have no doubt that
my presence would, reciprocally, inspire the same
feeling in him. If, therefore, he is to be a member,
I should prefer to stand out. Should I continue
to take a part, it would (since you, my dear
Marshal, are to retire) be a source of keen regret
that I should no longer have the pleasure of
meeting you.

Pray, Monsieur le Maréchal, accept these
assurances of the high esteem and of the sincere
friendship which I feel towards you, and believe
me to be your devoted servant,

FLAHAULT.* [1]

Flahault thus ceased his official connection with the
Commission, which, with an entirely new personnel, carried
on its work for the next five years under the Presidency of
Prince Jérôme Napoleon. To what extent the new Commission exercised their powers of censorship cannot be precisely known, but the non-publication of Napoleon's second
letter to Flahault of February 27, 1814 (*supra*, Part IV.
p. 63), may perhaps be cited as an example of their
methods.

(ii.) AN UNPUBLISHED LETTER

Amongst the Flahault papers there is another unpublished
letter from Napoleon of peculiar interest. We will insert
it here, though by order of date it should have come at
the beginning rather than at the end of this volume.

---

[1] Appendix No. 24, pp. 335-341.

Liberté et Égalité.

HEAD QUARTERS, MILAN, 18 *Thermidor.*

5th year of the Republic, one and indivisible.

[5 *August* 1797.]

* Bonaparte — General Commanding - in - chief the army of Italy,

To Citizen Talleyrand—Minister of Foreign Affairs.

* The choice made by the government in appointing you Minister of Foreign Affairs does credit to its discernment. It has found in you one whose abilities are outstanding, whose citizenship is unalloyed, and who has kept aloof from the excesses which have discredited the Revolution.

I am proud to think that it will be my privilege to be in constant communication with you, and that I shall thus be in a position to prove both the respect and high esteem in which I hold you.* 1

Salut et fraternité,

BONAPARTE.

This letter was written a month before the Coup d'État of the 18th Fructidor (September 4, 1797) which gave to Napoleon, in fact though not yet in name, the supreme control in French affairs. Talleyrand, who had returned from America at the beginning of 1796, had just been appointed Minister for Foreign Affairs, and it was desirable to secure his goodwill before the impending revolution. Hence the compliments which 'General Bonaparte' lavished upon 'Citoyen Talleyrand'. The Emperor Napoleon was later on to speak in a very different strain of the Prince of Beneventum.

1 Appendix No. 25, p. 341.

Au 2.e q.r de Milan le 18 Thermidor
an 5 de la République Une et Indivisible

Bonaparte, g.al en chef de
l'armée d'Italie

Au Citoyen Talleyrand, M.tre des
Relations Extérieures.

Le choix que le g.t a fait de
vous pour Ministre des Relations
Extérieures fait honneur à son
discernement. Il trouve en
vous de grands talens, un civisme
éprouvé, et un honneur étranger
aux egaremens qui ont déshonoré
la Révolution.

Je suis flatté de devoir correspondre
souvent avec vous et vous mettre
par là à même de vous convaincre
de l'estime et de la haute considération
que j'ai pour vous.

Salut et fraternité
Bonaparte

A LETTER FROM NAPOLEON TO TALLEYRAND
(August 5, 1797)

It may be noticed in the original document (*see* illustration) that Bonaparte had added—as an afterthought—the heading —*Liberté et Égalité*. It is interesting to note that the Republican professions of faith could not be ignored, even by these correspondents—to whom they meant nothing.

The letter must have been given by its recipient either to Madame de Flahault or to her son. Talleyrand's earlier relations with both were sufficiently close to explain so signal a mark of confidence. Though he is generally believed to have been incapable of the tenderer emotions, there can be no doubt that he cherished a real affection for Charles de Flahault. "Tu es un des premiers intérêts de ma vie," he wrote to him in March 1807, "et quand je dis cela, je les réduis à deux ou trois. Je t'embrasse et te presse contre mon cœur." Charles sent this on to his mother with the comment: "Je t'envois une lettre de M. de T. Elle te touchera, j'en suis sûr"—and though she had long since quarrelled with her quondam admirer, Madame de Souza was so far touched by the sentiments expressed that she kept the letter.[1]

Charles de Flahault, as his letters show, at first reciprocated Talleyrand's attachment, and friendly relations were always maintained between them ostensibly. But the Emperor was Flahault's idol, and in after years he found it hard to forget that Talleyrand had betrayed his master, or to forgive him for his share in bringing about the downfall of Napoleon.

[1] Bowood Papers.

APPENDIX

Original French Versions of Translated Documents

No. 1 (pp. 4-10)

Minute d'une conversation avec l'Empereur Napoléon
Ier au retour d'une mission dont il m'avait chargé
près de l'Empereur d'Autriche dont le Quartier
Général était à Dotis.

L'Empereur. Que disait-on de nous ?

Flahault. Ils parlaient de vous, Sire, avec la plus grande admiration et disaient que jusqu'à ce que la nouvelle de votre arrivée à l'armée fut parvenue, on entretenait les plus grandes espérances sur les résultats de la guerre et que l'Archiduc Charles lui-même paraissait les partager, mais qu'en apprenant que vous vous étiez mis à la tête de l'armée, tout cela avait changé, et que l'Archiduc avait passé de ces grandes espérances au plus grand découragement, montrant par là l'ascendant qu'exerçait votre génie.

L'Empereur. C'est une bêtise, dont l'Archiduc est incapable, mais il croyait que toutes mes forces étaient en Espagne et que je n'en aurais aucune à leur opposer et s'il en était ainsi, il jugeait que je ne prendrai pas le commandement de l'armée et quand il a appris le contraire, il y a vu la preuve que j'aurais les forces suffisantes pour lui faire craindre des revers.

Il est du reste tout simple qu'ils fassent mon éloge, car ils croient par là diminuer le mérite de mon armée en m'attribuant tout l'honneur des succès.

Ils cherchent à prouver que sans moi, ils seraient vos égaux, mais ce n'est pas vrai. Ils disent que notre armée est plus forte d'un [quart] d'hommes, cela est peut-être vrai, mais ce qui l'est aussi, c'est qu'elle est plus forte d'un quart, homme par homme.

Flahault. Tous ceux que j'ai vus à Dotis, se plaignent avec la plus grande vivacité de la conduite de l'Archiduc Jean, à qui on reproche la lenteur de sa marche, qui l'a empêché de se trouver à la Bataille d'Essling [Wagram]; et ils disent que si un de nos généraux s'était conduit comme cela, vous l'auriez fait fusiller.

L'Empereur. Il faudrait savoir jusqu'à quel point les reproches qu'on adresse à l'Archiduc sont fondés, et il faudrait pour cela connaître les circonstances dans lesquelles il a eu à agir ; certainement, j'aurais fait passer à un conseil de guerre un général qui eût mérité les reproches qu'on lui adresse, mais le tort véritable est d'avoir confié un pareil commandement à un prince du sang. Les Princes ne sont bons qu'à chasser dans leurs terres. Ou ils ont du talent et deviennent de grands généraux et alors sont dangereux, ou ils sont ineptes et alors il ne faut pas les employer. Il faut qu'un souverain puisse toujours mettre en jugement, faire fusiller les généraux qu'il emploie. Un prince cela ne se peut pas. Mettre en jugement, fusiller un prince, c'est mettre en danger la monarchie.

L'histoire n'est pleine que de princes qui ont inquiété des rois. Je le répète, pour une dynastie établie les princes ne peuvent qu'être inutiles ou dangereux.

Mon frère montrait de la nonchalance, je lui ai ôté son commandement. Je suis fâché que le roi Joseph ait celui de mon armée d'Espagne, mais c'est une chose faite. Les princes, s'ils ne sont pas assez forts pour se former des partis, ont toujours assez d'ambition pour se mettre à leur tête.

Flahault. On se plaignait beaucoup à Dotis des conditions dures du traité et on disait que ce n'était pas une crainte personnelle qui vous engage à les affaiblir autant, mais le désir de ne pas laisser une puissance à craindre à la France après vous.

L'Empereur. Cette idée prouve en eux l'intention de l'attaquer dès que l'occasion s'en présentera. Ils n'oublieront jamais qu'ils ont eu l'Allemagne et l'Italie. La France et l'Autriche ont toujours été deux taureaux qui se sont battus pour ces deux prairies. Je veux avoir l'Allemagne, je veux avoir l'Italie parce que lorsqu'on a l'Italie, on a l'Espagne, et l'Espagne est la continuation de la France.

Je ne me fie plus à leurs promesses ; on en est dupe

quelquefois, mais pas longtemps. L'Empereur d'Autriche—
après m'avoir dit qu'il voulait tenir son trône de moi, m'avoir
juré une amitié éternelle,—venir m'attaquer, parce qu'il me
croyait si occupé en Espagne, que je ne pourrai pas me
défendre ! Je ne m'en méfie pas, je le méprise trop pour
cela. Ce n'est pas un méchant homme ; au contraire, c'est
un bonhomme comme Louis XVI, mais le dernier qui lui a
parlé a toujours raison. On ne peut pas compter sur lui.
Sa seule passion est sa jalousie de l'Archiduc Charles, et c'est
le seul homme *là*. Il est venu me voir à R[aab] après
Essling. Il a proposé de me renvoyer Durosnel, mais cet
imbécile n'a pas voulu. J'ai causé avec lui et je le répète,
c'est le seul homme là. Qu'il prenne sa place et je leur
rends tout. Ils feront la paix à toute condition pour la
rompre dans six ans. Je l'ai fait dire aux plénipotentiaires.
S'ils avaient le moyen de me chasser de Vienne, ils seraient
les plus lâches des hommes ; il serait infâme à eux de traiter,
et dès qu'ils traitent, c'est la preuve qu'ils n'en ont pas le
moyen. Ils feront donc la paix. Qu'est-ce que cela leur fait
de donner quelques provinces qu'ils soulèveront aussitôt
que leur mauvaise foi le voudra ? Or, la Gallicie, à la bonne
heure, c'eût été une vraie perte pour eux. Là, on les déteste.
Là, ce serait parmi une nation, leur ennemie irréconciliable.
Si j'avais eu mon armée d'Espagne, j'aurais insisté pour
l'avoir, j'aurais séparé les trois royaumes, mais cela m'eût
demandé du temps. Mes affaires m'appellent ailleurs—je
ferai donc la paix—j'ai tort—mais je la ferai : d'ailleurs, c'est
du laisser aller, cela convient aux Français.

 Flahault. Ces pauvres Polonais seront bien maltraités.

 L'Empereur. Oh, pour cela il y aura des conditions,
mais d'ailleurs je suis Français avant tout—j'ai eu de grands
succès en Pologne : cela m'a amusé de former ce grand
duché, mais ce n'est pas là mon affaire.

 Vous ont-ils parlé de la Hollande ?

 Flahault. Non.

 L'Empereur. Ce Monnet est un polisson qui a perdu la
tête. Il n'y avait pas de brèche. Du reste, mes vaisseaux
sont sauvés ; mais si les anglais font assez de mal à la
Hollande pour qu'elle ne puisse plus former un royaume,
j'en ferai une province française ; sans eux je ne l'aurai pas
pu. Détrôner mon frère, c'eût été affreux, mais s'ils affai-

blissent trop ce pays, il ne sera plus digne de former un état
—je le réunirai à la France—j'y introduirai les douanes et
les employés de Mr. Callin et ils verront ce qu'ils y auront
gagné. Mon frère n'avait ni mon caractère ni ma volonté
—leur expédition m'aura rendu service—ils voudraient faire
un bon traité pour dire après cela qu'ils m'ont battu. Ils
rompront la paix dans 6 ans, mais cela donnera le temps à
la Westphalie de se former. Naples n'aura plus besoin
d'une armée française et l'Italie me donne déjà 60,000
hommes.

* * * * * *

Telle a été la minute de la conversation de l'Empereur,
à mon retour du Quartier Général Autrichien, où j'avais
été envoyé par lui et où j'avais passé 8 jours au milieu de
toute la Cour de l'Empereur d'Autriche—j'étais alors (en
1809) Colonel et aide de camp du Prince de Neuchâtel.

No. 2 (pp. 13-15)

Napoléon sur la Pologne (7 Juin 1812)

Flahault. Oui, Sire, il y a beaucoup d'enthousiasme et
par-dessus tout un sentiment national qui se manifeste par
la haine des Polonais contre les Russes, par leur admiration
pour votre Majesté et l'espoir qu'ils fondent sur Elle pour
recouvrir leur patrie.

L'Empereur. L'amour de la patrie est ce qu'il y a de
plus durable chez les hommes. Il naît avec l'enfant et
meurt avec le vieillard ; c'est le sentiment le plus difficile à
déraciner. Les Romains seuls ont compris l'art de le détruire chez les nations qu'ils ont vaincus, en employant des
moyens qui ne sont plus dans nos mœurs ; ils transportaient
toute la population d'un pays dans un autre, mais qui est-
ce qui aurait le pouvoir aujourd'hui d'exécuter une pareille
opération ? Je me crois assez puissant ; pourtant si j'ordon-
nais une pareille mesure, il n'est pas un colonel qui voulût
m'obéir, qui résistât aux larmes des vieillards, des femmes,
des enfans qu'il faudrait arracher à leurs foyers. Même les
Russes reculeraient devant une pareille violence, et cependant

quel pays se prêtait plus que la Pologne à une telle opération? Il ne s'agissait que de forcer quelques familles puissantes et propriétaires du sol à s'expatrier ; le reste n'est qu'un troupeau qui se serait laissé transporter ou traiter comme on aurait voulu. Les Russes aussi sont peut-être le seul peuple en Europe qui eût été capable d'exécuter un ordre aussi barbare et de prendre volontiers la place de ceux qu'ils auraient arraché à leur pays—et pourtant ils ont reculé devant un tel moyen. Aussi qu'est-il arrivé, c'est que *depuis 40 ans qu'a eu lieu le premier partage de la Pologne* la nationalité polonaise est restée ce qu'elle était, et chaque fois qu'il se présente une chance de rétablir la Pologne, tout le pays est prêt à se soulever pour une cause aussi sainte. Du reste cette guerre ne se terminera pas en une campagne ; je vais chasser les Russes et me *porter sur La Dwina et le Dnieper* ; je construirai une espèce de tête de pont entre ces deux rivières derrière lesquelles j'établirai 120,000 Français— je lèverai 200,000 Polonais, car puisqu'il s'agit de rétablir la Pologne, c'est avec le sang polonais que je ferai la guerre— mais je ménagerai le sang français qui est trop précieux.

No. 3 (pp. 31-34)

Ordres dictées par Napoléon
La Cavalerie

7 *Mars* 1813.

Flahault prendra aux bureaux de l'administration de la Guerre l'état de la Cavalerie. La cavalerie doit être envisagée sous 4 rapports—hommes, chevaux, selles et harnassement, et habillements.

Hommes : savoir quelle étoit à la dernière situation, la situation de chaque régiment. Combien ils ont reçu de conscrits de 1813 ? Combien des 4 années ? Combien des compagnies de réserve ? Combien des cohortes ? Combien chaque régiment devoit recevoir de volontaires donnés gratuitement ? Combien ils avoient reçu et combien ils avoient à recevoir aux derniers états de situation ? Il demandera le même état au Ministre de la Guerre. Il demandera également la distribution des officiers et sous-officiers de gendarmerie dans les corps. A quelle époque sont partis ceux qui y ont été envoyés ? Enfin des renseignemens sur la force et l'arrivée des cadres de la Grande Armée, et les cadres d'Espagne qui étoient organisés, et ceux qu'on a dû organiser.

Les *Chevaux* se composent de 3 élémens. Un marché conclu pour 4000 chevaux — est-il rempli ? Savoir sa distribution par régiment. Les 15,000 chevaux des Départemens—savoir dans quel département chaque régiment devoit prendre ? Dans quel lieu ? A quel dépôt on devoit les amener ? Enfin la même chose pour les dons de 16,000 chevaux des villes et cantons. Indépendamment il y a eu 3200 chevaux offerts par les particuliers—où et comment s'en fait la distribution ? Ces 4 élémens forment une masse de 38,000 chevaux, qui joint à ceux des dépôts font plus de 40,000 chevaux. Il faut comprendre dans ces derniers non seulement les dépôts de la Grande Armée, mais ceux de l'armée d'Espagne, c'est-à-dire les 88 régimens. Le Ministre de la Guerre et de l'Administration de la Guerre doivent avoir des renseignemens très précis là-dessus. Voir le Ministre de l'Intérieur pour savoir des renseignemens sur ceux qui ont donné et à qui ils ont donné.

Enfin les *Selles*. Quelle est la quantité de selles partis de France pour Magdebourg ? Quel jour cela partira de Mayence ? Cela est nécessaire à savoir, sans quoi si des coureurs ennemis passoient l'Elbe tout cela seroit perdu. Enfin quand seront terminées les 40,000 selles de l'intérieur ?

La même chose pour *l'Habillement* jusqu'à concurrence des 500 habillements par régiment en France. Enfin avoir des renseignemens sur les différens dépôts de la Grande Armée. Quand ont-ils envoyé des effets aux escadrons de guerre ? A quel époque sont-ils partis ? Quand les régimens les recevront-ils ?

Dire au Ministre de l'Administration de la Guerre at aux employés, que je n'ai pas été satisfait de leurs rapports : (1) Quand le ministre a-t-il écrit à l'Intendant Général de disposer des effets de Magdebourg et quels effets y étoient ? (2) Le ministre a prescrit aux conseils d'Administration le 17 d'expédier des effets aux escadrons de guerre. Qu'ont-ils répondu ? et comment se sont faites les expéditions ? Comment vont-ils de Mayence à Magdebourg ? Il est

nécessaire de le savoir, car la route peut être interruptée.
Me remettre les lettres du Général Duverger qui annoncent
que la plus grande partie des effets d'habillement du Hanovre
sont déjà disponibles. J'ai des lettres toutes opposées.
Quand aura-t-on l'habillement des 500 hommes ? On a le
tems pour les 900. Le 4 mars le train d'artillerie de l'armée
d'Italie n'avoit encore rien reçu. Quand ces effets seront-
ils arrivés ? Aller au bureau de la diligence le savoir. Ces
retards arrêtent le départ du Corps d'Observation d'Italie.
Le 9ᵉᵐᵉ battalion des équipages ne servira à rien, parce que
les draps pour l'habillement ne sont pas encore partis.
Envoyez par estafette l'ordre de s'en procurer à Plaisance.

No. 4 (pp. 34-35)

L'ARTILLERIE

ce 7 Mars à 7 hr. du soir 1813.

Il faut que le Ministre de la Guerre réitère ses ordres pour
le rappel des 17 compagnies d'artillerie qui se trouvent à
Magdebourg. Il les enverra par une estafette extraordinaire
qui partira demain matin et qui passera par Wesel. Ces
mesures ne sont pas suffisantes. Il faut qu'il y ait 2 compagnies d'artillerie à Mayence pour faire le service des
2 premières divisions du Corps d'Observation du Rhin. Il
faut donc que le 10 mars il y ait 2 compagnies et 4 batteries
pour les 2 divisions. Il est contraire aux règles de l'artillerie
de mettre le matériel d'un côté et le personnel de l'autre :
tout cela doit être ensemble. Il est donc de la plus haute
importance que ces 17 compagnies arrivent. S'il arrivoit
que la route d'Erfurt fut inquiétée et que des partis ennemis
eussent passé l'Elbe, il faudroit que ces compagnies se
rendissent sur Cologne et dans tous les cas repassassent le
Rhin. Puisqu'elles ne mènent avec elles aucune voiture, il
leur sera facile de voyager—il y a là assez de chemins.

Il me faut des états à colonnes pour l'artillerie, que je
puisse voir jour par jour où se trouvent les convois. On ne
me les remet de manière que je ne puis pas savoir quels sont
les convois qui peuvent être coupés. Il est probable qu'au

premier moment rien ne pourra passer de Magdebourg sur l'Oder, et il est possible que bientôt on ne puisse plus communiquer de Francfort avec Magdebourg. Il faut donc que les 2 Corps d'Observation ne dépendent absolument que de Mayence, et que l'artillerie et le génie, les généraux et officiers, tout cela vienne de l'intérieur.

No. 5 (pp. 52-55)

INSTRUCTIONS POUR LE GÉNÉRAL FLAHAULT, AIDE-DE-CAMP DE L'EMPEREUR

(Correspondance de Napoléon Ier No. 21359)

BOURG DES NOËS, À TROYES,
24 *février* 1814.

Flahault se rendra à Lusigny avec des pouvoirs du major général pour négocier, conclure et signer un armistice entre les deux armées.

Il est bien entendu que, pendant la durée des conférences, il n'y aura pas d'armistice, de sorte que les troupes françaises et alliées pourront se battre et aller où elles voudront. Ce ne sera que du moment de la signature et de l'échange des ratifications que l'armistice aura lieu. Ceci est important, car je n'entends pas être lié par ces pourparlers.

Dans l'état actuel de mes affaires, où un plan général se développe, je ne puis accorder d'armistice qu'autant que je serai certain de la paix. Je ne puis être certain de la paix qu'autant qu'on aura consenti à admettre les bases proposées à Francfort par le prince de Metternich, en présence du comte Nesselrode et de lord Aberdeen.

Le général Flahault a lu le *Moniteur* supprimé ; ainsi il connaît ces bases. Le premier article est celui-là.

Le général Flahault doit s'appuyer sur la lettre par laquelle le prince de Schwarzenberg demande un armistice en disant que la paix doit être conclue, sur la réponse du prince de Neuchâtel, et sur la lettre du prince de Schwarzenberg qui réitère la demande d'un armistice. Le général Flahault sera muni de cette correspondance.

Le préambule devra être rédigé à peu près en ces termes :

"Les hautes parties contractantes, ayant réuni leurs plénipotentiaires au congrès de Châtillon-sur-Seine pour traiter de la paix sur les bases proposées à Francfort, ont résolu, pour faciliter ladite négociation et épargner aux peuples la prolongation des maux de la guerre, de conclure une suspension d'armes, et ont nommé à cet effet les sieurs tels et tels pour commissaires."

Cet article souffrira difficultés. Le général Flahault dira que sans cet article il n'y a rien à faire ; que ce n'est pas dans un moment où une organisation secrète sur les derrières est au moment d'agir, et où différentes armées pèsent sur leurs flancs, qu'on peut nous arrêter, si on ne veut pas avoir la paix : or on ne peut avoir de paix que sur les bases de Francfort.

Le général Flahault n'entrera dans aucune discussion que cet article ne soit d'abord arrêté. Ces messieurs pourront envoyer chercher des pouvoirs s'ils n'en ont pas. Le général Flahault n'ouvrira pas même la bouche tant que ce ne sera pas fait. Cela une fois fait, le général Flahault proposera une suspension d'armes d'après laquelle les alliés évacueront les 18e, 19e et 7e divisions militaires, ainsi que le département de l'Aube, et se concentreront en Franche-Comté, en Alsace et en Lorraine ; ils évacueront toute la Belgique, et leur ligne sera la Meuse depuis son embouchure jusqu'à sa source, et, depuis là, une ligne qui passera entre Vesoul et Langres et qui viendra mourir par la Franche-Comté sur la Suisse.

Pendant tout le temps que durera la suspension d'armes, les places seront approvisionnées. Les places du Nord devant être dégagées, leur approvisionnement est donc hors de question. Quant aux places de la Meuse, nous pourrons y pourvoir par la rive qui nous sera rendue. Restent donc les places de la Lorraine, de l'Alsace et de la Franche-Comté. Des commissaires français seront chargés d'y faire entrer des vivres. Genève, étant de la 7e division, sera évacuée.

Le général Flahault doit avoir un langage honnête, mais ferme : "Nous connaissons les forces de l'ennemi, pourra-t-il dire, mais on ne connaît pas assez les nôtres. Tous les jours nous recevons de Paris 10,000 hommes habillés et armés, dont 2000 hommes de cavalerie ; notre armée est de 300,000 hommes. La vieille Garde, qui est composée d'hommes qui n'ont pas moins de seize ans de service, est

triplée et forme trois divisions, chacune de seize bataillons.
Tous les hommes qui ont servi dans la Garde et ont été con-
gédiés, y ont été rappelés ; ce qui a augmenté la Garde et
l'a portée à 30,000 hommes. Il est vrai que nous avons près
de 50,000 hommes qui ne sont pas habillés ; mais la plupart
des effets d'habillement vont arriver, on les attend à chaque
instant ; mais ces hommes ont de bons fusils et servent
assez bien. Enfin les horreurs que les Cosaques ont com-
mises, et qui n'ont pas de nom, ont excité au dernier point
toute la population en France, et tout le monde est sous les
armes. Aussi croyons-nous que toutes les chances sont pour
nous, et n'est-ce que la résolution où nous sommes de faire
la paix, à la condition qu'on traitera sur les bases de Francfort, qui peut nous porter à une suspension d'armes.''

Quant aux prisonniers, il faut dire que jusqu'à cette
heure nous en avons fait 50,000, que nous avons pris quatre-
vingts pièces de canon et 800 voitures.

Quand tous ces articles auront passé, le général Flahault
y ajoutera, que les capitulations de Dresde et de Danzig
ayant été faites selon toutes les lois de la guerre, elles seront
ratifiées, et qu'en conséquence les garnisons seront ramenées
sur le Rhin pour être échangées, conformément auxdites
capitulations, contre un pareil nombre d'alliés.

(D'après la copie. Archives de l'Empire.)

No. 6 (pp. 56-61)

ANALYSE DE LA NÉGOCIATION DE L'ARMISTICE DE LUSIGNY
(*Février* 24-28, 1814)

Les premières communications pour la négociation de
l'armistice eurent lieu le 24 février 1814. Le commissaire
français, le Comte de Flahault, n'avait reçu que des instructions verbales et de la bouche même de l'Empereur. Il lui
était enjoint expressément de déclarer aux Commissaires
Alliés, qu'il n'était autorisé à traiter qu'à la condition que
le préambule de l'armistice déclareroit que cette convention
avait pour objet de faciliter la conclusion de la paix sur les
bases proposées à Francfort. Mais les commissaires des

armées alliées répondirent que cette proposition dépassait leurs instructions et qu'une telle condition ne pouvait trouver sa place dans un traité d'armistice, qui n'avait d'autre but que de régler la suspension des hostilités et la ligne occupée par les armées pendant la durée de cette suspension.

Ce ne fut cependant qu'après une discussion, dont la longueur prouva au commissaire français leur vif désir d'arriver à un arrangement, qu'ils se décidèrent à refuser de négocier sur ces bases et à envoyer un courrier à leur quartier général pour mander cet incident inattendu et demander de nouvelles instructions. Le courrier revint le 25 et rapporta aux commissaires l'ordre de repousser la proposition du préambule, comme étant d'une nature diplomatique, et de se borner à traiter la question militaire de la suspension d'armes, lui faisant observer que cela paraissait d'autant plus convenable qu'il n'y avait pas de commissaire anglais présent à cette négociation.

L'Empereur Napoléon se rendit à cette observation et envoya alors au commissaire français l'ordre d'entrer en négociation ; mais des momens précieux avaient été perdus. Les craintes soulevées par nos succès à Champaubert et Montereau, etc. avaient eu le tems de se calmer, tandis qu'il est probable que si le comte de Flahault avait eu des pouvoirs plus étendus pour traiter dès l'ouverture de la négociation, il eût obtenu de meilleures conditions : mais l'Empereur lui avait donné l'ordre le plus formel de ne pas même entrer en pourparlers que le préambule sus-mentionné n'eût été consenti.

La discussion ayant commencé sur la ligne de démarcation, les commissaires ont proposé la ligne suivante :— L'ancienne frontière entre la France et les Pays-Bas depuis la mer jusqu'à Maubeuge ; la route de cette ville à Laon, en passant par Avesne ; de là à Rheims ; de Rheims à Châlons, d'où elle aurait remonté la Marne jusqu'à St-Dizier, etc. ; de là elle serait descendue à Colombey, où elle aurait traversé la route de Troyes à Chaumont ; aurait passé de là par Châtillon-sur-Seine, Montbard et Autun ; aurait de là été rejoindre la Saône à Chalon ; aurait suivi cette rivière jusqu'à Macon et la route de cette ville à Bourg ; aurait été de là rejoindre le Rhône à Lagnieu, et l'aurait suivi jusqu'à St-

Genix, où ce fleuve rejoint les anciennes frontières de la Savoie, qui par cet arrangement aurait été occupée par les troupes alliées. Quant à la durée de l'armistice, ils proposaient 15 jours et 6 jours de délai à partir de celui de la dénonciation.

On différait avec eux sur ce point important, que S.M. voulait que la ligne de démarcation ne donnât aux alliés ni la Belgique, ni la Savoie. Les commissaires, après une discussion de cinq heures dans laquelle on n'avoit pu s'accorder, se sont encore décidés à envoyer un courrier pour demander des nouvelles instructions sur ce point. Le courrier parti le 25 est revenu le 28. Il a rapporté aux commissaires des alliés de nouvelles instructions, qui ne changeaient rien aux conditions relatives à la Belgique et à la Savoie repoussées par l'Empereur, qui modifiaient à peine la ligne de démarcation proposée en l'établissant de la manière suivante :—Les anciennes frontières des Pays-Bas depuis la mer jusqu'aux environs de Maubeuge, de là une ligne passant la Sambre près de cette place en regagnant la route d'Avesnes, laissant cette place à la droite, pour gagner la route de Paris et la suivre jusqu'à Laon ; de Laon la grande route à Rheims ; de Rheims la route jusqu'à Châlons-sur-Marne ; de là remontant la Marne et passant près Vitry, St-Dizier et Joinville jusqu'à Chaumont ; de Chaumont la route à Langres ; de Langres la route à Dijon ; de Dijon le canal jusqu'à Macon ; de Macon la route à Bourg-en-Bresse ; de cet endroit gagner le Rhône par Pont-d'Ain à Lagnieu, le remonter jusqu'à St-Genix ; de là la ligne irait rejoindre les anciennes frontières de la Savoie, qui séparaient autrefois cette province de la France, et suivant cette frontière le long des Alpes et celle du Valais jusqu'aux frontières de la Suisse.

Tous les endroits qui se trouvent sur la ligne de démarcation devaient être occupés par les troupes des Puissances Alliées. L'armistice devait s'étendre également aux armées d'Italie et à celles du Maréchal Lord Wellington ; dans ces armées on devait régler la ligne de démarcation sur le *status quo* des choses à l'arrivée du courrier. L'armistice devait être de 15 jours, plus 6 jours après la dénonciation. Cette ligne aurait pu être adoptée pour la plus grande partie, mais quant à sa terminaison en Suisse, jamais on n'a pu la faire passer d'une manière qui convînt à l'Empereur, dont l'ordre formel au comte de Flahault était de ne céder dans aucun cas des pays occupés par les troupes françaises (tels que Bourg, Macon, Chambéry, Chalon-sur-Saône). Dans les départemens qui avoisinaient la Suisse, les efforts des habitans contre les troupes alliées avaient obtenu des succès, dont ils auraient été punis, si l'armistice les avait de nouveau livrés à des troupes.

Sur ces entrefaites, l'Empereur se décide de se porter sur le Gal Blücher, et écrivit le 27 février au Général Flahault la lettre suivante : [*v.* No. 8, *infra*].

* * * * * *

L'éloignement de l'Empereur eut deux inconvénients : celui de laisser le commissaire français sans instructions, et celui plus grave de faire passer le commandement des troupes opposées au Prince de Schwarzenberg et à l'armée principale des alliés, des mains de l'Empereur à celles d'un de ses maréchaux. Le secret dont il voulait couvrir ce changement ne put être gardé, et la manière molle dont les troupes attaquèrent à Bar-sur-Aube, dévoila sur-le-champ aux généraux ennemis l'absence de l'Empereur. Les Alliés reprirent l'offensive, repoussèrent les troupes françaises, et le Prince Schwarzenberg étant rentré à Troyes mit un terme à la négociation. Ainsi s'évanouit la dernière espérance du rétablissement de la paix et du maintien du gouvernement impérial.

Le Général Ducca, commissaire autrichien, a eu des communications confidentielles fréquentes avec le Général Flahault. Il a exprimé le désir sincère de la part de l'Empereur d'Autriche de mettre un terme à la guerre. Il a dit que son maître n'a jamais eu l'idée, ni le désir, d'aller à Paris. Il en a donné pour preuve la lenteur avec laquelle le Prince Swarzenberg a marché. Il a répété plusieurs fois qu'il ne doutait pas que la paix ne fût conclue sous peu, si on parvenait à faire cesser les hostilités ; que l'Empereur d'Autriche le désirait et qu'il était très modéré. Il est revenu chaque jour sur ce sujet, demandant en propres termes que l'on aidât l'Empereur d'Autriche à faire la paix. " Faites ", a-t-il dit encore, " que le 28 les hostilités cessent, facilitez-nous le moyen de faire la paix. Je vous jure que l'Empereur

d'Autriche et l'Angleterre la veulent *honorable* pour la France."
Il y avait eu des explications antérieures avec le Général
Ducca, qui ne laissaient aucun équivoque à ce mot sortant
de sa bouche. Enfin, en remettant leurs dernières propositions
le 28 au soir, les commissaires ont dit en commun que la paix
ne dépendait que d'un armistice et qu'ils ne doutaient pas
qu'elle ne fût faite d'une manière qui convînt à l'Empereur.

No. 7 (p. 62)

Napoléon à Flahault

(*Correspondance de Napoléon Ier No.* 21389)

TROYES, 27 *Février*, 1814, 7 *hr.*

Monsieur le Comte Flahault,
    Vous ne m'avez pas donné de vos nouvelles hier. Faites-
moi connoître où vous en êtes. Je suppose que les commissaires de l'ennemi se seront rapprochés de votre ligne ; vous
ne devez dans aucun cas leur céder des pays que nous occupons
tels que Bourg, Mâcon, Chambéry, Chalon-sur-Saône. Ces
messieurs le comprendront facilement : quel effet cela ferait-
il aux yeux des habitans qui se verraient abandonnés ?
Cependant si les difficultés tenaient à ce qu'ils gardassent
Langres et Chaumont, comme ils les occupent, vous devriez
y consentir. Tâchez de conclure : c'est le seul acheminement
à la paix.
    Je vous ai fait connoître que vous pourriez les laisser faire
passer la ligne de manière qu'ils gardent Bréda et tout le
Brabant hollandais. Enfin si en concluant quelque chose,
vous êtes obligé de vous éloigner de la ligne indiquée, faites
le valoir auprès de l'aide de camp de l'Empereur d'Autriche,
et tâchez d'en tirer la promesse positive, ou à peu près, que
son maître veut la paix sur les bases de Francfort.
    Sur ce, je prie Dieu qu'il vous ait en sa sainte garde.
    Troyes : le 27 février 1814 : à 7 heures du matin.

N. I.

(D'après l'original communiqué par M. le Comte de
Flahault.)

No. 8 (p. 63)

Napoléon à Flahault

TROYES, 27 *Février*, 1814, 9 *hrs.*

Monsieur le Général Flahault.

Tâchez de faire croire aux plénipotentiaires que je suis passé cette nuit pour porter mon quartier général à Bar-sur-Aube. Je me rends à Arcis-sur-Aube pour manœuvrer sur les derrières de Blücher, d'York, et de Wintzinzerode, qui marchent sur La Ferté-Gaucher. Vous sentez combien il est important que les commissaires et l'ennemi ne se doutent pas de ce mouvement. Aussitôt que vous aurez reçu cette lettre, envoyez-moi un courrier pour me faire connoître où en sont *les choses* : sur ce je prie Dieu qu'il vous ait en sa sainte garde.

Troyes : le 27 février 1814 : à 9 heures du matin.

N. I.

No. 9 (pp. 67-72)

Lettres de Flahault à Madame de Souza.
Fontainebleau 1814. (*Extraits*)

[*March.*]

Mon Dieu, que je suis inquiet de ce qui se prépare ! Je ne puis croire que les ennemis n'entrent pas dans Paris. Que feront-ils ? Que ferons-nous ? Nous les avons bien battus, mais ce n'est qu'une partie de leur armée. Au moins nous leur avons montré qu'il y avait encore de bons Français, car nos soldats se sont vaillamment conduits. . . . Que ce mois est long ! . . . Je te quitte pour dormir un peu.

[? 4 *Avril.*]

Il se passe un grand événement. Puisse-t-il rendre le repos à ma malheureuse patrie ! Si les étrangers sont de bonne foi, cela sera. Je me suis conduit dans cette circonstance comme je ferai toujours, avec honneur, et en disant de dures vérités. . . . J'ai été témoin oculaire et partie dans de bien grands événements. Le grand Écuyer a déployé le plus beau caractère qu'il y ait jamais eu. Quelle âme élevée !

Enfin nos efforts, notre courage n'auront servi à rien. Après avoir décidé l'Empereur au plus grand sacrifice qu'un homme puisse faire, nous courbons la tête sous le joug de l'étranger, et déshonorons la nation. On ne peut plus dire : " J'ai l'honneur d'être Français ". Aussi suis-je bien décidé à n'en conserver que la naissance, mais à n'occuper aucun emploi dans un pays aussi avili. . . . Envois cette lettre à Henriette comme tu le pourra, dans de la soie—enfin tâches qu'elle lui arrive.

L'Empereur aura donné toute liberté pour servir le nouveau gouvernement. Mais comment servir quand un crêpe couvre nos drapeaux et que nous avons joint à la haine qu'on nous portait un mépris mérité ? Enfin je m'en rapporte à toi pour faire que je puisse vivre dans mon pays et près de vous. C'est là le nécessaire. Je ne sais si M. Bégo voudra m'être utile pour cela, car depuis tous ces évènements il ne m'a rien fait dire par nos amis communs. Je ne lui en veux pas, puisqu'il est heureux. Je désire qu'il le soit toujours—mais j'en doute ! Nous nous livrons pieds et poings liés à l'ennemi.

Je suivrai l'Emp. probablement jusqu'à sa destination. Je crois le devoir faire et je n'ai point d'arrière-pensée quand il s'agit de mon devoir. Quant à la fin de tous ces évènements—de toutes ces trahisons, de toutes ces infamies, (selon les uns), ces belles actions (selon les autres), on sera arrivé irréprochable, on pourra se trouver heureux.

Je n'ai point donné ma démission, et puisque vous le voulez—malgré le deuil qui couvre nos drapeaux, malgré l'abaissement honteux de la patrie—je porterai encore mon uniforme et servirai encore mon pays. Je l'ai bien servi dans tous ces évènements. J'ai contribué à le sauver d'une guerre civile, quoique cela soit contraire à mon intérêt personnel. Mais qu'est-ce que l'intérêt personnel auprès de celui de la patrie ? J'aurai donné ma vie pour la sauver de l'humiliation où elle est tombée. Malheureusement elle est complète.

Je reste ici jusqu'au départ de l'Empereur. Je l'accompagnerai même, s'il le désire, jusqu'au lieu de son embarquement. Après cela je reviendrai auprès de vous. Je lui ai demandé (j'ai cru le devoir)—je lui ai demandé, quelle était son opinion, son intention, sur la conduite que devraient tenir ceux qui lui ont été personnellement attachés. "Comme je désire conserver votre estime, Sire, je voudrais avoir une règle de conduite que Votre Majesté peut seule me donner." Il m'a répondu qu'il " désirait que nous fussions heureux ; que tout ce qui s'y opposerait, serait contraire à ses intentions ; que tout ceci était fini, et que tout homme se doit à son pays " . . . J'ai écrit à M. de T[alleyrand] une lettre courte, mais bien. Je lui demande d'arranger ma position la meilleure possible. Je ne sais s'il prend encore quelque intérêt à moi—le bonheur n'éveille pas beaucoup sa sensibilité pour les autres ! Enfin, il n'est personne que je ne puisse regarder en face et je puis marcher la tête haute—c'est une démarche qui n'est pas commune !

[15 *Avril.*]?

Voici mon adhésion. Je ne ferai le voyage que s'il l'exige absolument, mais il est difficile de se refuser à faire une chose qu'un sentiment intérieur vous ordonne de faire, et qu'un honnête homme, qui ne m'aimerait pas, me blâmerait de n'avoir pas fait. . . .

Quelle agonie que ce séjour, ma chère Maman. Tu ne peux t'en faire aucune idée. Enfin cela passera.

[16-19 *Avril.*]?

Tu vas voir Girardin, qui, j'espère, te portera cette lettre lui-même, ma chère Maman. J'aurais aussi pu te voir il y a trois jours, mais il m'eût été trop affreux de voir les Russes dans Paris.

Je crois que j'accompagnerai l'Empereur, soit jusqu'à la frontière, soit jusqu'au lieu qu'il doit habiter. C'est un devoir que je remplirai, car le malheur ne m'éloigne pas. Il avait pensé et désiré me garder auprès de lui. J'ai répondu que je me devais à toi avant tout. Toutes les injures dont on l'accable dans les feuilles publiques m'attachent à lui. J'ai passé avec lui la plus grande partie des nuits depuis ces derniers jours, et jamais je n'ai vu plus de calme et de

courage. " Je ne regrette rien," m'a-t-il dit, " et j'aurais
été plus malheureux si j'avais dû signer le traité qui aurait
diminué la France d'un village qu'elle possédait le jour où
j'ai juré de maintenir l'intégrité de son territoire."

Enfin, ma chère Maman, lorsque j'aurai rempli ce dernier
devoir, je reviendrai—si les Russes nous ont délivrés de
leur odieuse présence—je reviendrai près de toi, sans honte
et sans regret, prêt à jouir d'un grand bonheur si Henriette
se décide à le faire. Lui as-tu envoyé ma lettre ? Écris-
lui, fais-lui dire de toutes les manières que tu pourras (envois-
y Morel), fais-lui dire qu'elle doit faire ses arrangements
avec sa famille, que celle de son mari ne doit pas l'occuper.
La séparation qui existait doit être la base de ses raisons.
Qu'elle se rattache aux siens ; ils sont aimés, estimés. Aucun
reproche ne s'adresse à eux, et d'ailleurs, elle n'aurait que
toutes sortes de peines à attendre des autres. Enfin, ma
chère Maman, une campagne avec elle et toi, mon bonheur
sera parfait. Papa me serait aussi bien nécessaire ; il
viendrait nous voir quelquefois.

Adieu, ma chère Maman, cherche, je t'en supplie, les
occasions d'avoir des nouvelles d'Henriette et de lui faire
dire tout ce que je viens de te mander, et de me dire si elle
l'approuve.

Adieu. Je t'embrasse de tout mon cœur, et t'aime bien
de toute mon âme, ma chère et bonne mère. Mille affections
à Papa. Embrasse *ma passion*.

Girardin te remettra ma montre. Faites que Bréguet y
mette un verre, et renvoie-la moi par Girardin, si tu le peux.

No. 10 (pp. 88-96)

PART OF THE CONVERSATION BETWEEN NAPOLEON AND MESSRS. VENABLES-VERNON AND FAZAKERLEY AT ELBA.

(*November* 18, 1814.)

" Je suis bon catholique, mais pas un bigot, et il fallait faire
quelque chose pour concilier ces gens-là—quelques-uns entre
eux étaient plus difficiles que les autres.—Il y a des Jansé-
nistes et des Molinistes parmi les Turcs comme autrefois en
France—mais ils furent tous d'accord, délibération faite, de

nous proposer deux conditions :—l'une était, que toute l'armée française renoncerait à l'usage du vin, l'autre, que nous serions tous circoncis. Je leur répondis, que l'habitude de boire du vin l'avait rendu nécessaire à la santé des Français, et pour ce qui était de la circoncision, c'était déjà perfection, il ne fallait pas nous couper. Je les priai de se rassembler de nouveau, et de songer à d'autres moyens d'accommodement. Il résulta de cette nouvelle delibération qu'on renonça au projet de nous circoncire, et qu'on insista seulement, que chaque Français serait tenu de faire une bonne œuvre pour chaque bouteille de vin qu'il lui serait permis de boire. ' Volontiers, Messieurs, je ne demande pas mieux ', et sur cela je commençai à bâtir une Mosquée."

He inquired about the recent massacre of the Mamelukes, which had happened when Mr. F. was at Cairo, and then informed us how he had quelled an insurrection there :

" Il fallait prendre des mesures vigoureuses pour l'étouffer dans le commencement. Je sçavais que c'étaient les prêtres qui avaient suscité le peuple à la révolte.—J'en fis assembler dèux cens (c'étaient des Abbés turcs, de la Prêtraille) ; je les fis fusiller dans 24 heures, et quand on vit qu'il n'y avait pas de mollesse dans ma manière de gouverner, on s'attacha beaucoup à moi."

Having dwelt some time on the subject of Egypt, he said to mè—" De quel parti êtes-vous au Parlement—"

" J'ai été de celui, Sire, qui a été opposé au Ministère actuel."

" Vous n'avez pas donc grand' chose à faire, votre parti ne peut rien aujourd'hui contre le Ministère."

" Il est vrai, Sire, que les derniers évènemens l'ont beaucoup fortifié, et de l'autre coté le parti de l'Opposition a été un peu décrédité par les prédictions qu'il avait faites sur le résultat probable de la guerre d'Espagne, et qui heureusement n'ont pas été vérifiées ; ils croyaient que nos troupes seraient chassées de la Péninsule."

" Cela aurait dû être—mes Maréchaux se sont mal entendus entre eux."

" On a cru que V.M. y serait allée elle-même pour commander ses troupes."

" Il y a eu des évènemens, qui m'ont empêché d'y aller."

"Je sçais, Sire, que V.M. a porté la guerre d'un autre côté, mais on avait été persuadé qu'Elle aurait fait tous ses efforts pour nous chasser de la Péninsule, avant que d'attaquer les Russes."

"L'Empereur de Russie m'a forcé de lui faire la guerre—c'était un article secret du traité de Tilsit, qu'il devait rompre avec l'Angleterre—il ne l'a pas fait, il m'a manqué de parole."

"V.M. lui accorde des talens ?"

"Il ne manque pas d'esprit, mais il est faux et fin. Il paraît qu'on lui suppose aujourd'hui l'intention de rétablir la Pologne. Il n'y a que des hommes ignorans qui puissent s'y attendre. L'Empereur n'oserait jamais le faire, s'il le voulait même ; il n'oserait jamais céder à la Pologne les provinces russes, pour cela il faudrait lui rendre Smolenske. Il ne le fera jamais, mais il ne le veut pas non plus, au contraire on verra qu'il va donner la loi en Pologne plus que jamais. J'aime les Polonais, ils sont braves, loyaux, bons militaires. Je désirais beaucoup de les rétablir en nation. C'est pour cela que j'ai ôté à l'Autriche les Provinces Illyriennes, elles n'étaient pas nécessaires à la France ; mais j'ai voulu avoir quelque chose que j'aurais pu changer ensuite avec l'Autriche contre la Gallicie, que j'avais le projet de lui ôter un de ces jours pour rétablir la Pologne dans toute son intégrité."

"Peut-être si V.M. était restée en Pologne l'hiver dernier, au lieu d'aller à Moscou, les choses auraient tourné autrement." He hesitated, and I continued—"V.M. a cru peut-être, qu'Elle pourrait dicter la paix à Moscou, que l'Empereur aurait été effrayé ?"

"Il est vrai que j'aurais pu compter un peu sur cela, et puis je ne pouvais pas m'attendre à l'incendie de Moscou, c'est un évènement inconnu dans l'histoire. Ce sont les Cosaques qui l'ont brûlé, ils n'aiment pas les Russes. Ils ont mis le feu aux villages partout."

"Je crois, Sire, que le Gouvernement l'a voulu ; au moins je sçais, que le Gouverneur de la ville, Rostopchin, a donné l'exemple aux autres. Un général anglais, qui était avec lui dans ce temps-là, m'a dit, qu'il l'a vu lui-même mettre le feu à sa propre maison, qui était richement meublée. Il est allé d'abord dans la chambre de sa femme, dont il incendia le lit, et après cela il fit de même dans les autres appartemens."

" Je le sçais, c'était le Général Smith (I did not interrupt him, but it was Sir R. Wilson), je le sçais bien—le Gouverneur s'entendait avec les Cosaques ; il avait fait enlever toutes les pompes. J'ai fait mon possible pour arrêter l'incendie ; j'étais sur le Kremlin, mais le vent était trop fort."

" J'ai vu, Sire, à Paris l'Abbé de Pradt, qui était, je crois, le Ministre de V.M. en Pologne dans ce temps-là. Il racontait un soir, chez Mme de Staël, que dans une conversation qu'il a eue avec V.M., quand Elle s'est arrêtée à Varsovie en retournant de Wilna à Paris, V.M. lui a dit, ' Un homme de moins, j'étais le maître du monde '—que cet homme c'était lui-même ; qu'il aurait dû mettre plus d'activité à remuer la Pologne ; qu'il n'avait pas assez fait pour profiter des ressources qu'on aurait pu tirer de ce pays-là, que c'était à lui enfin que le mauvais succès de la campagne devait s'attribuer."

" Il est vrai que lorsque je me suis arrêté à Varsovie pour écrire des lettres, cet homme est venu me rendre compte des affaires dont je l'avais chargé—et puis il m'a parlé de guerre, à moi M. l'Abbé ! Je ne lui dis rien du tout. J'écrivais toujours à mon Ministre à Paris, et entre autres choses que je lui mandai, je lui donnai l'ordre de rappeler M. l'Abbé—peut-être j'ai parlé après à Paris de son incapacité. Vous l'avez vu chez Mme de Staël ? "

" Oui, Sire."

" Que dit-elle de moi aujourd'hui ? Peut-être à cette heure elle fait mon éloge, et des reproches aux Bourbons."

" Elle ne m'a jamais parlé de V.M., et il est de son intérêt de ne pas déplaire au gouvernement. Elle lui fait des réclamations pour récouvrer de l'argent qui était dû, je crois, à son père."

" Mais il faut être juste, ce n'est pas une femme qui cherche son intérêt."

" Je le sçais bien, Sire ; et ses amis se fiaient si peu à sa discrétion, qu'ils l'ont priée de s'éloigner de Paris pendant les discussions sur la liberté de la Presse ; c'est une question beaucoup agitée en France."

" Je le sçais, mais ce qui est bon pour vous autres ne l'est pas pour la France ; votre Constitution ne lui conviendrait pas dans son état actuel. Je voulais faire de grandes choses pour la France, mais j'ai toujours demandé 20 ans ; il me fallait 20 ans pour mon système. Votre Gouvernement est essentiellement aristocratique. C'est l'aristocratie qui dirige le Parlement, et même l'opinion publique, c'est elle qui a soutenu le Duc de York contre les Libellistes. En France la même chose n'aurait pas pu arriver; elle n'a pas une aristocratie capable d'influer sur l'opinion. Je voulais en former une ; mais pour cela il faut du temps. Les chymistes ont une espèce de poudre dont ils peuvent faire du marbre, mais il faut du temps pour lui donner de la solidité. L'aristocratie en Angleterre est respectable et puissante en elle-même, et si toute la Chambre des Pairs était anéantie subitement, la perte serait bientôt réparée par leurs enfans, la nation n'y perdrait pas beaucoup.—En France la queue est bonne, la tête est mauvaise ; en Angleterre la tête est bonne, la queue est médiocre. Puis il y a une différence de l'esprit national dans ces deux pays ; les Anglais sont orgueilleux, les Français sont vaniteux. Je voulais trop faire pour leur gloire—ils ne m'ont pas soutenu. C'est vous, Messieurs, qui avez réussi. L'Angleterre n'a jamais été si grande qu'elle l'est aujourd'hui, c'est elle qui joue le premier rôle ; mais son tour viendra, elle tombera comme tous les grands empires."

"V.M. ne croit pas que ce tour-là viendra bientôt ? "

"Je ne connais pas assez l'état politique de l'Angleterre pour juger de cela ; mais en attendant vous allez devenir fort riches. La paix vous donnera le moyen de payer vos dettes ; mais ne comptez pas trop sur cela, elle ne durera pas long-temps. Pour faire une paix durable il aurait fallu laisser la Belgique à la France."

" Mais V.M. conviendra qu'une frontière contre la France a toujours été regardée comme une chose essentielle pour l'indépendance de la Hollande ? "

" Cela n'est pas nécessaire. Les Prussiens seront toujours avec les Hollandais contre la France ; et puis vous pouvez y envoyer des troupes. Une armée de quarante mille Anglais dans ce pays-là ne serait pas une chose indifférente. Ce sont des braves troupes, les troupes anglaises ; elles valent beaucoup mieux que les autres. Après celles-là je regarde les prussiennes comme les meilleures, mais j'ai toujours pu battre toutes les troupes continentales avec des forces très inférieures—combien de fois j'ai battu les Alliés entre le Rhin et Paris avec une poignée d'hommes ! C'est malheureux pour l'Europe que votre Ministère ne soit pas plus fort—si vous aviez eu un homme de talens comme Ld Chatham à la tête des affaires, il aurait compris qu'il ne fallait pas trop humilier la France. Vous l'aviez déjà assez humiliée en lui imposant les Bourbons. Elle ne renoncera jamais à l'espoir de regagner la Belgique. Vous verrez ! il sortira un de ces jours du fond des villages un vent de Libeccio qui bouleversera tout. Cela ne me regarde pas moi, mon rôle est fini, mais vous verrez. Il y a cinq cens familles en France que l'on n'aime pas ; pour assurer son repos, vous auriez dû lui donner ses limites naturelles. Vous savez que quand l'air a été trop comprimé il rompt tout quelquefois pour s'échapper. Vous verrez la guerre se renouveler pour la Belgique."

" Il me paraît, Sire, que la France est fatiguée de la guerre ; elle peut regretter la Belgique, mais la paix lui est plus nécessaire."

" Vous vous trompez. La France n'est pas épuisée ; j'ai toujours ménagé ses ressources. J'ai tiré des soldats de l'Allemagne, de l'Italie, de l'Espagne, pour épargner la France. J'ai levé des contributions partout pour le même objet. J'ai fait porter en France deux milliards des pays étrangers. Vous aurez vu dans les provinces une jeunesse abondante, l'agriculture améliorée, les manufactures florissantes." . . .

No. 11 (p. 111)

NAPOLÉON ET LE XME RÉGIMENT

14 *Mai* 1815.

Le 10ème Régiment avait suivi Monsieur le Dauphin dans le Midi et avait tiré sur les troupes qui, ayant pris le parti de l'Empereur, lui étaient opposées. Venu à Paris, l'Empereur devait en passer la revue dans la cour des Tuileries, et il avait reçu l'avis qu'un projet avait été formé dans le but de le tuer d'un coup de fusil. Il fit former le carré au régiment, y entra suivi seulement de son aide de camp, le Général Flahault et de son officier d'ordonnance, M. de la Riboisière,

et se plaçant au milieu lui tint le discours suivant. Le
discours prononcé, les soldats se prosternèrent devant lui,
aux cris mille fois répétés de " Vive l'Empereur ".

" Soldats—vous êtes les seuls qui ayez refusé de reconnaître et ayez tiré sur les couleurs qui pendant 25 ans vous
avaient conduit de victoire en victoire, de capitale en
capitale. Je devrais rayer votre numéro du cadre de l'armée
—je devrais couvrir vos drapeaux de crêpe et vous faire
décimer ; mais je veux vous donner l'occasion de réparer
votre faute et de faire votre paix avec l'armée. On m'a dit
que vous aviez de mauvais chefs. Je vous en donnerai de
bons, et je vous placerai à l'avant-garde. Il ne se tirera pas
un coup de fusil que vous n'y soyiez, et vous laverez votre
honte avec votre sang."

No. 12 (pp. 115-117)

Flahault à Brialmont

Monsieur, [1857]

Je viens de lire la relation de la campagne de 1815, qui
termine le 2e volume de votre histoire du Duc de Wellington,
et je ne puis résister au désir de vous exprimer la satisfaction
que, malgré la tristesse de ces souvenirs, j'ai éprouvé à la
lecture de ce morceau d'histoire, qui se distingue par l'im-
partialité avec laquelle vous racontez les évènemens et jugez
les hommes qui y ont pris part. . . . J'espère que vous ne
trouverez pas mauvais que je vous fasse connaître quelques
faits qui ne pouvaient pas être parvenus à votre connaissance
et qui sont de nature à modifier l'opinion que vous avez
exprimée sur la part qu'ont eue les Maréchaux Ney et
Grouchy dans les résultats de cette campagne.

Peut-être le meilleur moyen de parvenir au but que je me
propose est-il de vous faire le récit de ce qui s'est passé sous
mes yeux, ou dont j'ai eu connaissance personnelle. L'Empereur m'a, comme vous le dites, dicté à Charleroi entre
8 et 9 hes du matin, une lettre pour le Maréchal Ney, dans
laquelle il lui fesait connaître la manière dont il avait dis-
tribué l'armée sous ses ordres et ceux du Maréchal Grouchy,
et l'informait (autant que je puis m'en souvenir) de l'opéra-

tion qu'il allait entreprendre avec ce dernier, le corps du
Comte de Lobau, et la Garde Impériale, contre l'armée
prussienne : mais quant aux ordres de mouvements, je fus
chargé de les porter verbalement au Maréchal Ney. Je
lui donnai donc de la part de l'Empereur l'ordre de se
porter sur les Quatre-Bras, d'occuper fortement ce point
important, et (si les forces qu'il rencontrerait le lui permet-
taient) d'appuyer le mouvement de l'Empereur sur l'armée
prussienne avec toutes les troupes dont il pourrait disposer.

Après lui avoir donné cet ordre vers onze heures, ainsi
que je l'ai dit dans ma lettre au Duc d'Elchingen que vous
citez, je me portai en avant et je rencontrai assez près des
Quatre-Bras le Général Lefèvre Desnouettes avec sa cavalerie.
Je restai avec lui en attendant l'arrivée des troupes du
Maréchal Ney, et nous vîmes, assez loin, en face de nous, des
états-majors anglais qui paraissaient examiner la position.
Le Général Lefèvre Desnouettes fit tirer quelques coups de
canon sur eux, bien qu'ils fussent hors de portée.

Enfin, le Maréchal Ney parut et l'affaire s'engagea, mais
il n'y eu point d'ensemble dans les dispositions. On attaqua
comme on dit, le taureau par les cornes, lançant les troupes
successivement à mesure qu'elles arrivaient, et malgré la
bravoure qu'elles déployèrent, on n'obtint aucun résultat.

La nuit venue, chacun garda sa position. Je soupai avec
le Maréchal Ney et me mis ensuite en route pour rejoindre
l'Empereur. J'arrivai à Fleurus entre 6 et 7 heures du
matin. Le Maréchal Ney n'ayant pas eu le temps de faire
son rapport, m'avait chargé de rendre compte à l'Empereur
de ce qui s'était passé. Mon récit ne lui causa pas une
grande satisfaction.

Vers 10 heures nous montâmes à cheval et après avoir
parcouru le champ de bataille, nous rejoignîmes la chaussée.
Là, l'Empereur prit congé du Maréchal Grouchy en lui
adressant ces paroles, dont je me souviens comme si cela
s'était passé hier. " Allons Grouchy, poursuivez les Prussiens, l'épée dans les reins ; mais communiquez toujours
avec moi par votre gauche."

Vous voyez donc, Monsieur, que quant au M^{al} Grouchy,
il était impossible de chercher à le pénétrer davantage de la
nécessité de ne pas perdre de vue l'armée prussienne et de
se tenir, le cas échéant, en mesure de se porter vers l'Em-

pereur ; et l'on comprend que Sa Majesté ne dut pas s'attendre à voir arriver les Prussiens sans être suivis par Grouchy. Quant au Maréchal Ney, il a su le 16 à 11 heures du matin, l'importance que l'Empereur attachait à ce qu'il s'emparât de la position des Quatre-Bras.   Et quant au mouvement de cavalerie, que vous signalez avec raison (page 422) comme ayant eu une influence funeste sur l'issue de la bataille de Waterloo, j'ai l'honneur de vous envoyer copie d'une réclamation contre des assertions mensongères du Maréchal Marmont que j'ai cru devoir faire publier dans le *Moniteur* et qui vous dira la manière dont cela s'est passé. . . .

No. 13 (pp. 118-122)

Flahault à Lavalette

LONDRES, *ce* 27 *Octobre* 1861.

Mon cher Félix,

Savez-vous quelque chose de M. Edgar Quinet, auteur des articles sur la campagne de 1815 qui ont paru dans la *Revue des Deux Mondes* ?   Tout à fait entre nous et pour vous seul, il me fait l'effet d'un cuistre qui écrit sur un sujet dont il n'a pas la première idée, qui a été mal renseigné, qui veut établir la mémoire de Ney et pour cela faire, porte contre l'Empereur les accusations les plus absurdes.

Ainsi il dit qu'il était 2 ou 3 heures quand Grouchy put se mettre en marche, et en même temps il dit que les premières colonnes de Napoléon parurent aux Quatre-Bras à 2 heures.   Ainsi il fallait qu'il eût quitté Fleurus depuis longtemps, après avoir pris congé de Grouchy, car il y a une bonne distance d'un endroit à l'autre.

Il dit aussi que le Maréchal Ney m'avait envoyé à l'Empereur pour avoir des renseignemens sur ce qui s'était passé à Fleurus.   Si c'est le duc d'Elchingen qui lui a donné ses informations, cela prouve qu'il était aussi ignorant que celui à qui il les donnait !   J'ai assisté près de Ney à toute l'affaire des Quatre-Bras.   On ne saurait montrer plus de courage, je dirais même plus de mépris de la mort.   Mais là finira mon éloge ; car l'affaire s'est bornée à des attaques décousues, et l'absence de toutes dispositions.   Enfin, après

avoir soupé avec le maréchal, je suis parti, vers 1 heure du
matin, non pas chargé d'une mission par lui, mais pour
rejoindre l'Empereur à Fleurus, où j'arrivai avant déjeuner,
et où je lui rendis compte de ce qui s'était passé la veille.
Peu après déjeuner nous montâmes à cheval pour parcourir
le champ de bataille, après quoi nous nous rendîmes à la
grande route qui mène de Namur aux Quatre-Bras, et là
l'Empereur donna ses dernières instructions à Grouchy.
Quant à ce que dit M. Quinet qu'il ne fut pas question d'une
route intermédiaire, je puis sur ma parole d'honneur affirmer
que l'Empereur dit à Grouchy " Allons Grouchy, poursuivez les Prussiens, l'épée dans les reins ; mais communiquez
toujours avec moi par votre gauche ". Or n'était-ce pas lui
dire que cette communication était un point essentiel de ses
instructions ?

Que M. Quinet, qui paraît avoir eu beaucoup de rapports
avec le Duc d'Elchingen, ait fait tous ses efforts pour rétablir
les faits d'une manière favorable au Maréchal Ney, je le
conçois ; et je ne voudrai rien dire contre cette grande
victime.   Mais pourquoi se montre-t-il aussi injuste, et
s'écarte-t-il autant de la vérité, en ce qui concerne l'Empereur ?   Ainsi il loue Ney, ou au moins trouve tout simple
qu'il n'ait pas voulu attaquer les Anglais avant d'être rassuré
sur ce qui se passait du côté des Prussiens.   Mais pourquoi
alors fait-il un si grande reproche à l'Empereur de n'avoir
pas voulu se lancer tête baissée sur les Prussiens, sans savoir
ce qui se passait du côté des Anglais ?   Si l'un était bien,
pourquoi blâmer l'autre ?

Quant à tout ce qu'il lui reproche le lendemain matin du
retard dans la poursuite de l'armée de Blücher, il n'y a pas
un mot de vrai.   Une armée ne peut pas, après une bataille
rangée et des marches comme celles que la nôtre avait faites
la veille, se mettre en mouvement à l'aube du jour.   Le fait
est que ce qui est incompréhensible, c'est que les forces de
l'Empereur aient suffi à tout ce qu'il a fait à cette triste
époque, et M. Quinet aura beau faire et aura beau compulser
tous les papiers qu'aura laissés le Maréchal Grouchy, il ne
le lavera jamais de la faute (je ne dis point intentionnelle) de
n'avoir pas constamment gardé ses communications avec
nous par sa gauche ; et il y a de plus que Gérard et Excelmans l'en ont supplié.

On a beau être républicain et libéral outré ; quand on se mêle d'écrire l'histoire il faut dire la vérité ; c'est le seul irritable devoir de l'historien !

Du reste dans ces descriptions il y a des choses qui font mourir de rire. Ainsi il dit (page 35 du numéro du 1er septembre) que des lanciers français vinrent intrépidement planter en terre les hampes de leurs lances, en guise de jalons sur le front des bataillons ennemis, à peu de distance des baïonnettes ! Voulez-vous quelque chose de plus absurde ?—C'est une imitation burlesque de " Tirez Messieurs les Anglais " de Voltaire !

Et plus loin (page 37) se trouve : " Kellerman, à la tête de ses cuirassiers, charge sur la route qu'enfile une batterie anglaise. Il perce plusieurs lignes et bientôt la route est couverte des cadavres des assaillants. Ce grand effort a été inutile, la charge se rompt. Kellerman dont le cheval a été tué, reste quelque temps à la merci des ennemis. Il leur échappe à pied, en se suspendant aux mors des chevaux de deux de ses cuirassiers." Vous figurez-vous cette manière adroite de se faciliter la retraite ! De se suspendre à quoi ? Aux crins, aux bottes, à la queue des chevaux ? Non,—aux mors, qui était un moyen inévitable d'arrêter leur course et de les faire se cabrer ! C'est vraiment burlesque, mais il est affligeant de voir la *Revue des Deux Mondes* admettre dans ses colonnes de pareils articles. Grâce au Ciel, j'espère que, malgré l'esprit de parti, le bon sens public fera justice de pareilles sottises.

Du reste je tiens que l'Empereur ait connaissance de tout ce que je viens de vous dire, et je vous autorise à lui lire ou lui donner cette lettre écrite à la hâte. . . .

No. 14 (pp. 125-127)

Flahault à Thiers

LONDRES, *le* 27 *Août* 1862.

Mon cher Thiers,

Je viens de terminer la lecture de votre livre LX, contenant le récit de la campagne de 1815 ; elle a réveillé en moi tous les tristes souvenirs de cette douloureuse époque et c'est le

cœur encore tout gros, que je veux vous dire les impressions
qu'elle m'a causée.

A moins d'être historien infidèle, vous aviez une pénible
tâche à remplir et je dois dire que vous l'avez accomplie,
tout en gardant pour la mémoire de ceux dont vous aviez à
relever les fautes, le respect que leurs services antérieurs et
leurs grandes infortunes depuis, doivent inspirer.

Votre devoir envers la mémoire de l'Empereur vous
imposait aussi celui de faire retomber nos malheurs sur la
tête de ceux qui en étoient les véritables auteurs, et vous
l'avez merveilleusement fait, et également bien fait de dire
qu'à aucune époque de sa vie l'Empereur n'a montré plus
d'énergie, plus d'autorité, et une plus grande capacité comme
chef d'armée.

Grouchy a, comme vous le dites, été dans une sorte
d'aveuglement pendant les deux jours où il auroit pu sauver
l'armée et la France, du moins pour quelque temps, et c'est
d'autant plus inconcevable que les paroles que lui a adressées
l'Empereur au moment de le quitter et que Gérard vous a
répétées, sont textuelles. Je les ai entendues et elles sont
gravées dans ma mémoire.

Quant au Maréchal Ney, sa conduite aux Quatre-Bras est
celle que vous lui prêtez et mon rapport à l'Empereur quand
je l'ai rejoint le lendemain matin est aussi tel que vous le
représentez.

Venant maintenant à la bataille de Waterloo elle-même,
vous en faites une description vraie, et si nous avions causé
ensemble de toutes ces malheureuses affaires, je vous aurais
raconté une circonstance qui confirme ce que vous dites à
propos de l'attaque de la cavalerie, ordonnée par Ney.
Voyant la position de l'ennemi dégarnie, il a cru que le duc
de Wellington avait commencé son mouvement de retraite,
ne se rappelant pas que les Anglais ne couronnent jamais les
hauteurs et placent toujours leurs troupes en arrière du
rideau. J'étais auprès de l'Empereur sur le tertre où il s'est
placé pendant une grande partie de la journée, lorsqu'il a vu
Ney commencer son mouvement et faire passer le ravin à un
corps de cavalerie, et il s'est écrié, " Voilà Ney, qui d'une
affaire sûre, fait une affaire incertaine " (ces mots aussi sont
stéréotypés dans ma mémoire), " mais il n'y a plus d'autre
chance que celle d'appuyer le mouvement "—et alors,

s'adressant à moi, il me chargea de porter à toute la cavalerie que je rencontrerais, l'ordre d'appuyer les troupes que Ney avait lancées au travers du ravin contre l'ennemi.

Tristes souvenirs, et qu'il ne faut pas vous le dissimuler, vous attireront probablement des rancunes et du mauvais vouloir de la part de ceux qui, ayant hérité d'un nom glorieux, seront blessés des justes remarques qui sont de nature à en diminuer l'éclat : mais lorsqu'on a entrepris la tâche de raconter l'histoire de son pays, on ne doit jamais oublier que le premier devoir de l'historien est de dire la vérité.

FLAHAULT.

P.S. J'ai eu entre les mains l'autre jour toute la correspondance du gouvernement anglais et de l'amirauté avec mon beau-père Lord Keith et Sir H. Hotham et le Capitaine Maitland pendant cette abominable et cruelle conduite, si dépourvue de tout sentiment de générosité, que l'on a tenue envers l'Empereur quand il s'est livré lui-même en 1815. Vous parlez dans votre histoire de ceux qui lui ont conseillé de ne pas se rendre aux Anglais.   Personne ne l'a fait avec plus d'insistance que moi. Je lui ai dit qu'il ne fallait attendre aucun sentiment généreux d'un gouvernement collectif et responsable, et je lui ai non seulement conseillé de donner la préférence à l'Empereur Alexandre, mais je me suis offert pour aller auprès de ce monarque. Je lui ai dit que l'Empereur Alexandre sentirait qu'il serait responsable devant l'histoire de la conduite qu'il tiendrait envers lui et que je ne doutais pas qu'il ne lui offrît un asile sûr.

No. 15 (pp. 128-131)

Flahault au " Moniteur "

LONDRES, ce 6 Avril, 1857.

Monsieur Le Directeur,

Déjà plusieurs réclamations soulevées par les *Mémoires* du Maréchal duc de Raguse, ont été publiées dans le *Moniteur*, et j'espère que vous voudrez bien accorder la même faveur à celle que j'ai l'honneur de vous adresser.

Recevez, monsieur le directeur, l'assurance de ma parfaite considération,

COMTE DE FLAHAULT.

Le Maréchal *Marmont* dit à la page 121 du tome VII, en rendant compte de la bataille de Waterloo :

" Pendant le cours de la journée, Napoléon s'était trouvé si éloigné du champ de bataille, qu'il n'avait pu modifier l'exécution de ses projets, et particulièrement faire soutenir à temps ce mouvement de cavalerie qui aurait pu produire un effet si utile et si décisif ; prématuré et exécuté d'une manière isolée, il devint inutile ; et cependant si, quand il commença, on eût fait donner la garde, on aurait remédié au mal.

" Au moment du désordre, la terreur s'empara de l'esprit de Napoléon, il se retira au galop à plusieurs lieues, et à chaque instant (il était nuit), il croyait voir sur sa route ou sur son flanc de la cavalerie ennemie, il l'envoyait reconnaître."

Il est impossible de ne pas remarquer la haine qui perce dans tout ce récit, que le maréchal prétend tenir du général Bernard ; ce qui est impossible, car le général Bernard était un brave et honnête homme, et par conséquent incapable de lui avoir raconté un tel tissu de faussetés.

L'Empereur s'est placé, pendant la bataille, sur un mamelon, au centre de la position d'où son regard embrassait l'ensemble des opérations et d'où il aperçut le mouvement de la cavalerie qu'avait ordonné le Maréchal Ney, qui lui parut en effet prématuré et intempestif ; aussi s'écria-t-il : " Voilà Ney qui d'une affaire sûre en fait une affaire incertaine ; mais maintenant, puisque le mouvement est commencé, il n'y a plus autre chose à faire qu'à l'appuyer ". Et il m'ordonna de porter l'ordre à toute la cavalerie de soutenir et de suivre celle qui avait déjà passé le ravin qui la séparait de la position occupée par l'ennemi. Ce qui fut fait. Malheureusement le moment n'était pas arrivé pour qu'un tel mouvement pût réussir, et l'Empereur l'avait bien senti ; mais on ne pouvait pas arrêter et rappeler les corps déjà engagés, et il y a à la guerre des fautes qu'il n'y a moyen de réparer qu'en y persévérant.

Je laisse au Maréchal Marmont, sans le lui envier, l'honneur du parallèle (voyez page 125) qu'il cherche à établir entre les chefs des deux armées et la part qu'il fait à chacun dans le résultat de la bataille ; il se complait à faire le panégyrique du général anglais aux dépens de l'Empereur, mais au lieu de prendre tant de peine pour l'accuser de fautes auxquelles il attribue l'issue funeste de cette journée, il aurait pu sentir que l'arrivée inattendue sur notre flanc d'un corps de 30,000 Prussiens, dont l'artillerie traversait et labourait de ses boulets notre ligne d'opérations, a été la véritable cause de la perte de la bataille et de ses suites désastreuses. Dans son rapport à son gouvernement, le duc de Wellington a la justice d'en convenir.

Quant à la terreur que le maréchal prétend s'être emparée de l'esprit de l'Empereur au moment du désordre, je ne puis mieux faire pour réfuter cette assertion mensongère, que de raconter les faits tels qu'ils se sont passés sous mes yeux, et par conséquent personne n'est plus en état de le faire que moi.

Après avoir assisté à l'attaque de la cavalerie et à celle de la garde, et lorsque le mouvement de retraite se fut prononcé, je suis revenu chercher l'Empereur. Il était nuit ; je l'ai retrouvé dans un carré et je ne l'ai plus quitté ; après y être resté quelque temps, et la bataille étant perdue sans ressource, il en est sorti pour se porter sur la route de Charleroi.

Nous avons suivi cette direction, *non pas au galop*, comme on a l'infamie de le dire dans ces *Mémoires*, mais au pas, et aucune poursuite de l'ennemi n'a pu inspirer à l'Empereur les craintes que le maréchal, dans sa haine, voudrait lui attribuer. Loin d'avoir l'esprit troublé d'aucune crainte personnelle, et bien que la situation ne fût pas de nature à lui inspirer une grande quiétude, il était tellement accablé par la fatigue et le travail des jours précédents, qu'il n'a pu s'empêcher plusieurs fois de céder au sommeil qui s'emparait de lui, et il serait tombé de cheval si je ne l'avais pas soutenu.

Nous sommes arrivés le lendemain matin à Charleroi, où nous avons pris la poste pour nous rendre à Laon ; il s'y est arrêté pour écrire le bulletin dans lequel il rend compte de cette fatale journée, et s'est ensuite mis en route pour Paris ; voilà la vérité. Qu'on la compare avec le récit haineux et mensonger du Maréchal Marmont, et qu'on juge.

Mais quel sentiment d'indignation et de dégoût n'éprouve-t-on pas en voyant un homme, dont tous les efforts auraient dû tendre à se faire oublier ou au moins pardonner, venir ainsi attaquer celui qui avait été son bienfaiteur, et, après l'avoir trahi vivant, le calomnier après sa mort !

Cte DE FLAHAULT.

Y

No. 16 (pp. 133-134)

Flahault à Larabit

Mon cher collègue,

J'ai lu le discours que vous avez prononcé à l'inauguration de la statue du M^{al} Davoust à Auxerre. On ne saurait louer en termes plus justes et plus dignes la mémoire d'un homme qui a rendu de si éclatants services à l'Empereur et au pays, et qui a déployé pendant les guerres de la Révolution et de l'Empire tant de talent, de bravoure et de stricte probité.

J'ai regretté toutefois qu'amené à parler d'une anecdote racontée par Fleury de Chaboulon, vous ayez placé la scène décrite par lui comme s'étant passée dans le cabinet de l'Empereur sans témoins, tandis qu'elle a eu lieu dans le cabinet du gouvernement provisoire en présence de tous ses membres, de plusieurs ministres, du duc de Vicence et plusieurs autres personnages—en tout une vingtaine de personnes.

J'avais été envoyé de la Malmaison par l'Empereur pour demander au Gouvernement un ordre aux commandants des frégates alors à Cherbourg de se mettre à sa disposition ; il m'avait chargé de lui déclarer qu'il ne quitteroit les environs de Paris que lorsqu'on le lui aurait envoyé. Je venais de faire cette déclaration au Duc d'Otrante, lorsque le Maréchal Davoust, qui était debout près de la cheminée, prit la parole sans que quoique ce soit l'y obligeât et s'adressant à moi, me dit " Général, rendez-vous auprès de l'Empereur et dites lui qu'il parte, que sa présence nous gêne et est un obstacle à toute espèce d'arrangements et que le salut du pays exige son départ—sans quoi nous serons obligés de le faire arrêter ; que je l'arrêterai moi-même ".

Ces paroles me consternèrent, et je lui répondis sur le champ à haute voix : " Monsieur le Maréchal, il n'y a que celui qui donne un pareil message qui soit capable de le porter : quant à moi je ne m'en charge pas et si pour vous désobéir il faut donner sa démission, je vous donne la mienne ".

Cette scène me laissa durant quelques minutes en proie à une émotion très vive, pendant laquelle le Duc de Vicence et plusieurs autres personnes vinrent m'exprimer leur sympathie et leur indignation,

Je me rendis alors à la Malmaison où je trouvai l'Empereur couché. Il me fit entrer, mais je m'étais décidé à ne pas lui faire part de la scène à laquelle j'avais assisté, craignant d'ajouter à ses douleurs. Avec sa perspicacité ordinaire, il s'aperçut qu'il y avait quelque chose que je ne lui disais pas. Il me demanda de ne rien lui cacher, cherchant en même temps à me faire comprendre combien il lui importait de tout savoir. Alors, je lui racontai tout ce qui s'était passé, et il porta la main à son cou en disant, " Eh bien, qu'il y vienne ".

Voilà l'exacte vérité. Je ne cherche pas à revenir sur ce triste sujet, car il m'en coûte de rien dire qui soit de nature à porter atteinte à une des gloires de la France ; mais seulement je ne peux pas consentir à ce que l'on nie ce qui n'est malheureusement que trop vrai.

No. 17 (p. 166)

Napoléon à Keith

[BELLEROPHON], *July* 31, 1815.

Milord,

J'ai lu avec attention l'extrait de la lettre que vous m'avez communiqué. Je vous ai fait connaître tous mes sentimens. Je ne suis point prisonnier de guerre, mais je suis l'hôte de l'Angleterre. Je suis venu dans ce pays sur le vaisseau de guerre le *Bellerophon,* après avoir fait communiquer au Capitaine la lettre que j'écrivais au Prince Régent, et en avoir reçu l'assurance qu'il avoit des ordres qui lui prescrivaient de me recevoir à son bord pour me transporter en Angleterre avec ma suite, si je me présentais pour cela. L'amiral Hotham m'a depuis réitéré les mêmes choses. Du moment que j'ai été reçu librement sur le *Bellerophon*, je me suis trouvé sous la protection des loix de votre pays. Je préfère la mort à aller à St. Hélène, ou à être enfermé dans une citadelle quelconque. Je désire vivre libre dans l'intérieur de l'Angleterre, sous la protection et la surveillance des loix, et en prenant tous engagements et mesures qui pourraient être jugés convenables.

Je ne veux entretenir aucune correspondance avec la France, ni me mêler d'aucunes affaires politiques. Depuis

mon abdication, mon intention a toujours été de me domi-
cilier dans le sein d'un des deux états—les États-Unis, ou
l'Angleterre.

Je me flatte que vous, Milord, et le sous-Secrétaire d'État,
ferez un récit fidèle de tous les détails dans lesquels je suis
entré pour vous prouver les droits de ma position. C'est à
l'honneur du Prince Régent et à la protection des loix de
votre pays, que j'ai mis, et que je mets, ma confiance.

NAPOLÉON.

No. 18 (pp. 211-215)

L'Impératrice Joséphine

L'Impératrice Joséphine était d'une jalousie toute créole,
et que son mari excitait encore, soit par l'humeur qu'il
avait lorsqu'elle le tourmentait, soit par la confiance qui
suivait leurs raccommodemens; car c'est la seule femme qu'il
ait véritablement aimée. Dans ces momens d'abandon il
lui avouait ses infidélités, ses larmes le touchaient, sa colère
l'amusait. Il lui fesait les plus étranges confidences, son
âme devenait alors comme un transparent à travers lequel
elle connaissait tous ses sentimens. Quand la jalousie la
travaillait, personne n'avait d'empire sur elle; son fils, sa
fille, ses meilleurs amies lui semblaient liguées contre elle, dès
qu'on voulait lui parler raison.

Je me rappelle qu'un jour je voulais lui faire entendre
indirectement que, comme l'année était partagée par saisons,
la vie devait être séparée par volumes; que dès que son mari
avait des maîtresses, elle devrait lui laisser passer cette folie
et ne plus être que son amie; que peut-être même revien-
drait-il de ses égaremens, s'il trouvait toujours chez elle la
plus tendre amitié, la plus douce indulgence, un zèle attentif
et soutenu pour tous ses intérêts; que la grande affaire du
mariage n'était point de chercher une félicité qui n'existait
pas, mais de se plaire assez pour qu'on ait plus de plaisir à
revenir chez soi qu'à aller dans une autre maison. Enfin
que passé 30 ans, on ne pouvait prétendre qu'à la seconde
place dans l'affection de ceux qu'on aimait; mais qu'à tout
âge, et de tout le monde, je croyais qu'on pouvait obtenir

cette seconde place en renonçant volontairement à la première, se promettant d'offrir toujours tous les sentimens qui donnent du charme à la vie.

J'étais à m'évertuer ainsi sur la pointe de mon éloquence, lorsqu'elle me regarda avec ses yeux noirs et passionnés en me disant : " Cette première mort est pire que la dernière ". Elle me tourna le dos et fut 8 jours sans me parler : cependant elle profita de mes conseils. L'Empereur en rentrant chez elle, lui trouva l'air calme et doux. Il s'était monté à la colère parce qu'il s'attendait à une scène qu'il fut étonné de ne pas trouver. Fort méfiant de son naturel, l'étonnement l'inquiétait. Il lui dit qu'il venait de chez Madame Duch[âtel] —elle leva les yeux au ciel sans répondre un seul mot. Il cherche à la piquer, sans lui inspirer un mouvement d'humeur. Encore plus surpris, il parla de Mlle Georges dont il avait la fantaisie—un grand soupir et pas un mot. Troublé, il lui demande si elle ne l'aimait plus ? " Je serai toujours votre meilleure amie ", répondit-elle, " mais je tremble pour votre bonheur, je crains pour votre santé ; car si vous ne m'aimez plus, du moins aimez-vous vous-même ". Elle pleurait (car elle était réellement malheureuse) ; il en fut touché, la chargea de déclarer à Mme Duch[âtel] qu'il ne la reverrait plus, renvoya Mlle Georges, et fut pendant quelques jours le plus tendre et le meilleur des maris. Ce moment de bonheur suprême fit oublier à l'Impératrice Joséphine son âge, ses douces résolutions. Le sang créole commença encore à la tourmenter, et la jalousie revint troubler ce ménage—qui n'avait que des instants de calme et des mois de tourment.

Je suis encore persuadée que si elle avait voulu n'être que son amie, il n'aurait jamais divorcé, parce qu'il lui aurait ouvert toute son âme, et qu'elle aurait vu venir toutes les intrigues contre elle, et les aurait déjouées. La situation d'une Impératrice menacée continuellement d'un divorce, ayant pour époux un homme plus jeune qu'elle, brillant de gloire et de puissance, environné de parens qui détestaient Joséphine et offraient à l'Empereur tous les genres de séduction, était bien difficile. Dès qu'il eut pour ses fantaisies d'amour des confidences dans sa propre famille, il en aurait eu aussi pour les affaires, et ce fut elle qui lui apprit qu'il pouvait se passer d'elle. En général il versait du côté où il penchait. Mécontent de Joséphine, il se jetait vers sa famille, et c'était avec les Bonapartes qu'il frappait les Beauharnais, se raccommodait-il avec sa femme. C'était avec des comparaisons offensantes pour eux sur le mérite d'Eugène et d'Hortense qu'il blessait ses frères et ses sœurs ; et cependant il était faible pour tous, faisait le bien de tous, mais ne pouvait dissimuler son humeur. Malheureusement pour lui il offensait souvent, et ne punissait jamais. Cette disposition a été la cause de ses plus grands ennemis en France.

*   *   *   *   *   *

La famille Beaunaparte (*sic*) était fort jalouse des Beauharnais. Elle détestait l'Impératrice Joséphine et avait grand tort ; d'abord parce que c'était une excellente personne, mais encore parce que le divorce dont elle était toujours menacée lui donnait le désir de leur plaire, de les obliger, de les gagner enfin, ce qui est déjà une sorte de dépendance.

No. 19 (pp. 222-228)

Louis Bonaparte à Madame de Flahault

PARIS, 1er *fructidor* : *l'an* 8
[18 *August* 1800].

Je ne puis accepter la *Belle normande* de votre Charles, Madame, parce que de tous les défauts possibles, celui que je crains et que je hais le plus c'est l'égoïsme. Il est plus juste qu'un dragon ait un bon, beau, et solide cheval, qu'un colonel (*sic*) qui doit en avoir plusieurs. Ainsi vous ne me l'offrirez pas—ou en traduisant cet offre à la manière de Sterne, je croirai que vous me jugez mal. Vous me voyez avec des yeux trop beaux et trop flatteurs, pour que je ne désire pas d'être meilleur autant que possible. Je vous demande de me faire acheter par votre parent la jument qui va le Diable, dont vous m'avez déjà parlé, et celle dont vous me parliez aujourdhui, qui est dressée ; cette qualité est précieuse pour moi dans ce moment-ci. Je prends ici les eaux minérales artificielles, cela m'oblige à une vie réglée.

Je veux vous faire part, madame, d'un projet qui sera exécuté si je m'en sens les forces. Nous jouons à la Malmaison la comédie tous les decadis. Nous sommes fort embarrassés de trouver des pièces. Nous jouons celles que l'on donne au Français, et quoique nous n'ayons pour spectateurs que des gens fort légers, il y a éclipse. Tout le monde pense que si nous donnions des pièces tout à fait nouvelles, cela nous sauverait la comparaison. J'ai donc formé le projet d'une comédie ; depuis longtemps je mets mes délices à me voir jouer. Le sujet, et le plan m'embarrassaient également. Je veux y mettre un peu de morale, pas de pédanterie, et de la nouveauté—c'est beaucoup, mais enfin c'est quelque chose que la volonté. J'ai trouvé le sujet, il n'y a plus que le reste qui m'embarrasse, mais je prends patience, comme un roi déchargé du poids de mon gouvernement pour tout le mois prochain. J'espère qu'une fois reposé, ma tête et mon cœur pourront s'entendre pour l'exécution de mon grand projet. J'ai bien résolu de ne la lire qu'à vous et aux artistes de la Malmaison. Si vous me promettez de l'écouter je me mettrai à l'ouvrage de suite, mais ne divulguez pas mon secret. Je ne suis encore auteur que dans l'avenir, et en vérité c'est beaucoup que l'espoir, quand on songe que tant de savants et d'*instituts* ne peuvent plus en avoir, et qu'en voulant enforcer les portes du temple de mémoire ils s'y sont écrasés. Pardonnez-moi cet anathème ; il me prouve déjà que je réussirai, car c'est ainsi que débutent les hommes savants de nos jours !

Pardon, Madame, de mes jeux de mouche, de mon bavardage. Ne voyez, je vous en supplie, que l'hommage de mon admiration et de ma vive reconnaissance.

Louis Bonaparte.

Burgos, *le* 26 *Floréal, an* 9
[*May* 16, 1801].

J'ai reçu, Madame, la lettre qu'il vous a plu m'écrire (*sic*). S'il ne falloit pas me servir d'expressions tant de fois prodiguées, je vous renouvellerai l'assurance de mes sentiments, mais vous me permettrez de me taire. Il me siérait mal de croire que vous doutez de toute ma reconnaissance ; après m'avoir enorgueilli par votre amitié et votre estime, vous ne voudriez pas m'ôter l'idée que j'en suis desormais digne.

Votre dragon est officier depuis un mois. Lorsqu'il s'y attendait le moins je l'ai fait recevoir par le chef d'escadron qu'il redoutoit tant. Je l'ai fait passer dans une compagnie dont le capitaine est très sévère, mais mon intention n'a nullement été remplie ; au lieu de maîtriser le novice, c'est celui-ci qui s'est emparé de l'esprit du capitaine ! Je ne le vois pas votre dragon plus souvent qu'un autre officier. Quand il a tort je le gronde et le punis comme un autre. J'ai été traité ainsi à son âge et je crois que cela lui est aussi nécessaire, qu'il est impossible que je fasse autrement. Mais soyez tranquille en outre que je compte avec raison le soin de veiller sur les hommes confiés à mon intelligence comme mon premier et plus sacré devoir. Je n'oublierai ni la surveillance que je dois exercer sur mon jeune ami, ni ce que je dois à votre fils. Madame, je ne puis lui servir de mentor, mais je puis veiller à ce qu'il s'accoutume graduellement et sans trop de peine réelle à son métier, si dur pour les hommes faits et surtout pour les enfants gâtés comme lui. Je vous supplie de vous rappeller que tout ceci me regarde et que c'est doublement mon devoir. Pour de l'argent vous lui en donnez trop. Permettez-moi de vous dire que ce que vous faites pour lui peut exactement se comparer à ce que font de vieilles nourrices qui, lorsque les enfans sont malades, leur donnent beaucoup de dragées, qui sont tôt ou tard la cause d'une maladie. Puis j'ajouterai que jeune et enfant comme il est, ayant à camardiser à d'anciens militaires, pour la plus part cicatricés, il n'est pas bien qu'il s'élève trop au-dessus d'eux par des moyens pécuniaires.

Le jeune Meulan a de l'esprit, des moyens, mais il a le tort de se croire fait pour être officier d'armée, et il auroit dû cacher cela aux yeux surtout de ses camarades, qui ne peuvent voir en lui qu'une recrue—permettez-moi ce mot de caserne. Il est en effet très nouveau au service, il n'a point fait la guerre, il ne monte pas bien à cheval, il se tient très mal sous les armes, mais de manière à être remarqué par le général à chaque revue. Il n'a point de fermeté, et puis plus que tout cela, il fait fi de ses camarades. Il est toujours avec les officiers, il vit avec eux, ce qui est contraire à la discipline militaire, et m'a obligé à le tancer à l'ordre ; sans cela les autres sous-officiers auroient fait comme lui et il n'y auroit plus de subordination—en effet pourquoi les autres sous-officiers ne feroient-ils pas ce que fait un d'eux ? Je ne puis le souffrir, sans trahir mon devoir et me faire haïr avec raison de tout le monde. J'ai fait mettre à l'ordre du régiment que " celui qui vouloit s'élever au-dessus de ses camarades, au lieu de prouver qu'il étoit fait pour des grades supérieurs, prouvait qu'il n'étoit pas digne de celui qu'il avoit ", et cela à propos de lui. Il devoit se rappeller que votre fils a été un an dragon et qu'il a eu le bon esprit de se mettre à leur niveau. Mais M. Meulan se rangera. Il apprendra son métier ou quittera le régiment, et au retour de Portugal ce sera un bon officier ; pour cela il faut qu'il travaille. Mes promesses, quand elles ne sont pas officielles, n'obligent à l'exécution que Louis Bonaparte, mais il faut que le commandeur d'un régiment fasse son devoir aussi strictement que qui ce soit. Les préférences trop marquées au lieu de faire . . .

[*January* 3, 1802.]

Ce sera bientôt mais pas encore—après demain. J'aurais été vous annoncer le 1er de l'an, si je n'avais un grand nombre de petits affaires. Je ne pourrai avoir l'honneur de vous voir qu'après demain.

J'attends mon ami d'un instant à l'autre. Il vient du régiment, il seroit possible que votre fils profite de sa voiture pour arriver ici. Je suis bien content pour vous et pour lui.

Veuillez recevoir tous mes remerciements pour toutes vos marques d'amitié. Au commencement du nouvel an on dit adieu à une assez bonne partie de la vie, on salue le 1er jour de l'avenir. Dans l'une et l'autre période, j'ai vu avec joye l'amitié que vous voulez me rendre et je me suis applaudi d'y pouvoir ajouter ces sentiments d'admiration et de dévouement que vous me connaissez pour vous, Madame.

PARIS : *le* 13 *Nivôse, an* 10.

À Charles de Flahault

[13 *January* 1802.]

Je n'ai jamais été fâché de votre silence, mon cher Flahault. Il n'y avait là qu'un peu de négligence à accuser ; mais ce qui m'a peiné c'est que vous avez écrit que vous ne saviez que me dire, par où commencer. J'ai pour vous une amitié vraie fondée sur vos qualités. Vos défauts passent aisément, avec elles j'en suis sûr, je crois d'avantage que je n'y ferais double attention parce que ce ne sont pas eux qui frappent le plus en vous. J'en veux à Dommanizet de ne pas vous avoir envoyé de suite, j'avais des raisons pour cela. Dans votre état la meilleure manière de bien raisonner c'est de bien obéir.

Adieu, mon jeune ami. Vous n'avez plus 15 ans, mais j'ai et j'aurai toujours pour vous les mêmes sentiments.

LOUIS BONAPARTE.

PARIS, 23 *Nivôse, an* 10.

À Madame de Flahault

[*April* 19, 1801.]

Je viens tenir la promesse que votre obligeante amitié a exigée de moi. J'ai retrouvé ma solitude avec plaisir ; et quoique Paris, ce séjour de tant de choses opposées, renferme quelques amis que je sais plus aimer que je ne sais leur dire, j'y resterai content et occupé toute la semaine.

Veuillez me permettre de ne rien ajouter—Pourquoi finir par des phrases insignifiantes abîmées par l'usage ? Une lettre n'a-t-elle pas pour but de rappeler à la personne à qui l'on parle les sentiments que l'on a pour elle ?

Ce mardi, 29 *g*[l].

à Madame Flahault, rue d'Anjou,
  St. Honoré, près le chantier : Paris.

No. 20 (pp. 230-232)

"LES GRENOUILLES QUI DEMANDENT UN ROI"

Lorsque l'Empereur Napoléon voulut établir son frère Louis, Roi de Hollande, il eut soin de se faire demander ce nouveau souverain par une députation des États. Depuis longtems la Hollande, conquise par la France, était en quelque sorte administrée suivant les volontés de l'Empereur. Elle avait bien encore un Grand Pensionnaire et le nom de République, mais elle était absolument soumise à la France. Ainsi il fut très facile à Napoléon d'obtenir cette démarche par laquelle il prétendait dissimuler son ambition aux yeux de l'Europe, et cacher son autorité derrière ce fantôme de

Roi, dont, comme frère, il espérait plus d'obéissance que d'aucun autre de ses Préfets.

Les Stadthoudériens qui ne voulaient qu'une cour, des cordons, une noblesse, furent satisfaits de voir ce pays érigé en royaume, et le parti Républicain qui s'était livré à la France, lorsqu'elle même était une République, n'avait pas la force ni les moyens de s'y opposer. Toutes ces réflexions appartiennent à l'histoire, mais ce qui frappe les femmes, ce sont les petites circonstances ridicules qui viennent se joindre aux plus grands évènements.

Lorsque Napoléon, en grand costume, eut accueilli la demande des États, il fit venir le Prince et la Princesse Louis, qui furent reconnus pour Roi et Reine de Hollande.

La nouvelle Reine tenait par la main son fils, âgé de cinq ans, devenu Prince héréditaire—enfant charmant, mort depuis, et dont on soignait beaucoup l'éducation. Sa mémoire était fort cultivée, il apprenait chaque matin des vers que l'Empereur lui fesait souvent répéter.

Quand la cérémonie de cette présentation du nouveau Roi aux États et des Députés au Roi fut finie, on se mêla un peu dans le salon. L'Empereur s'assit, et je crois, pour distraire tout le monde, il se mit à jouer avec l'enfant. Tout en jouant il lui dit, " Qu'as-tu appris aujourd'huy ? "—" Une fable, mon oncle."—" Dis-nous-la "—et le petit de partir avec cette voix grèle et pointue des enfans :

> " *Les Grenouilles qui demandent un Roi.*"

L'étonnement causa un silence général ; le petit continua :

> *Les grenouilles se lassant*
> *De l'état démocratique*
> *Par leurs clameurs firent tant*
> *Que Jupin les soumit au pouvoir monarchique,* &c. &c.

La nouvelle Reine était rouge, embarrassée. Napoléon garda son sérieux quelque tems, mais il finit par de ces rires fols qu'on ne peut contenir ; et le soir on ne parlait pas d'autre chose. Le grand changement du Gouvernement Hollandais n'occupait personne.

Je crois que les Français s'en amusèrent fort indiscrètement, que les Hollandais en furent peut-être trop choqués, car c'était réellement un hazard—mais quel hazard !

No. 21 (pp. 261-263)

Testament de Jean de Morny

Ceci est mon testament.

Je soussigné Auguste Jean Hyacinthe de Morny, propriétaire à St-Dominique, voulant prévoir le cas où mon épouse Louise Émilie Coralie Fleury, partie depuis huit mois pour Philadelphie, sans que j'aye reçu de ses nouvelles depuis son départ, y étant allée pour tâcher d'y recouvrer les débris de ma fortune perdue par les désastres arrivés dans la colonie. Au cas où elle reviendroit avec des recouvrements certains, je lui recommande d'en faire le placement en France de la manière la plus solide, de s'en conserver la jouissance, et d'en assurer la propriété à notre fils, Charles Auguste Louis Josephe, né le vingt et un Octobre mille huit cent onze à Paris : et afin d'être parfaitement tranquil sur ce placement, je la prie de ne rien faire sans les avis de Monsieur don Josephe Marie de Souza, à qui nous devons notre existence depuis nos malheurs.

Dans le cas où ma femme viendroit à mourir, ayant perdu tous mes parens lors du désastre arrivé à St-Dominique, je fais choix pour tuteur de mon fils de la personne de Monsieur de Souza ci-dessus nommé. Dans le cas où il quitteroit la France, ou dans le cas où il viendroit à mourir, je choisis pour tutrice de mon fils l'épouse de Monsieur de Souza, Madame Adélaïde Marie Émilie Filleul, veuve en première noce de Monsieur de Flahault, dont la bienfaisance nous a si souvent secourus ; et dans le cas du prédécès de Madame de Souza, ou dans le cas d'absence ou empêchements, je choisis pour tuteur de mon fils, Monsieur Auguste Charles Joseph de Flahault, actuellement aide de camp de S.A.I. Monseigneur le Prince de Neuchâtel.

J'espère que toutes les personnes ci-dessus dénommées ne refuseront pas de me rendre ce dernier service et d'accorder à mon fils, s'il devenoit orphelin, tous les soins et les secours que son âge et notre ancienne position réclameront, et en attendant le retour de mon épouse, je leur donne toute autorité et tous droits sur mon enfant.

Dans ce dernier moment j'ordonne à mon fils de témoigner

par son obéissance et sa gratitude tout ce que je dois, et tout ce qu'il devra, à Monsieur et à Madame de Souza, dont je prie la Providence de récompenser la bonté et la bienfaisance.

Je révoque tout autre disposition dernière que j'aurois pu faire avant le présent testament auquel seul je m'arrête comme contenant mes dernières volontés.

Fait à Paris ce treize Novembre, mille huit cent douze.

AUGUSTE JEAN HYACINTHE DE MORNY.

No. 22 (pp. 266-267)

Duchesse de St. Leu à Madame de Souza

Je vous ai écrit par Gabriel pour vous dire combien j'avais partagé votre malheur ; je n'ai reçu aucune réponse de vous. Cependant vous connaissez mes sentimens ; comment ne m'aviez-vous pas donné de vos nouvelles, et en détail, de votre santé, de votre position ? Ce n'est pas bien à vous, car tous les détails que d'autres m'ont donnés ne me suffisent pas.

Je vais entreprendre un long voyage à la fin d'Octobre. J'espère que l'année prochaine si vous avez besoin des eaux, que nous nous y réunirons. Écrivez-moi par Gabriel. Croyez que je serai bien heureux de vous revoir. Nous sommes bien vieillies toutes deux et bien isolées, mais on se rapproche par la pensée, par les lettres, et quoiqu'il faille toujours s'imaginer qu'on est souvent lu par des curieux, n'importe. Il est naturel de parler de sa famille, et quand on n'a rien de mal à cacher on ne doit pas se gêner, c'est trop attrister sa vie.

Adieu ; je vous embrasse tendrement. J'ai eu tant de visites cette année que j'ai besoin de me retrouver un peu seule.

Quand on a quitté le monde on a de la peine à s'y habituer, et il a fallu bien de la peine aussi pour se résigner à vivre seule et sans un ami pour vous entendre et vous consoler ! Mais pour moi telle a été ma destinée et j'ai dû m'y résigner.

J'ai appris avec bien de la peine qu'il n'y avait que des filles dans votre famille, c'est réellement un tort. Je n'ai jamais sçu comment le grand-père avait laissé sa fortune et si un fils auroit eu l'espoir de l'avoir. Mais avec tant de filles on doit être gêné, et cette idée est affligeante.

Adieu ; mille tendresses pour vous et votre enfant.

Ce 20 Sept. 1825.

No. 23 (pp. 274-276)

CORRESPONDANCE DE NAPOLÉON IER

Flahault à Laborde

Mon cher L.

Je partage entièrement votre manière de voir sur les inconvénients et les dangers qui résulteraient de la continuation du système adopté par la Commission pour la publication de la Correspondance de l'Empereur.

Parmi les premiers je place le principe qui paraît prévaloir d'imprimer même les lettres ou pièces les plus insignifiantes, du moment où l'on peut tracer leur origine comme venant de l'Empereur ou de son cabinet. Si nous continuons ainsi il en résultera que nous publierons un ouvrage interminable et terriblement ennuyeux, dont personne ne voudra, et qui ne se trouvera que dans les bibliothèques publiques auxquelles l'Empereur en aura fait présent. Je n'ai pas reçu une épreuve dans laquelle je n'eusse désiré supprimer bon nombre de lettres, tout en en conservant assez pour prouver qu'aucun détail n'échappait à l'infatigable attention du grand homme.

J'arrive maintenant aux dangers qui découleraient des pièces semblables à celle (10,060) que vous m'avez envoyée, et je n'hésite pas à dire que sa publication ferait un grand tort à la mémoire de celui à qui l'Empereur s'est proposé d'élever un monument ; car une politique semblable justifierait celle adoptée contre lui en 1814 et 15, alors et depuis si généralement blâmée par tous les hommes honnêtes et impartiaux. Je n'ai point reçu la pièce 10,138, et ne puis par conséquent exprimer aucune opinion.

Quel but s'est proposé l'Empereur Napoléon III en ordonnant cette publication, et en instituant cette Commission ? A-t-il entendu que l'on imprimerait aveuglément tout ce qui serait sorti du cabinet de son oncle ? Ce serait la première fois que l'héritier et le successeur d'un grand homme aurait voulu une telle chose. Aussi n'est-il pas évident que ce n'est pas là son intention?—mais qu'il a cru que la commission, composée d'hommes éclairés et dévoués à la gloire impériale—ne donnerait pas de publicité à des pièces qui n'y étaient pas destinées et qui avaient été écrites ou dictées dans des moments ou des circonstances où le génie le plus puissant, le plus fort, et le plus élévé, n'est pas toujours maître de lui-même.

En ce qui touche au mérite de l'ouvrage et aux intérêts de l'Empereur Napoléon III et de la France dans la publication de la Correspondance de Napoléon Ier, je ne prétends à exercer d'autre influence que celle qui appartient à tous mes collègues, certain que ces intérêts leur sont aussi chers qu'à moi-même. Mais sa Majesté l'Empereur ayant été consultée et ayant déclaré que la commission était souveraine, je crois devoir lui dire qu'ayant eu l'honneur d'être aide de Camp de l'Empereur Napoléon Ier, et pénétré d'un profond respect pour sa mémoire, s'il arrivait qu'elle autorisât l'impression d'une pièce confidentielle—écrite dans un moment d'irritation et qui n'était pas destinée à devenir publique et qui fut de nature à porter atteinte à la considération du grand homme duquel elle serait émanée—quel qu'honneur que ce soit de compter dans ses rangs, je me croirais obligé de prier l'Empereur de me permettre de ne plus m'en faire partie.

Vous connaissez, mon cher Léon (?), tous les sentimens que je vous ai voués.

No. 24 (pp. 277-285)

Vaillant à Flahault

PALAIS DES TUILERIES,
le 27 Novembre 1863.

Ministère de la Maison de l'Empereur et
    des Beaux Arts
        Secrétariat Général
            Bureau du Personnel.

Monsieur le comte et cher collègue,

S.M. l'Empereur vient de décider que la Commission, chargée de publier la Correspondance de Napoléon Ier, cesserait ses travaux. J'extrais de la lettre par laquelle Sa Majesté a bien voulu me faire connaître sa décision, un passage qui vous expliquera quelles sont les intentions de l'Empereur relativement à la continuation de la grande œuvre napoléonienne qui nous avait été confiée. Voici ce passage :

" Remerciez de ma part les membres de la Commission, en leur disant que, si je mets un terme à leurs travaux, c'est pour chercher un moyen de rendre la publication plus prompte et basée sur un nouveau plan."

Si vous le voulez bien, nous nous réunirons mardi prochain, une dernière fois, pour nous faire nos adieux.

Recevez, Monsieur le Comte et cher collègue, l'assurance de mes sentiments dévoués.

Le Maréchal de France,
Président de la Commission,
VAILLANT.

Monsieur le comte de Flahault, Sénateur
  Membre de la commission de la correspondance de
    Napoléon Ier.

Flahault à l'Empereur Napoléon III

Nov. 1863.

La commission dont j'avais l'honneur de faire partie et aux travaux de laquelle Votre Majesté vient de mettre un terme a apporté, dans l'accomplissement de la tâche dont vous l'avez chargé, tout le zèle dont elle était capable ; et il ne lui a manqué, pour que ses efforts fussent couronnés de succès, qu'une bonne direction, que Votre Majesté seule était en position et en état de lui donner. Il fallait qu'elle apprît de vous, Sire, ce que je me suis souvent permis de lui dire, qu'au lieu de ce respect aveugle dont elle était animée pour tout ce qui lui paraissait émané du grand homme, elle aurait dû ne reproduire que ce qui était de nature à rendre, s'il était possible, sa mémoire encore plus illustre ; enfin ce qu'il aurait publié lui-même, s'il eut pu être consulté.

Pardonnez-moi, Sire, si j'ai pris la liberté de vous écrire à cette occasion ; mais resté seul de tous ceux qui ont eu l'honneur d'approcher ce grand homme, et sa mémoire ayant toujours été ce que j'ai de plus cher, j'ai cru que vous me permettriez de vous soumettre ces courtes observations, qui pourraient encore être utiles si vous vouliez bien les adresser à mes successeurs.

Je suis, Sire, avec le plus profond respect, de Votre Majesté le très obéissant serviteur et fidèle sujet,

FLAHAULT.

L'Empereur Napoléon III à Flahault

COMPIÈGNE, *le 3 Décembre* 1863.

Mon cher Comte de Flahault,

J'ai arrêté la publication des lettres de l'Empereur, parce que je me suis aperçu qu'on avait publié des lettres qu'on aurait aussi bien fait de supprimer. En dernier lieu le Prince Napoléon m'a cité plusieurs faits qui ont attiré mon attention et m'a remis le rapport ci-joint. Je vous prie de le lire avec attention et de me dire votre avis. La chose qui me paraît grave serait, comme me le propose mon cousin, de recommencer la publication.

J'ai mis au crayon le nom des personnes qui pourraient faire partie de la commission. J'espère que vous voudrez bien encore en faire partie, car le Prince Napoléon se plaît à reconnaître que vous êtes le seul qui ayez mis dans ce travail un discernement éclairé, basé sur un véritable dévouement à la mémoire de l'Empereur.

Je saisis avec plaisir cette occasion pour vous renouveler l'assurance de ma sincère amitié.   NAPOLÉON.

Note sur la Correspondance de Napoléon Ier

[*Dec.* 1863.]

But de la Publication

Je partage entièrement les opinions à ce sujet exprimées dans la note.

Caractère de la Publication

Il me semble qu'il y a dans cette partie de la note des opinions avancées un peu légèrement sur quelques membres de la commission, et je dois dire que je ne me suis jamais aperçu qu'aucun d'eux ait essayé de dénaturer ou écarter aucun des documens qu'on proposait de publier.

z

S'il y a un reproche à leur faire, c'est d'avoir, par un respect aveugle pour tout ce qui leur semblait émané de l'Empereur, été trop inclins à admettre dans ce recueil des pièces qui n'auraient pas dû s'y trouver.

Modifications à introduire dans cette Publication
Diviser le contenu en quatre grandes Catégories

Je crois que ce serait un très mauvais arrangement, et qui ôterait à la publication son caractère le plus remarquable.

N'est-ce pas, en effet, cette correspondance, traitant à la fois des sujets les plus divers : la grande politique générale, la guerre, l'administration de l'armée, l'administration intérieure de la France, les questions de morale philosophique et de morale religieuse, les relations de famille et d'affection, les établissemens de diverses sortes (comme cette lettre sur l'institut fondé à Écouen pour l'éducation des filles des membres de la Légion d'honneur), qui est un chef-d'œuvre par le soin et l'habileté avec lesquels tout y est prévu et discuté.

Je le répète donc, ce qui est surtout remarquable, outre le génie et l'habileté avec lesquels ces sujets sont traités, c'est de voir qu'ils forment son occupation de chaque jour, à toutes les heures ; et ce cachet se perdrait (indépendamment de la difficulté de la classification) si on voulait adopter le système proposé, et au lieu d'un tableau synoptique de la vie journalière de l'Empereur, on aurait quatre recueils de pièces historiques, pour servir à l'histoire de son règne.

Un autre inconvénient encore qui résulterait de ce plan serait la nécessité de détruire tout ce qui a été fait jusqu'ici. Il faudrait redemander à tous les souverains, à toutes les bibliothèques, à tous ceux enfin qui les possèdent, les exemplaires qu'ils ont reçus.

Ne serait-il pas à craindre que cela n'inspirât l'idée que trop de franchise avait présidé à l'œuvre supprimée, et qu'on se propose d'être plus réservé à l'avenir ? Ce qui ne manquerait pas de jeter du doute et de la défaveur sur la nouvelle commission et publication.

L'Empereur m'ayant permis de lui dire mon avis, j'ai l'honneur de le lui soumettre en toute sincérité, et je le prie de me permettre d'attendre sa résolution, avant d'accepter la proposition de faire partie de la commission, que j'ai reçue avec une profonde reconnaissance.

Vaillant à Flahault

Monsieur le comte et cher collègue,

Avant de signer le Décret, qui va reconstituer la Commission chargée de continuer la publication de la Correspondance de Napoléon Ier, *on* désire savoir si vous accepterez de faire partie de cette Commission. Elle sera présidée par S.A.I^{le} le Prince Napoléon. Le comte Walewski sera sans doute au nombre des désignés ; le Prince a demandé son adjonction. Son Altesse m'a dit que probablement le général Troppard y sera aussi. M. de Laborde a vu le Prince ; son acceptation est assuré si on le choisit. Moi, j'ai demandé la permission de me retirer. Soyez assez bon pour me répondre le plus promptement possible. *On* m'a bien recommandé de vous faire cette prière.

Je ne dois pas oublier que le mode de publication sera le même que précédemment. On a renoncé à l'*ordre des matières*. Toute la différence sera, je pense, qu'on ira plus vite et que l'adoption ou le rejet des pièces sera fait dans un esprit, je ne dirai pas mieux intentionné, mais peut-être plus éclairé que celui qui a guidé l'ancienne Commission.

Veuillez me croire, ce que je suis depuis bien des années,
Votre bien dévoué serviteur,
M^{al} VAILLANT.

M. le Comte de Flahault, Sénateur, &c.

Flahault à Morny

Mon cher A.,

J'ai reçu la lettre copiée ci-dessous du Maréchal Vaillant, et je ne comprends pas bien qui il veut désigner par *on*. Il est clair que c'est l'Empereur qui doit signer le décret, mais d'un autre côté, je serais surpris que ce fut lui qui fut indiqué. J'attendrai donc votre réponse pour faire la mienne. Ce serait avec une peine bien véritable que je me verrai dans le cas de ne pas accepter les fonctions qui me sont offertes par l'Empereur, mais certainement l'adjonction du Cte

Walewski à cette commission me fait désirer de n'en pas faire partie moi-même.

Dites-moi ce que vous en pensez, si vous trouvez l'occasion d'en parler à l'Empereur.

Adressez votre réponse à Londres, où nous serons lundi. Ne faites pas usage de la lettre de Vaillant auprès de l'Empereur, car je ne voudrais rien faire qui pût lui être désagréable.

Morny à Flahault

Lundi 18 [*Janvier* 1864.]

Mon cher ami,

J'ai reçu votre lettre hier, et n'ai pu voir l'Empereur que ce matin. C'est lui qui [doit] signer le Décret, et "*on*" l'a beaucoup amusé. Il attend votre réponse.

Je lui ai dit que si Valewski devait faire partie de la Commission vous ne consentiriez pas à en être—" C'est justement pour cela que j'attends la réponse de M. de Flahault. Parce que naturellement, si M. de Flahault accepte, je n'y mettrai pas Valewski que Napoléon désire y faire entrer." Si vous voulez mon sentiment, l'Empereur aimera mieux que vous acceptiez et n'est pas fâché d'en exclure Valewski.

Vous pouvez, si vous voulez, mettre dans cette lettre l'acceptation conditionnelle, afin que si jamais par un coup de fureur le Prince Napoléon voulût vous jouer un tour, vous eussiez à l'avance fait vos conditions.

Quant à l'Empereur c'est convenu. J'espère que vous accepterez cela, et la Légion d'Honneur. L'Empereur m'a dit ce matin : " J'ai dit à Rouher d'offrir la Légion d'Honneur à M. de Flahault. Je serais bien heureux qu'il voulût l'accepter."

Je vous embrasse, MORNY.

Flahault à Vaillant

LONDRES, *ce* 19 *Janvier*, 1864.

Monsieur le Maréchal et cher Collègue,

J'ai reçu la lettre que vous m'avez fait l'honneur de m'adresser le 13 cour^t, lorsque j'étais à la campagne, et je ne me rendais pas bien compte de ce que je devais entendre par l'*on*, que vous me disiez désirer savoir si j'accepterais de faire partie de la commission chargée de continuer la publication de la correspondance de l'Empereur Napoléon Ier. Cette publication est pour moi un objet de premier intérêt. Tout ce qui est de nature à contribuer à la gloire du grand homme que j'ai eu l'honneur de servir personnellement, me touche au plus haut point, et je ne voudrais pas perdre l'occasion d'y vouer mes faibles efforts.

Je suis donc disposé à accepter ; mais puisque vous avez l'obligeance de me prévenir que le Comte Walewski sera du nombre des désignés et que le Prince désire son adjonction, je ne vous cacherai pas qu'il me serait extrêmement pénible de me trouver fesant partie de la même réunion que lui, comme je ne doute pas que ma présence ne lui inspire réciproquement le même sentiment. Si donc il doit en être, je préférerais n'en être pas.

Si je dois en faire partie, je regretterai, mon cher Maréchal, puisque vous vous en retirez, de ne plus avoir le plaisir de vous rencontrer.

Veuillez, Monsieur le Maréchal, agréer l'assurance des sentimens de haute considération et de sincère attachement avec lesquels je suis

Votre dévoué Serviteur,

FLAHAULT.

No. 25 (p. 286)

Bonaparte à Talleyrand.

Liberté et Égalité

Au Q^r G^{al} DE MILAN,
Le 18 Thermidor, an 5 de la République,
Une et Indivisible.
[5 *August* 1797.]

BONAPARTE, G^{al} en chef de l'armée d'Italie
Au citoyen TALLEYRAND, M^{tre} des Relations Extérieures.

Le choix que le g^t a fait de vous pour ministre des Relations Extérieures, fait honneur à son discernement.

Il trouve en vous de grands talens, un civisme épuré, et un homme étranger aux égaremens qui ont déshonoré la Révolution.

Je suis flatté de devoir correspondre souvent avec vous, et vous mettre par là à même de vous convaincre de l'estime et de la haute considération que j'ai pour vous.

Salut et fraternité,

BONAPARTE.

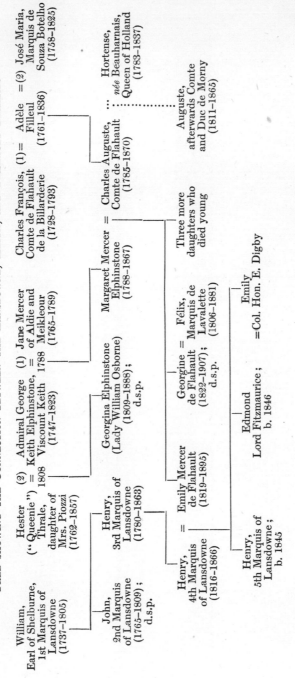

INDEX

ABERDEEN, George Hamilton Gordon, 4th Earl of. Ambassador Extraordinary and Minister Plenipotentiary to Vienna, 1813–14 : 52

ABOUKIR BAY, the landing at (1801) : 138

ADAM, General Frederick. Son of William Adam, M.P. : 144

ADAM, William, M.P. Chief Commissioner of the Jury Court in Scotland : 144, 162, 187

ADDINGTON, Henry, afterwards Lord Sidmouth. Prime Minister, 1801 to 1804 : 96

D'ALBANY, Comtesse. Widow of Charles Stuart, the " Young Pretender ". She lived at Florence : 74, 243, 247 n.

ALEXANDER I., Emperor of Russia from 1801 to 1825 : 23, 76, 90, 127, 249

AMHERST, William Pitt, Earl. Ambassador Extraordinary to China in 1816, afterwards Governor-General of India : 200

AMIENS, Treaty of (March 1802) : 96

D'ANGIVILLERS, Madame. Elizabeth de Laborde, widow of Charles Claude de Flahault, comte d'Angivillers : 236 n., 238

ANGOULÊME, Duke of. Eldest son of the Comte d'Artois and nephew of Louis XVIII. : 110

D'ARBLAY, Madame (Fanny Burney), novelist : 220, 221

ARENENBERG, near Constance. Queen Hortense's residence after 1817 : 255, 266

D'ARTOIS, Comte, afterwards Charles X. Brother to Louis XVIII. : 71 n.

ASPERN-ESSLING, battle of (1809) : 2, 5, 7

AUGUSTE : see de Morny

BAGRATION, Prince Peter, Russian general : 18

BALCOMBE, Mr. Owner of " The Briars ". A " general purveyor " at St. Helena : 189, 193, 194

BALCOMBES, the Miss : 195

BALMAIN, Comte de. Russian Commissioner at St. Helena : 188, 189 n., 196

BARCLAY DE TOLLY. Russian general : 18

BASSANO, duc de : see Maret

BATHURST, Henry, 3rd Earl. Secretary for War and Colonies under Lord Liverpool : 154, 161, 176

BAVARIA, Maximilian I., King of. He joined the Allies against Napoleon in October 1813 : 34

BEAUHARNAIS, Eugène, Viceroy of Italy : 26 n., 28, 36, 84, 99, 214, 250, 258, 259, 276
Napoleon's orders for : 35–47

BEAUHARNAIS family, the : 211 et seq., 251

BEDFORD, John Russell, 6th Duke of, and Georgina, Duchess of. She was a daughter of the Duke of Gordon : 105, 254

" BÉGO, Monsieur " : see Talleyrand

BERNARD, Simon. General of engineers and aide-de-camp to Napoleon I. : 129

BERRI, Charles Ferdinand, duc de. Second son of the Comte d'Artois (afterwards Charles X.) and father of the Comte de Chambord : 75

BERTHIER, Alexandre, Prince de Neuchâtel. Napoleon's chief of the staff : 3, 10-12, 16, 25, 26, 39, 44, 53, 237, 239, 242, 262

BERTRAND, General Count Henri. Napoleon's companion in exile: 84, 160, 167, 169, 171, 173, 174, 177, 181 et seq.

BERTRAND, Madame. Fanny, daughter of Hon. Arthur Dillon and grand-daughter of the 11th Viscount Dillon : 159, 160, 174, 182 et seq.

BERTRAND, the Abbé. Tutor to Queen Hortense's children : 244 et seq.

BESSBOROUGH, Henrietta, Countess of. Daughter of John, 1st Earl Spencer : 76

BILLARDERIE, Marquis de La. Uncle to Charles de Flahault : 237

BINGHAM, Sir George Ridout, Colonel. Second in command to Sir Hudson Lowe at St. Helena : 182

BINGHAM, Lady. Wife of Sir George Bingham : 182

BLACAS, duc de. The favourite adviser of Louis XVIII. during the First Restoration and later Ambassador at Rome : 75, 77

BLÜCHER, General : 60, 63, 64, 101, 120

BOLINGBROKE, Henry St. John, Viscount : 66 n.

BONAPARTE, Jérôme, King of Westphalia. Napoleon's youngest brother : 18, 42, 219

BONAPARTE, Eliza. Wife of Baciocchi, Prince de Lucques : 259

BONAPARTE, Joseph. Elder brother of Napoleon, who placed him first on the throne of Naples (1806) and afterwards on that of Spain (1808–1813) : 6, 97

BONAPARTE, Louis, younger brother of Napoleon. King of Holland from 1806 to 1810 : 6, 97. Part XI. (218-224), 235, 249

BONAPARTE, Napoleon Louis Charles (1803–1807). Eldest son of Louis Bonaparte and Queen Hortense : 230

BONAPARTE and Beauharnais families, the : 211-215

BONNEFOUX. Préfet maritime at Rochfort in 1815 : 157 n.

BORGHESE, Princess Pauline. Sister to Napoleon : 104, 276

BORINGDON, John Parker, Lord (afterwards 1st Earl of Morley) and Lady Boringdon : 156

BORODINO, battle of the (September 7, 1812) : 23

BOUCHEPORN, Madame de : 241

BOULAY DE LA MEURTHE. A leading orator during the Revolution and afterwards an adherent of Napoleon : 132

BOURBONS, the : 76, 93, 95, 101, 141 n., 233, 249

BOURCIER, François Antoine, Comte, General. Entrusted with the reorganisation of the Cavalry in 1813 : 41

BRIALMONT, Alexis Henri. Belgian general and writer on military topics : 114

" BRIARS, THE ". Sir Pulteney and Lady Malcolm's residence at St. Helena : 189

BROWNE, General. Military commander at Plymouth, August 1815 : 153, 162

BUFFON, Georges Louis Leclerc. French naturalist : 208

BÜLOW, Count von. Prussian General : 64

BUNBURY, Sir Henry. Son of W. Bunbury the caricaturist. Under-Secretary for War, 1815 : 160-165, 176

BURDETT, Sir Francis. Member of Parliament for Westminster, 1807–37 : 184

BURDETT, Lady. Daughter of Thomas Coutts, the banker : 184

BYNG, General Sir John. Afterwards Earl of Strafford : 176

CALLIN, Monsieur. Comptroller of Napoleon's household at Elba : 9

CAMOËNS, The Lusiads of. Edited by M. de Souza, 1817 : 66, 256

CAMPAN, Madame. The mistress of the school at which Hortense Beauharnais was educated : 244

CAMPBELL, Colonel, afterwards General Sir Neil. British Commissioner at Elba : 80, 83

CAPE EXPEDITION (1795) : 138

CASTLEREAGH, Robert Stewart, Lord, afterwards Marquis of Londonderry. Foreign Secretary from 1812 to 1822, and Plenipotentiary Extraordinary at the Congress of Vienna, 1814 : 150, 151

CAULAINCOURT, Armand de, duc de Vicenza. General, Minister for War, and *premier écuyer* to Napoleon : 50, 68, 73, 133

" CHAMBRE INTROUVABLE ", La, of 1815–16 : 259

CHAMPAUBERT, battle of (February 10, 1815) : 57

CHARLES, the Archduke. Charles Louis de Lorraine, son of the Emperor Leopold II. and brother of Francis II. of Austria : 2, 4-8

CHARLOTTE, Princess, of Wales. Only child of George, Prince of Wales (afterwards George IV.). Married in 1816 Prince Leopold of Saxe-Coburg and died the following year in child-birth : 156, 162, 257

CHATHAM, William Pitt, Earl of : 95

CHÂTILLON, Congress of (February and March 1814) : 51, 53, 101

CHEVERT, François de. A French general in the 18th century : 22

CINTRÉ, Marquis de. The husband of Henriette de Capellis : 237

CLARENCE, William Duke of, afterwards William IV. : 163

CLARKE, Henri Jacques Guillaume, duc de Feltre. Napoleon's Minister for War : 31, 32, 34

COCHRANE, Captain. (?) Thomas John Cochrane, afterwards an admiral and K.C.B. : 198

COCKBURN, Admiral Sir George. Governor of St. Helena, 1815–1816. Afterwards M.P. and a lord of the Admiralty : 157, 161, 168 *et seq.*, 180, 195, 201

COMMISSION, for the publication of the correspondence of Napoleon I. : 272 *et seq.*

CONDORCET, Marquis de. Philosopher and social reformer. He killed himself by taking poison when arrested by the Revolutionaries (1794) : 73

CONSTANT, Benjamin. Orator and author. His conduct in 1815 made it necessary for him to leave France after the Second Restoration : 259

CORNWALLIS, Admiral Sir William (1744–1819). Younger brother of General Lord Cornwallis : 187

" COUSINE, MA " : see Hortense, Queen

CRAONNE, battle of (March 1814) : 64

DAVOUT, Prince D'Eckmuhl. Marshal of France and Minister for War in 1815 : 3, 18, 37, 42, 109, 110, 132 *et seq.*

DEADWOOD CAMP (St. Helena) : 202

DECRÈS, Denis, duc de, Admiral. French Naval Minister from 1801 to 1814 : 132

DELESSERT, Gabriel. Banker : 266, 268

DENON, Baron. Director-General of Museums. He wrote a book about Napoleon's Egyptian campaigns : 87

DEVON, Captain and Mrs. : 199

DIGBY, Lady Emily. Granddaughter of the Comte de Flahault : 268, and Table, 343

DOMMANIZET. (?) An officer in the Ve *Dragons* : 227

DOMMERGUE (?), Madame : 268

DOUGLAS, Frederick Sylvester North. His interview with Napoleon : 80

DROUOT, General Count Antoine. Governor of Elba during Napoleon's stay on that island : 84-86, 103, 104

DUCCA, General. Aide-de-camp to the Emperor of Austria in 1814 : 51, 60, 62

DUCHÂTEL, Madame. Her liaison with Napoleon : 213

DUCKWORTH, Sir John, Admiral. He appears to have held an independent command in the Channel in the summer of 1815, though Keith was Commander-in-Chief of the Fleet : 142, 146, 151, 153, 154, 155

DUCKWORTH, Lady. A daughter of William Buller, Bishop of Exeter : 162

DUNCAN, Captain, of the *Glasgow* : 147

DUNDAS, Henry, 1st Viscount Melville : 145 *n.*

DUNDAS, Robert Saunders, 2nd Viscount Melville. First Lord of the Admiralty in 1815 : 145 *n.*, 166 *n.*
Letters from : 145, 150, 157, 158, 160, 161
Letter to : 163

DUROC, Marshal, *Grand Maréchal du Palais*. Killed at the battle of Wurtzschen in 1813 : 84 *n.*

DUROSNEL, Antoine Jean Auguste, General. Napoleon's favourite equerry. Wounded and taken prisoner at Essling : 7

DUVERGIER, General. His letters as to cavalry stores, 1813 : 33

EBRINGTON, Hugh Fortescue, Viscount, afterwards 2nd Earl Fortescue : 80

D'ÉCOUEN, " La maison imperiale " : 280

D'ELCHINGEN, duc : *see* Ney

D'ELCHINGEN, duc (1804–1854). Michel Louis Félix Ney, brother to Marshal Ney : 119, 120

ELPHINSTONE, Anne. Daughter of William Fullerton Elphinstone : 167, 175

ELPHINSTONE, Clementine. A daughter of John, 11th Lord Elphinstone : 198

ELPHINSTONE, Georgina. Daughter of Lord Keith by his (second) marriage with Hester Thrale : 154, 168, 193, and Table, 343

ELPHINSTONE, James Drummond. Son of William Fullerton Elphinstone : 144 *n.*, 156

ELPHINSTONE, Sidney Herbert. Sixteenth and present Lord Elphinstone : 144

ELPHINSTONE, Margaret Mercer. Daughter of Lord Keith and wife of the Comte de Flahault : 13, 108, 135, 139, 178, 180, 208, 234, 254, 256, 260, and Table, 343

ELPHINSTONE. Mary. Sister of Lord Keith : 180, 189
Letters to : 189, 193

ELPHINSTONE, William Fullerton. Brother to Lord Keith, and sometime chairman of the East India Company : 180

ESTERHAZY, Prince Paul Antoine. Austrian diplomat, afterwards Ambassador in London: 257, 259

EXELMANS, Remy Joseph Isidore, Comte. A French General and friend of Flahault : 121

FAIN, Baron. His *Manuscrit de 1814* : 73

FARNELL, Mrs. : 156

FAZAKERLEY, John Nicholas ; of Prescott, county Lancaster. Whig member of Parliament, a friend of Lord Holland : 80, 81 *et seq.*

FINGAL. A legendary hero of Scotland concerning whom James Macpherson published an epic poem in 1762 : 187

FITZMAURICE, Lord. Grandson of the Comte de Flahault : 268, and Table, 343

FLAHAULT, Adèle Filleul, Madame de : *see* Madame de Souza

FLAHAULT, Charles François, Comte de. Father of General Comte de Flahault : 208, and Table, 343

FLAHAULT, Charles Auguste, Comte de : *see* Introduction, etc., and Table, 343

FLAHAULT, Madame de : *see* Elphinstone, Margaret Mercer

FLAHAULT - SOUZA correspondence (Bowood papers) : 233
Quotations from: 16-28, 66, 67-72, 108, 114, 208, 219, 235-265, 287

FLEMING, Admiral Charles Elphinstone. Second son of 11th Lord Elphinstone : 142

FOLLIN, Capitaine. An officer in the *Vᵉ Dragons* : 219

FONTAINEBLEAU, Treaty of (1814) : 72

FOUCHÉ, duc d'Otranto. President of the Provisional Government in 1815 : 132, 133

FOX, Charles James. His negotiations with Napoleon in 1806 : 97, 196

Fox, Mrs. Elizabeth Bridget Cane, known as Mrs. Armistead. She was for many years Fox's mistress and eventually (1795) became his wife : 87

Francis II., Emperor of Austria from 1792 to 1835 : 2, 7, 10, 61

Frankfort, negotiations of (1813): 50, 52, 53, 55, 56, 63

Freemantle, Sir Thomas, Admiral. In 1815 he seems to have held a detached command for the purpose of intercepting Napoleon at sea : 146

" Furibonde, la " : 247

Gallatin, Albert. United States Envoy to France, 1813–1827 : 80 n.

Gallatin, James, son of Albert Gallatin. His Diary : 80 n., 95 n., 205 n.

Gardien, Claude Martin. Médecin accoucheur : 260

Georges, Mademoiselle, the actress : 210, 213

" Georgina "—" Georgie " : see Elphinstone, Georgina

Gérard, Comte Maurice Étienne. General and afterwards Marshal of France : 121, 126

Gérard, François. Historical painter. His portrait of the Comte de Flahault : 268

Girardin, Madame. Wife of General Comte Alexandre de Girardin : 77

Gourgaud, Gaspard, General. He helped Napoleon with the writing of his Mémoires at St. Helena : 174, 177, 185, 200, 202

Grouchy, Emanuel, Marshal of France : 115, 117 et seq., 119, 125, 148, 193

Guard, the : 24, 54, 85, 128, 130

Hallowell, Admiral Sir Benjamin. He held the Mediterranean command from 1812 to 1815. Afterwards took the name of Carew : 141, 169

Hanau, battle of (October 29, 1813) : 50, and illustration facing p. 48

Haxo, François Benoit. General of engineers : 39, 44, 46

" Henri " : see de Morny, Auguste

" Henriette " : see Hortense, Queen

Hippisley, Sir John Coxe (1748–1815). Political writer and sometime member of Parliament : 167

Hobhouse, John Cam, afterwards Lord Broughton-de-Gyfford— Recollections of a Long Life : 74-76, 80, 135-6 Letters from an Englishman resident in Paris during the Last Reign of Napoleon : 76, 135

Holland, Louis, King of : see Bonaparte, Louis

Holland, Henry Richard Fox, 3rd Lord, Whig statesman : 84, 87

Holland, Elizabeth Vassall, Lady, married (1st) Sir Richard Webster and (2nd) 3rd Lord Holland : 183, 184

Hood, Samuel, Viscount, the celebrated Admiral : 187

Hortense, Queen. Daughter of Joséphine Beauharnais : 69, 71, 72, 84, 214, 218 et seq., 230-268 (Part XII.)

Hotham, Admiral Sir Henry. Serving under Lord Keith in the Channel Fleet, 1815 : 127, 141, 147, 149, 152, 157-158, 166

Houssaye, Henri. French writer, his Waterloo, 1815 : 110, 122

Hubert, one of Napoleon's valets : 73

Jansenists, the followers of Cornelius Jansen in the famous controversy against the Jesuits : 88

De Jean's Hotel at Sécherons : 252

Jena, battle of (October 14, 1806) : 97

Jerningham, Lady Frances, widow of Sir William Jerningham, Bart. She was the daughter of Henry, 11th Viscount Dillon : 203

John, the Archduke. Brother of the Emperor Francis II. of Austria and of the Archduke Charles : 2, 5-6

Joséphine, the Empress : 84, 99,

Part X. (208-215), 218, 219, 235, 249

KEITH, Admiral Viscount : 127, Part VIII. (138-178), 254, and Table, 343

KEITH, Lady, Hester Maria (" Queenie ") Thrale. Second wife of Admiral Lord Keith : 139, 154, 180, 220, 267, and Table, 343

KEITH, James Francis Edward. Brother of the last Earl Marischal of Scotland, Field-Marshal in the Prussian service after 1715 : 138

KELLERMANN, Christophe François, duc de Valmy. He commanded the 3rd Cavalry Corps in the army of 1815 : 121

KOSSUTH, Louis. The leader of the Hungarian revolution of 1849 : 108

LA BÉDOYÈRE, Charles, Comte de, General. Executed August 1815 : 112-113, 136, 252

LABORDE, Léon Marquis de. *Directeur Général des archives* under Napoleon III. : 273, 282

LABORDE, Comte, Alexandre de. *Membre de l'Institut* : 273 n.

LACUÉE, General, Comte de Cessac. *Ministre directeur de l'administration de la Guerre* in 1813 : 32, 33

LA FONTAINE. *The Frogs ask for a King* : 232

LALLEMAND, General Baron. He was interned for a time after Napoleon's fall and subsequently went to America : 175 n.

LANGUENAU, DE, Austrian commissioner at Lusigny in 1814 : 51

LANSDOWNE, Henry, 3rd Marquis of : 81, 139, and Table, 343

LANSDOWNE, 4th Marquis of : 139, and Table, 343

LANSDOWNE, Henry, 5th Marquis of : 239, and Table, 343

LAON, battle of (March 1814) : 64

LARABIT. Senator and President of the *Conseil Général de l'Yonne* in 1867 : 132, 134

LAS CASES, Comte de. Accompanied Napoleon to St. Helena, where he wrote the *Mémorial de St. Hélène* : 174, 177, 185, 186, 189, 193, 195

LASCOURS, M. de. An officer in the *gardes du corps* of King Louis XVIII. : 256

LAUDERDALE, James Maitland, Earl of. Minister Plenipotentiary to France for the purpose of concluding a peace in 1806 : 196

LAURISTON, James Alexander Bernard Law, Comte de. Marshal of France : 38, 44, 47

LAVAL, Vicomtesse de. Friend of Talleyrand : 234

LAVALETTE, Madame de. Wife of Marie Chamans, Comte de Lavalette, *née* Emilie de Beauharnais : 199

LAVALETTE, Félix, Marquis de. Diplomatist, French Ambassador in London, 1869 : 118, and Table, 343

Letter to : 118-122

LAVALETTE, Georgine, Marquise de. Flahault's younger daughter : 3, 110, 123, 268, and Table, 343

LECESTRE, Léon. His *Lettres inédites de Napoléon* : 272

LECLERC, Charles Emanuel, General. Died of yellow fever at St. Domingo, 1801 : 219

LEFÈBRE - DESNOËTTES, Charles, Comte, General. He commanded a light cavalry division at Fleurus and at Waterloo : 116

LE HON, Comtesse. The wife of the Belgian Ambassador in Paris under Louis Philippe : 269

LE HON, Mlle. Louise. Married (in 1856) Prince Stanislas Poniatowski : 269

LETORT, Louis Michel, Baron. Killed at Fleurus, June 15, 1815, while in command of the *Dragons de la garde* : 114

LEVESON-GOWER, Lord Granville, First Earl Granville. Diplomatist, friend of Lady Bessborough : 76

LIECHTENSTEIN, Prince Wenceslas of. Sent as emissary to Napoleon during the campaign of France : 51

LIGNY, battle of (June 16, 1815):
114 *et seq.*

LIVERPOOL, Earl of. Prime Minister, 1812 to 1826 : 145 *n.*

LOBAU, Count Mouton, Marshal. He commanded the Sixth Corps in 1815 : 115

LOIRE, the army of the, 1815 : 149, 251

"LONGWOOD", St. Helena : 181 *et seq.*

LOUIS XVI. : 208

LOUIS XVIII. : 108, 110, 142, 151

LOUIS NAPOLEON, afterwards Napoleon III. : 122, 124, 235, 272 *et seq.*
  Letter to : 278
  Letter from : 279

LOUIS PHILIPPE, King of the French : 124

"LOUISE". Mlle. Cochelet, the writer of *Mémoires sur la Reine Hortense* : 256

LOWE, General Sir Hudson. Governor of St. Helena during Napoleon's captivity : 135 *n.*, 151 *n.*, 180 *et seq.*

LOWE, Lady. Wife of Sir Hudson Lowe : 197, 200

LOWTHER, William, 2nd Earl of Lonsdale : 176

LYTTELTON, William Henry, 3rd Lord : 176

MACDONALD, Étienne Jacques Joseph Alexandre, Duke of Tarentum. Marshal of France : 77, 101

MACKENROT, Antony. A messenger from the Court of King's Bench : 168

MACLEAN, (?) Sir Hector. Baronet of Morven. He had been an army officer : 167

MACNAMARA, John. His interview with Napoleon at Elba (January 1815) : 80

MACPHERSON, James. Published a series of poems alleged to be translated from Ossian. It was, however, subsequently decided that they were for the most part from Macpherson's pen : 186

"MADELEINE". (?) Auguste de Morny's nurse : 246

MAINGAUD. The doctor who accompanied Napoleon, in a temporary capacity, from Rochefort to Plymouth : 175

MAITLAND, Frederick Lewis, Captain (of the *Bellerophon*). Afterwards Admiral and Commander-in-Chief in East Indies : 127, 151 *et seq.*, 162, 166, 170, 171, 172, 177

MAITLAND, Mrs. Wife of Captain Maitland : 155, 162

MALCOLM, Admiral Sir Pulteney. Commander-in-Chief at St. Helena, 1816–17 : Part IX. (180-205)

MALCOLM, Lady (Clementine Elphinstone). Wife of Admiral Sir Pulteney Malcolm : 180
  Letters from : 181-205

MALCOLM, Sir John. Indian administrator and diplomatist : 197

MALMAISON, theatricals at : 222-3

MALO - JAROSLAVETZ, battle of (October 1812) : 25

MAMELUKES, in Napoleon's body-guard at Elba : 86, 87, 88

MARET, Hugues Bernard, duc de Bassano. Napoleon's Minister for Foreign Affairs from 1811 to 1813 : 30, 50, 73, 113

MARIE LOUISE, Empress. Daughter of the Emperor Francis II. of Austria. Married Napoleon in 1810 : 108

MARISCHAL, George Keith, 10th Earl. Jacobite and favourite of Frederick the Great, *d.* 1778 : 138

MARMONT, duc de Raguse. Marshal of France : 100, 102, 117, 128
  His *Mémoires* : 128-131

MARS, Mlle. Actress at the *Français* : 77, 253

MASSON, Frederic. His brochure *Le Général Comte de Flahault* : 118 *n.*, 122, 132, 209
  Napoléon et sa famille : 241, 249, 252, 255, 265

MEEK, Mr., secretary to Lord Keith in 1815 : 140, 171

MELVILLE, Lord : *see* Dundas

MÉNEVAL, Baron de. *Secrétaire du portefeuille* to Napoleon : 31

MERCER, Jane, of Meikleour and Aldie. First wife of Admiral Lord Keith : 139, and Table, 343

METTERNICH, Clement Prince de. Austrian Chancellor : 12, 50, 52, 82, 98, 268

MEULAN, Théodore, Comte de. An officer in the Ve Dragons (1801). He later became a General of some distinction : 225-6

MOLÉ, Comte Louis Mathieu de. His *Mémoires* : 6, 31

MOLINISTES. The followers of Luis Molina, the Spanish Jesuit (1535–1601) : 88

Moniteur, Le : 52
Flahault's letter to : 114, 128-131

MONNET, General, Baron. Commanding at Flushing, 1809. Condemned to death for its surrender : 9

MONTAGU, Lady. (?) The wife of Henry James (Montagu-Scott) Baron Montagu of Boughton : 105

MONTCHENU, Marquis de. French Commissioner at St. Helena : 188, 191, 196

MONTEREAU, battle of (February 18, 1814) : 51, 57

MONTHOLON, General Comte. One of Napoleon's companions at St. Helena : 174, 184 n., 185, 199, 201

MONTHOLON, Madame. Wife of General Montholon : 159, 173, 187, 195, 201, 202

MONTROND, Casimir, Comte de. A friend of Flahault and later the *âme damné* of Talleyrand : 237 n., 268

MOORE, Rear-Admiral Sir Graham. Afterwards Admiral and Commander-in-Chief in the Mediterranean : 141

MORNY, Auguste de, afterwards duc de : 232-234, 241-269
Letter to : 282
Letter from : 283

MORNY, Jean Hyacinthe de. *Propriétaire à St. Dominique*. The putative father of duc de Morny : 260-265

MORNY, Louise Émilie Coralie Fleury de, wife of Jean Hyacinthe de Morny : 261-3

MOSCOW, the great fire of (1812) : 24, 91

MOSTYN, Mrs. (Cecilia Thrale).

Daughter of Mrs. Piozzi : 150, 189

MUFFLING, Frederic Ferdinand Charles, Baron von. Prussian General. He was appointed governor of Paris by the Allies in 1815 : 251

MURAT, Joachim. Grand duc de Berg and King of Naples : 3, 18, 26 n., 28

NAPOLEON I. Letters from : 62, 63, 109, 113, 166, 285

NAPOLEON III. : *see* Louis Napoleon

NAPOLEON, Joseph Charles Paul, " Plon-Plon ". Son of Jérôme Napoleon : 279, 282, 285

NARBONNE-LARA, Louis, Comte de. Aide-de-camp to Napoleon : 15

NAVARRE. The residence assigned to the Empress Josephine by Napoleon after her divorce : 249

" NÉNÉ " : *see* Flahault, Charles de

NESSELRODE, Carl Robert, Count von. Russian diplomatist : 52

NEY, Michel, duc d'Elchingen and Prince de Moskowa. French marshal : 20, 43, 90, 101, 115 *et seq.*, 120

NEY, Madame (Eglé Augié). A niece of Madame Campan. Married Ney in 1802 : 77

NICOLAS I. Emperor of Russia from 1825 to 1855 : 108

NIEMEN, crossing of the (June 24, 1812) : 17, 25

O'MEARA, Barry, Dr. With Napoleon at St. Helena : 175, 202, 203, 204

ORANGE, William Prince of. Eldest son of William I., King of Holland, whom he afterwards succeeded : 156 n.

" ORDERS IN COUNCIL " (of 1807) and Napoleon's " Berlin Decrees " : 97

" OSSIAN " : *see* Macpherson

OTRANTO, duc d' : *see* Fouché

PALLISER, Captain, of the *Eridanus* (1815) : 175

" PAPA " : *see* Souza, M. de

PARIS, Second Treaty of (1815):
147
PIONTKOWSKI, Captain. Equerry
to Napoleon at St. Helena:
184 *n.*, 198 *n.*
PITT, William. Prime Minister : 96
PLAMPIN, Robert, Admiral. Suc-
ceeded Sir Pulteney Malcolm
at St. Helena, 1817 : 180,
199 *n.*
PLANAT. Accompanied Napoleon
to Plymouth, but was detained
and interned at Malta : 175 *n.*
" PLANTATION HOUSE ". Sir Hud-
son Lowe's residence at St.
Helena : 196, 197
POLAND, Napoleon on : 9, 12-16,
90-91, 92
POLYGAMY. Napoleon's views on :
102
POPE, Alexander. His *Essay on
Man* : 66 *n.*
POPPLETON, Captain. Orderly
officer to Napoleon at St.
Helena : 190 *n.*, 202, 204
POTOCKA, Comtesse. Anna Tysz-
kieuwicz, the wife of Comte
Alexandre Potocki. She after-
wards married a Comte Won-
sowicz : 243, 245
Her *Mémoires* published by
Stryenski, 1897 : 244
POZZO DI BORGO, Count. Corsican
diplomatist : 76
PRADT, Abbé Dominique de. Am-
bassador to the duchy of
Warsaw in 1812 : 13, 15, 92
PRÉGNY, near Geneva, Queen Hor-
tense's house at : 241, 242-243
PRETENDER, the young, Charles
Edward Stuart (1720–88): 74
PRÉVILLE, de (or Dépréville),
Madame. Sometime *première
femme* to Queen Hortense
(Cochelet, *Mémoires*, iii. 230):
255
PYRAMIDS, battle of the (July 20,
1798) : 88

QUATRE BRAS, battle of (June 16,
1815) : 114
QUINET, Edgar. Philosopher, poet,
and writer (1803–1875) : 118

RAGUSE, duc de : *see* Marmont
RAPETTI. His *La Défection de
Marmont* : 128

RAUCH, Prussian commissioner
at the Lusigny negotiations :
(1814) : 51
REGENT, the Prince, afterwards
George IV. : 156 *n.*, 161, 163,
166, 175, 255
REGNIER, Claude Ambroise, afterwards duc de Massa. Na-
poleon's Minister of Justice,
1802 to 1813 : 276
REILLE, General Comte. In command of the *Armée du Nord*
during the Hundred Days :
123
Revue des deux Mondes : 118-122
REYNIER, Jean Louis Ebenezer,
Comte. French General : 20,
41, 42, 44, 47
RIBOISIÈRE, Charles Honoré Bas-
ton, Comte de la. Orderly
officer to Napoleon during the
Hundred Days : 110, 111
RICHELIEU, Cardinal. First Minister of France under Louis
XIII. : 98 *n.*
ROME, King of. Napoleon's son
by Marie Louise : 103
" ROSEMARY HALL ", Baron Stür-
mer's residence at St. Helena :
196
ROSTOPCHIN, Féodor, Count. Gov-
ernor of Moscow, 1812 : 24, 91
ROUHER, Eugène. Minister under
Napoleon III. *Ministre d'État*
in 1863 : 284
RUSSELL, Lord John, M.P. After-
wards Earl Russell and Prime
Minister : 80, 105

ST. AIGNAN, Baron de. Minister at
Weimar, 1813. He acted as
French intermediary during
the conversations held at
Frankfort that year : 50
SAINTE-AULAIRE, Louis Clair de
Beaupoil, Comte de. His-
torian and politician. Cham-
berlain to Napoleon from
1809 : 25 *n.*
SAINTE-BEUVE, Charles Augustin,
1804–1869. His *Portraits de
Femmes* : 209
ST. LEU, Duchesse de : *see* Hor-
tense, Queen
Letter from : 265
" ST. MARTIN ". Napoleon's villa
on the island of Elba : 85, 86,
104

St. Vincent, John Jervis, Earl of. Admiral : 187

" Sally ", maid to Madame de Souza : see Hortense, Queen

Sardinia, King of, Victor Emmanuel I., in whose favour Charles Emmanuel IV. of Savoy abdicated in 1802 : 99

Sartorius, George Rose, Captain, commanding the Slaney. Afterwards Admiral and K.C.B. He brought the news of Napoleon's surrender from Rochefort : 152, 154

Savary, Anne René, Duke of Rovigo. General. He was refused permission to accompany Napoleon to St. Helena : 175 n.

Schönbrunn, Treaty of (1809) : 2, 4

Schouvaloff, Comte Paul. Distinguished Russian General. Aide-de-camp to the Czar : 51

Schwarzenberg, Carl Philip, Prince de. Austrian Field-Marshal : 12, 20, 51, 52, 53, 60, 61

Sébastiani, Horace François, Comte. General, afterwards Marshal of France : 77

Ségur, General Comte de :
His Histoires et Mémoires : 19, 23
Mémoires d'un aide-de-camp de Napoléon : 72

Sismondi, Charles Simonde de. Historian and political economist : 102

Slavery, Napoleon's views on: 102, 107

Smith, General : 92

" Sophie, ma cousine " : see Hortense, Queen

Soult, Nicolas Jean-de-Dieu. Marshal of France : 76, 90, 123

Souza, de Botelho, Don José Maria de. " Papa " : 66-209, 210, 221, 252, 255, 256, 257, 259, 262, 266, and Table, 343

Souza, Madame de, Adèle Filleul. Married (1) Comte Charles François de Flahault; (2) Marquis de Souza Botelho : 135, 185, 208 et seq., 262, and Table, 343
Her novels, Adèle de Sénange : 208; Eugène de Rothelin : 208, 236

Staël, Madame de. Daughter of Necker. She had to quit France in 1810 and only returned after Waterloo : 92, 93

States-General of Holland, the : 230-232

Sterne, Laurence, author of Tristram Shandy, etc.: 221, 222

Stöffel, Colonel, Baron. French military attaché in Berlin during the Second Empire : 123

Strachan, Admiral Sir Richard John. Commander of the Walcheren Expedition, 1809 : 141

Stürmer, Baron. Austrian Commissioner at St. Helena : 188, 196

Suchet, Louis Gabriel, duc d'Albuféra. Marshal of France : 76

Talleyrand, Prince of Beneventum : 69, 70, 76, 102, 209, 210, 234, 237, 286-7
Letter to : 286

Talma, François Joseph. The celebrated tragic actor : 77

Tettenborn, Frederic Charles, Baron. German cavalry leader, 37

Thiers, Louis Adolphe. Historian and politician : 55-6, 73-110, 124
His Histoire du Consulat et de l'Empire : 51, 55, 68, 73, 110, 126
Flahault's letters to : 110, 124

Thornborough, Sir Edward. Admiral (1754–1834) : 146

Thrale, Cecilia : see Mrs. Mostyn

Thrale, Hester Maria : see Lady Keith

Thrale, Susan. Afterwards Mrs. Hoare : 150, 168

Tilsit, Treaty of (1807) : 90

Toulon, the defence of (1793) : 138, 159, 177

Trafalgar, battle of (1805) : 139

Troppard, General. A member of the Commission for the Publication of the Napoleonic Correspondence, 1864 : 282

Ussher, Captain. Commanding the Undaunted. His conversations with Napoleon : 9, 73, 89, 95, 159, 187

UXBRIDGE, Henry William Paget, Earl of. Commanded cavalry at Waterloo, where he lost a leg. Afterwards Marquis of Anglesey : 144

VAILLANT, Jean Baptiste Philibert. Marshal of France, 1851 : 277, 283
Letters from : 277, 281
Letter to : 284

VAN DE WEYER, Sylvain. Belgian Ambassador in London under Queen Victoria : 80 n.

VAUGHAN, Sir Richard : 156

VENABLES-VERNON, George Granville, M.P. Afterwards Vernon-Harcourt, of Nuneham : 80, 81 et seq.

VERNON (Harcourt), Edward, Archbishop of York from 1807 to 1847 : 81

VICENZA, duc de : see Caulaincourt

VICEROY, of Italy, the : see Beauharnais, Eugène

VICTOR, Claude Perrin, duc de Bellune. Marshal of France : 42, 43

VIENNA, Congress of (1814–15) : 98, 147 n.

VILLEMAIN, Abel François, statesman and historian. His Souvenirs Contemporains : 15

VINCENT ROUSSEAU, Queen Hortense's foster-brother : 252, 257, 258 n., 260

VOLTAIRE, François Abouet de : 121

WAGRAM, battle of (July 6, 1809) : 2, 5 n.

WALCHEREN EXPEDITION (1809) : 4, 9

WALEWSKI, Alexandre, Count. Son of Napoleon I. by Marie Walewski. Minister for Foreign Affairs under Napoleon III. : 282, 283, 284

WATERLOO, battle of (June 18, 1815) : 124-131, 193

WELLINGTON, Duke of : 59-115, 126, 130, 143, 148, 193

WELLINGTON, Duchess of. Catherine Pakenham, daughter of second Lord Longford : 77

WILSON, Sir Robert, General. Attached to the Russian army during the 1812 campaign : 92

WINDSOR HOTEL, Plymouth : 148, 167

WINTZINGERODE, Ferdinand, Baron de. Russian General. In March 1814 he engaged Napoleon while the rest of the Allied army was marching on Paris : 63, 68

WOBURN ABBEY. Family seat of the Dukes of Bedford : 254

WRANGHAMS, the (of St. Helena) : 196

WYNYARD, Mrs. (at St. Helena) : 198

YORK, Frederick, Duke of. Second son of George III., Commander-in-Chief. Accused (in 1809) of having improperly disposed of commissions in the army : 93

YORK, VON WARTENBURG, Count. Prussian Field Marshal. He withdrew the Prussian forces from the French army in 1812: 63

YOUNGHUSBAND, Mrs. She incurred Sir Hudson Lowe's displeasure, by inviting General Gourgaud to meet the Allied Commissioners, before Napoleon had consented to receive them (A Voice from St. Helena, O'Meara, i. 507) : 191

ZIETHEN, John Ernest Charles, Comte de. Prussian General. Prominent during the Hundred Days and afterwards commanded the Prussian army of occupation in France: 11

ZNAIM, armistice of (July 11, 1809) : 2

THE END